OPEN SOCIETY UNRESOLVED

OPEN SOCIETY UNRESOLVED

The Contemporary Relevance of a Contested Idea

Edited by Christof Royer and Liviu Matei

Central European University Press
Budapest–Vienna–New York

©2023 by the contributors

Published in 2023 by
Central European University Press

Nádor utca 9, H-1051 Budapest, Hungary
Tel: +36-1-327-3138 or 327-3000
E-mail: ceupress@press.ceu.edu

Website: www.ceupress.com

This work is licensed under a Creative Commons
Attribution-NonCommercial-NoDerivatives 4.0 International License.

This publication is the result of research conducted for Central European University, Private University – CEU GmbH. It was made possible by the CEU Open Access Fund.

ISBN 978-963-386-589-7 (paperback)
ISBN 978-963-386-590-3 (ebook)

Library of Congress Cataloging-in-Publication Data
Names: Royer, Christof, editor. | Matei, Liviu, editor.
Title: Open society unresolved : the contemporary relevance of a contested idea / edited by Christof Royer, Liviu Matei.
Description: Budapest ; New York : Central European University Press, 2023.
| Includes bibliographical references and index.
Identifiers: LCCN 2022058516 (print) | LCCN 2022058517 (ebook) | ISBN 9789633865897 (paperback) | ISBN 9789633865903 (pdf)
Subjects: LCSH: Social sciences--Philosophy. | Social structure. |
Liberalism. | Universalism. | BISAC: SOCIAL SCIENCE / General |
PHILOSOPHY / Ethics & Moral Philosophy
Classification: LCC H61.15 O63 2023 (print) | LCC H61.15 (ebook) | DDC 300.1--dc23/eng/20230105
LC record available at https://lccn.loc.gov/2022058516
LC ebook record available at https://lccn.loc.gov/2022058517

Contents

Introduction: Open Society Unresolved: Charting the
Contested Terrain   1
Christof Royer

PART I
Philosophical and Theoretical Perspectives on Open Society   21

1. Human Nature and the Open Society   23
   Thom Scott-Phillips

2. In Praise of Coldness: The Open Neighborhood and Its
   Enemies   38
   Rachid Boutayeb

3. Against Identity: Individuality as the Foundation of
   Open Society   48
   Gregory Lobo

4. Empirical Embodiment of Critical Rationalism:
   Deliberative Theory and Open Society   59
   Gazela Pudar Draško and Predrag Krstić

5. Open Society as an Achievement: Popper, Gaus, and
   the Liberal Tradition   72
   Piers Norris Turner

6. Nozick's Meta-Utopia as an Open Society   83
   Avery Fox White

Contents

7 Hannah Arendt and Literary Pedagogy 94
   Andrea Timár

8 Can Bergson's Definition of Open Society Be Useful Today? 105
   Jean-Louis Fabiani

PART II
National and Regional Perspectives on Open Society 115

9 The Gender of Illiberalism: New Transnational Alliances against Open Societies in Central and Eastern Europe 117
   Katalin Fábián

10 Open Society Contested: Liberal Universalism versus Autocratic Functionalism in Hong Kong 132
   Kenneth Ka-Lok Chan

11 "Sorosoids": Uses of Labeling in Bulgaria 148
   Lubomir Terziev

12 An African Background to the Concept of Open Society: *Ikenga* and *Ofo* Cultic Figures as Structural Representations of the Enterprising Spirit of the Igbo of Nigeria 162
   Nwankwo T. Nwaezeigwe

13 Imagining the Future of Intelligence in Open Societies: Venturing beyond Secrecy and Scientific Prophecy as Totalitarian Modes of Modernity 174
   Anna Eva Grutza

14 Open Society in Crisis: Making Sense of Public Health and Expert Advice during Covid-19 190
   Tarun Weeramanthri

List of Contributors *207*
Index *211*

Introduction

Open Society Unresolved: Charting the Contested Terrain

Christof Royer

As the editors of this volume, Liviu Matei and I settled on the title "Open Society Unresolved" for two main reasons: One is that open society has always been a contested concept; it has been vaguely (if at all) defined by its original architects, and its precise meaning has remained elusive ever since. The second is that many of the questions that surround the idea of an open society are still—and will remain—unresolved. There is, in fact, a good reason why Karl Popper, the thinker who popularized the term "open society," was so smitten by Michael Oakeshott's expression of a "politics of conversation" to capture the open-endedness of open societies.[1] For in a genuinely open society, solutions to moral, social, and political questions can only be tentative and must remain open to contestation; there can, in other words, be no final "once and for all" solutions. Inevitably, then, the question(s) of open society will remain unresolved, and they will—as they always have been—be confronted on contested terrain.

It is, of course, true that in public discourses as well as in the academic literature, *open* societies are routinely portrayed as *liberal* societies. For better or worse, open society has, as Norbert Götz and Carl Marklund put it, "become a watchword of liberal democracy" (2014). Seen in this light, things, indeed, look rather dismal for open societies. History has returned with a vengeance. Russia and China have (re)emerged as authoritarian challengers of the liberal international order, with the Russian invasion of Ukraine only being the most extreme expression of this conflict. Populist movements around the world claim to defend "the people" against "elites" while, at the same time, hollowing out fundamental pillars of liberal democracy. Political polarization threatens to tear apart even established democratic societies. Capitalism has turned out to be unsustainable and—depending on the view of the respective author—needs to be either reformed or abolished. Evils such as racism and sexism have anything but disappeared from human relations. In response, advocates of critical social

---

1 For a splendid overview of this discussion, see Jacobs and Tregenza (2013).

justice have gone so far as to reject freedom of speech as an ideological weapon of powerful elites to oppress marginalized groups. Modern technologies such as artificial intelligence produce new forms of domination on a global scale. The climate disaster is no longer a distant dystopia but has become a present-day reality. And then there is, of course, Covid-19 with its double effect of producing new fault lines, precarities, and exclusions, while exacerbating previously existing ones.

Yet, even if we leave aside for the moment the objection that it is too simplistic to equate open society with liberalism (or liberal democracy), there remains a further problem: it is one thing to diagnose that liberal, open societies are under attack and quite another to take open society seriously as a philosophical and political idea. Indeed, there are several potential reasons to doubt the usefulness of the concept, perhaps even to "forget" open society altogether.[2] To start with, open society has always been a contested idea. It is, of course, true that most—if not all—of the concepts of the social sciences and humanities share this feature (Connolly 1993). In the case of open society, however, we face the problem that even its original architects (as will be seen in the next section) have left it rather underspecified. This "underspecification" invites radical criticism that questions the meaningfulness of the concept itself. Mark Lilla (2018), for instance, asserts that open society is an "oxymoron" as societies are by their very nature "closed"; unless one believes in the existence of a borderless world society, he thinks, open society is a contradiction in terms.

A second line of argument questions not so much the meaningfulness of the concept, but its normative desirability. Neil McInnes, in his criticism of Karl Popper, expresses this point most eloquently: "A society as open and abstract as the one Popper sought sounds like a cold, draughty place to those of us who come still trailing clouds of partisan loyalty from the old closed society" (2002, no pagination). No one really wants to live in such an environment.

Finally, it might be argued that a paradigm developed in the first half of the twentieth century is simply outdated. The world has radically changed, the challenges of today are unprecedented, and the enemies have changed their faces and tactics. Thus, rather than clinging to old ideas, we should focus our attention on developing new concepts and vocabularies better equipped to guide our thought and action in the twenty-first century.

To be sure, advocates of the open society need not be swayed by these criticisms. Lilla's accusation of the open society as an oxymoron might well be based on a conflation of open society with "open borders." The communitarian counter-argument wrongly assumes that theories of open society are necessarily oblivious to the importance of identification and belonging in social

---

2 "Forget Open Society? Critical Conversations on a Contested Concept" was the—deliberately provocative—title of the first annual conference of the Open Society Research Platform (OSRP) held on October 28–29, 2021. Many of the chapters in this volume were first presented at this conference.

and political life. And those who think that the idea of open society is outdated tend to underestimate the adaptability of this concept. Nonetheless, those who advocate open society today cannot simply take its relevance or usefulness for granted. For such a presumption of self-evidence would, in fact, go against the critical ethos that lies at the heart of the concept of open society, a critical ethos that rejects every form of dogmatism and does not shy away from radical self-criticism and self-questioning. As such, the best way to promote open society is to demonstrate why and how this concept still matters in today's world and, in doing so, take the self-critical ethos of the open society idea seriously.

This, indeed, is the purpose of the present volume. Its fourteen chapters bring together the theory of open society with the realities of social, moral, and political life. This, therefore, is a book neither on abstract philosophy nor on empirical social science; rather, it aims to bring to the fore the critical and constructive potential of open society to analyze, rethink, and address contemporary problems and challenges.[3] It should be made clear from the outset, though, that the authors do not draw on a uniform conception of open society. Indeed, given the concept's contested (or unresolved) nature, and the variety of possible interpretations, uniformity would be counterproductive and problematic. To impose uniformity would also contradict this volume's ambition to be the first geographically and intellectually global volume on open society in theory and practice. Individual authors hail from different geographical and cultural backgrounds, they come from a variety of academic disciplines and scholarly traditions, and they address themes as diverse as public health, cognitive science, African cosmology, colonialism, or deliberative democracy. Thus, the commitment to a genuine diversity and plurality of viewpoints is one that lies at the heart of this book as much as it lies at the heart of the open society concept itself. However, what unites the individual authors and chapters is an interest in open society's continuing usefulness and relevance to address contemporary problems.

In this introduction, I would like to set the stage for these contributions. As such, the introduction serves three purposes: The first is to give an overview of how the "original architects" (i.e., Henri Bergson, Karl Popper, and Friedrich Hayek) developed the concept of open society. Obviously, these "open society portraits" have to remain sketchy. Nonetheless, in the following section, my aim is not only to sketch out the basic contours of the three respective conceptions of open society but also to tease out some of the parallels and divergences between them. The second purpose is to map out the contested terrain of open society. In other words, I will give the reader a sense of how the concept of open society has (more) recently been used in the literature of the social sciences and the humanities. Again, this is not a comprehensive literature review but, rather, a critical overview of the state

---

3 This, of course, is a description of the broader orientation of the volume. Individual chapters might be more historically, or theoretically, or empirically oriented.

of the debate on open society.[4] The third purpose is to introduce the individual chapters of this book. This will not be done through a separate chapter outline, but as an integral part of the introduction. My aim is to show how the contributions to this volume relate to the existing literature on open society, how they push its boundaries, fill existing gaps, and open up further avenues for research.

Three Architects of Open Society: Bergson, Popper, Hayek

To be sure, the idea of open society long predates its coinage (Germino 1982). It is also not, as is often assumed, an exclusively "Western" concept. Echoes of this idea can be found in the philosophies of societies around the world, among others, as Nwankwo Nwaezeigwe demonstrates in this volume, in the Igbo culture of Southern Nigeria. This society, as Nwaezeigwe shows, is characterized by democratic structures and dispersed authority, high degrees of freedom and social mobility, and a strong egalitarian spirit.

As a philosophical concept, however, open society was introduced by the French philosopher Henri Bergson in his last major work (originally published in 1932)—*The Two Sources of Morality and Religion* (1977). *The Two Sources* is Bergson's attempt to bring his ideas and insights developed in earlier works (especially in *Creative Evolution*) to the moral, social, and political realm. Bergson distinguishes here between what he calls a "mystic" or "open" society and a "static" or "closed" society. The mystic or open society is characterized by the "strength to love mankind" (1977, 23)—this strength, indeed, is what openness means for Bergson. Such a passionate "love of mankind," according to Bergson, can be found in "open souls," that is, in the mystic figures that "are not simply humans of vision, raptures, and ecstasies, but figures of action" (Ansell-Pearson 2018, 123). These open souls can act as the "harbingers of humanity" (ibid.) as it is through their emulation that we can (perhaps) bring into existence the "open society." In the final chapter of *The Two Sources*, Bergson lays out the distinction between the open and the closed society in the following terms:

> [There is] a sharp distinction, in the sphere of society, between the closed and the open. The closed society is that whose members hold together, caring nothing for the rest of humanity, on the alert for attack or defence, bound, in fact, to a perpetual readiness for battle. Such is human society fresh from the hands of nature. Man was made for this society as the ant was made for ant-heap. (1977, 266)

While this brief discussion cannot do justice to Bergson's complex conception of open society, I want to draw attention to several features that I think are important: For Bergson, an open society is a form of democracy. It is not, however, an

---

4 For a comprehensive review of the literature on open society between 1989 and today, see the database of the OSRP (https://elkanacenter.ceu.edu/database).

already existing democracy but, rather, a "democracy to come" (Baugh 2016). Of course, it is anything but clear from Bergson's account if such an open society can ever be realized. For the realization of the open society depends, as we have seen, on the emergence of mystical figures who embody the (radically) cosmopolitan "strength to love mankind."[5] To be fair, for Bergsonians this is not necessarily a problem. Rather, they embrace the fact that "the vague, or indefinite, is a technical idea at work throughout his writings" (Mullarkey 2012, 71). But let us go a step further and ask: What if such an open society were realized? Bergson's open society, it seems, would have overcome many of the recalcitrant problems that have always haunted moral, social, and political life. Exclusion, struggle, and enmity would have been replaced by a love of mankind that would render politics obsolete. Obviously, the utopianism that undergirds this conception of open society is appealing to some and rejected by others. While prominent thinkers such as Eric Voegelin (1967) or Gilles Deleuze (1990) have found inspiration in Bergson's work, Judith Shklar diagnoses in Bergson a "desire to escape from politics, from the unpoetic realities of everyday social life" (1998, 335).

However, one of the most interesting recent developments in the literature on Bergson is that some authors have brought to the fore the "practical relevance" of his thought. Andrea Pitts and Mark Westmoreland, for instance, have recently edited a splendid volume that brings Bergson into conversation with critical scholars of race and decolonial theory (2019). While it is true that some attempts to use Bergson, and especially his conception of open society as a transcendent "democracy to come," have remained curiously abstract and somewhat detached from worldly realities, this volume demonstrates the radical potential of his thought for contemporary social, moral, and political questions. Jean-Loius Fabiani's contribution to this volume has a broadly similar purpose. Asking whether or not Bergson's definition of open society can be "useful today," Fábiáni thinks that Bergson's work can help us to alleviate one of the "major contradictions of our time": that we try to include the socially marginalized by relying on the tools of identity politics, which are based on the distinction of "us" and "them" and the radical critique of Western universalism. Bergson, then, despite his seemingly outdated vocabulary, might well be a valuable source of inspiration for a (more) critical universalism, based on a "radical questioning of the logic of identity."[6]

If Bergson introduced the concept of open society to philosophy, then Karl Popper popularized it in his *The Open Society and Its Enemies* (2020). Having

---

5 In their (excellent) entry on Bergson in the *Stanford Encyclopedia of Philosophy*, Leonard Lawlor and Valentine Moulard-Leonard contribute to the enigmatic status of Bergson's open society when they write that "perhaps in these ideas of an always still to be named coming community, we find the enduring influence of Bergson's 'open society.'"
6 For a similar argument, albeit developed through the lens of Karl Popper's conception of open society, see Gregory Lobo's chapter. Kenneth Ka-Lok Chan, on the other hand, argues in his chapter that a successful battle of Hong Kong against a repressive Chinese government requires a "generic identity" inspired by the values of open society.

penned this tome in exile in New Zealand, it was first published in 1945. Similar to Bergson's *The Two Sources*, *The Open Society* is Popper's attempt to apply his earlier ideas (in his case, in the philosophy of science) to social and political theory. As such, the book is driven by the epistemological outlook of "critical rationalism," which holds that knowledge claims should be subjected to rational criticism in a trial and error process that seeks to "falsify" rather than to confirm them. This epistemological position has crucial consequences for the concept of open society. On a fundamental level, it even establishes an important parallel between Popper and Bergson. For both thinkers had a strong aversion to "historicism"—that is, the idea that history has a purpose and is determined by underlying "natural laws." Popper expresses his aversion with characteristic lucidity: "History has no meaning," he asserts in the final chapter of *The Open Society*. There are no natural laws built into our unfolding history. But although history has no meaning, "we can give it a meaning" (Popper 2020, 482); we—as humans—have agency to "become the makers of our fate." Bergson, in a similar vein, rejects the idea of historicism: "If there were really a pre-existent direction along which man simply had to advance, moral renovation would be foreseeable; there would be no need, in each occasion, for a creative effort" (1977, 267).

In other respects, though, Popper's critical rationalism leads to a conception of open society that is strikingly different from Bergson's. Most obviously, Popper has little sympathy for Bergson's mysticism. "My terms," he announces,

> indicate, as it were, a *rationalistic decision*: the closed society is characterized by the belief in magical taboos, while the open society is one in which men have learned to be to some extent critical of taboos, and to base decisions on the authority of their own decisions (after discussion): Bergson; on the other hand, has a kind of *religious distinction* in mind.
>
> *(2020, 512, note 1 to introduction, emphases in original)*

Popper, in other words, contrasts "the magical or tribal or collectivist society [which] will also be called the closed society," with "the society in which individuals are confronted with personal decisions, the open society" (2020, 165). Again, I do not have space here to give a more detailed account of Popper's conception of open society; but it is worth teasing out some of the central elements. Since open society "sets free the critical powers of man," it is based on the idea that societal and political progress (just like progress in science) is linked to the critique of existing ideas, theories, taboos, and dogmas. For Popper, moreover, an open society is one in which the status of the individual is superior to the status of the collective (i.e., the community or the state). It is true that some commentators see this individualism as one of the salient strengths of Popper's open society concept, while others criticize it as its fundamental flaw. At any rate, for Popper, "the transition from the closed to the open society can be described as one of the deepest revolutions through which mankind has passed" precisely because it is marked by a "new individualism" (2020, 167). Finally, the combination of critical rationalism and the elevated position of the individual, leads Popper to the endorsement of a cosmopolitan position based on the idea of a "brotherhood of all men" (2020, 175). While this might seem to establish a further parallel between Popper and Bergson, it must be noted that this is a very different cosmopolitanism. Popper's open society, in contrast to Bergson's, is resolutely "anti-utopian" for two reasons: The first, and more obvious, is that Popper, throughout the book, rejects the utopian tendencies of thinkers like Plato, Marx, and Hegel (and their followers) to contrive "blueprints" for societies. Such a utopianism, Popper thinks, sets societies on a slippery slope toward totalitarianism and should be replaced with what he calls a "piecemeal approach" to social, moral, and political progress. The second (perhaps less obvious) reason is that Popper does not believe in the eventual overcoming of enmity. To be sure, the relationship between the open society and its enemies is more complex than most commentators tend to assume. At any rate, though, Popper believes that open society is not a normatively empty concept—and precisely because it stands for values such as openness, tolerance, or plurality, those who reject or violate these values are to be regarded as its enemies.

This normative thrust of Popper's conception of open society is pivotal but easily overlooked (or willfully ignored). Open society, after all, does not stand for "anything goes" relativism; open society stands for very specific values and it is of crucial importance to express these values as clearly as possible, to stand up for them, and, if necessary, to defend them. Perhaps the most sustained engagement with Popper's thought in this book is Gazela Pudar Draško and Predrag Krstić's chapter. Based on a careful and imaginative reading of *The Open Society*, they unearth the deliberative elements in Popper's thought and, more importantly, the reciprocal relationship between the traditions of open society and deliberative democracy. The one—deliberative democracy—institutionalizes what the other—open society—promotes: "a loud and well-founded protest against expectations, demands and, especially, against prescriptions of paths to social happiness." Deliberation, they emphasize, does not take place in a normative vacuum; deliberation, rather, can only take place against a relatively stable normative background, provided and sustained by a "unity of human reason," in which openness toward the voices and opinions of others is secured.

The third and final conception of open society I would like to sketch out is Friedrich Hayek's. This selection might seem a bit more controversial since Hayek preferred the term "great society" to "open society."[7] There is, however, renewed interest in Hayek's account (see below), which warrants a brief discussion of his

---

7 Hayek's use of the term "great society" is borrowed from Adam Smith; he sees it as a synonym to Popper's "open society" (1977, 2).

conception of open society. Hayek is, of course, known (and much criticized today) as one of the fathers of neoliberalism—an ideology that also shaped his idea of a spontaneously generated and self-generating order that should not be interfered with. Hayek shares with Popper the idea that the "closed society" holds an enduring (even perpetual) attraction and that a return to tribalism is an ever-present possibility. But Hayek's neoliberal principle of non-interference stands in marked contrast to Popper's "piecemeal engineering" approach—laissez faire instead of Popper's *peu à peu* or Bergson's "sudden leap."

Of crucial importance in understanding Hayek's idea is his distinction between a "spontaneous order" that leads to "rules of just conduct" and an "organized order" that decouples considerations of justice from a legal order. For Hayek, the open (or great) society is the outcome of the former, spontaneous order, based on rules of just conduct. He calls this order a "rule-connected" *nomocracy* that strictly applies the concepts of universalization and equality.[8] "The conception of justice as we understand it," he writes, "that is, the principle of treating all under the same rules . . . became the guide in the progressive approach to an Open Society of free individuals equal before the law" (1976, 39). An open society, therefore, is understood as an order "brought about by the observance of abstract and end-independent rules" (Hayek 1978, 39). The rationale behind this conception is clear enough: equality before the law is the central cornerstone of an open society; it is, indeed, the principle that made its emergence possible in the first place. For Hayek, this equality requires the abstract and universal application of the law; the law cannot—indeed, must not—take into consideration the peculiarities of individual cases lest it becomes arbitrary and, therefore, unjust. Hayek's insistence on "universalization" leads him to a cosmopolitan position that—albeit in different expressions—we also find in Popper and Bergson. As Calvin Hayes observes, "Hayek is amazingly lacking in chauvinism of any kind: national, racial, even cultural and he was cosmopolitan in the best sense of that much abused and contested term. This is what he means by the 'Great or Open Society'" (2008, 126). Now, the various criticisms of Hayek's neoliberalism are, I think, well-known and do not need to be ruminated here. But there is a further important point that Hayek's conception of open society finds difficult to account for. As Mark Notturno observes, one of the main differences between Popper and Hayek is that for the former, the recognition that the laws can be changed by the people marks the end of the *closed* and the beginning of the *open* society; for Hayek, on the other hand, a change of laws sounds the death knell of the *open* and ushers in the *closed* society. Indeed, what seems to be decisive for Hayek is the recognition that we are all equally bound by the same universal rules of conduct (Notturno 2014, 121). There is, then, a

---

8 In distinguishing between "teleocracy" (an end-connected tribal society) and a "nomocracy" (rule-connected open society), Hayek is inspired by Michael Oakeshott's distinction in *On Human Conduct*.

dynamic element built into Popper's conception of the open society that seems to be absent from Hayek's more static account.

Yet, Hayek's conception of open society has made a, perhaps surprising, recent comeback via the work of Gerald Gaus. Gaus accuses Popper of advocating a "sectarian" vision of open society, which is deeply flawed and inadvertently encourages a retreat to the very reactionary tribalism it opposes—the two most tangible manifestations of this mindset are Brexit and the election of Donald Trump (2017). Against Popper, Gaus advocates an account of open society inspired by Hayek. Hayek, he claims, conceived of the open society as "an evolving moral, legal, and economic framework that encourages toleration, trust, mutually advantageous interactions, and the flow of information." In contrast to Popper's "arrogant sectarianism," the core of Hayek's open society "is free and willing cooperation of strangers on the basis of rules that allow each space to effectively pursue her aims and values" (Gaus 2017, 2–3). Ultimately, as Gaus asserts in his posthumously published *The Open Society and Its Complexities*, what Hayek allows us to see is that the open society is "an ever-increasing and relentless engine of diversity and inclusivity" (2021, 248). In this volume, Piers Turner's chapter offers a powerful defense of Popper, arguing that Gaus wrongly associates Popper's fallibilistic problem-solving and piecemeal social engineering with hyper-rationalism and hubristic ideal theory. He also asserts that Popper is right that the preservation of open society depends on the development of norms and traditions that can sustain liberal attitudes and modes of interaction. Pace Hayek and Gaus, then, a diverse, open society does not sustain itself without effort: "To obtain the benefits of diversity and to avoid its pitfalls, we must cultivate certain norms within our social morality, and protect them once established." Hence Turner's conviction that open society is an "achievement."

Where does that leave us with the open society concept? As we have seen, the three "architects" of the idea have developed rather diverging notions of open society. Of course, it should not come as a surprise that differences arise between Bergson's mysticism, Popper's critical rationalism, and Hayek's neoliberalism. Moreover, "opening up" the idea of open society to thinkers beyond the original architects, a project that seems theoretically and practically useful, would complicate the picture even further. As Andrea Timár's Arendtian notion of open society or Avery White's bold assertion of Robert Nozick's metautopia as an expression of open society in this volume show, broadening the intellectual repertoire of open society invigorates the concept but surely does not render its terrain less contested. At the same time, though, there are family resemblances: a commitment to genuine human plurality and diversity, an aversion to all forms of authoritarian domination, a cosmopolitan conviction of the equal worth of individuals, a rejection of narrow ("tribal") attachments to collectives and uncritical groupthink. These family resemblances, to be sure, do not change the fact that open society has always been, and will always be, a contested concept. This, however, does not devalue the idea of open society; quite the contrary. For one of the most fundamental features built into the idea of open society is openness to contestation, which extends to the very concept of open society itself.

Open Society in Selected Thematic Areas

Turning away from the original architects of open society, I now want to offer a necessarily sketchy overview of several thematic areas in which open society has recently been used and link them to the contributions in this volume. Before doing so, allow me a more general comment. It is perhaps not too surprising that, in terms of sheer quantity, the literature on open society cannot compete with other concepts of the social sciences and humanities (e.g., democracy, liberalism, human rights, or globalization). Open society, however, also faces a more specific dilemma: the widespread unreflective use of open society as a mere slogan in book or article titles. Indeed, there are countless works out there that have open society in the title without ever discussing the concept—sometimes even without mentioning open society at all in the text. It is, thus, unfortunate but true that, as two perceptive commentators argue, open society is all too often "merely used as a catch phrase in political and social philosophy" (Armbrüster and Gebert 2002, 170). Yet, this is not to say that the contemporary literature on open society is generally dull or unsophisticated. In what follows, I will focus on the areas of authoritarianism, feminism, belonging and identification, education, and digital technology and public emergencies to introduce some of the most interesting works in these areas as well as the contributions of this volume to them.

Authoritarianism

One theme that has always been prominent in the literature is that authoritarian states reject (and violate) the values of an open society. But, of course, a direct analogy between the first half of the twentieth century (i.e., the historical background against which Bergson, Popper, and Hayek developed their conceptions of open society) and today is anything but straightforward. Michael Ignatieff (2018a and b) rightly argues that today's enemies of the open society are very different: we are today faced with closed societies that have "shed their totalitarian form" and "assumed new authoritarian guises" (2018a, 2). For Ignatieff, the "new" enemies of open societies are "authoritarian single party states that are actually parasitic on our freedoms" (2018b, 335). And it is important to understand that these are not the "closed societies" of the past as they are not in the grip of messianic, totalizing ideologies. Still, it is clear what kind of "enemies" Ignatieff has in mind: states and governments that are relying—once again—on nationalist sentiments, on a sense of unity and (internal) solidarity that questions and even rejects the liberal democratic and cosmopolitan outlook of the open society. In a similar vein, Mark Bovens (2020) stresses that authoritarian states like China or Russia, populist movements, and democratic backsliding around the world constitute a severe threat to the open society. This argument is also reiterated by those who focus on Hungary's eviction of Central European University, which they portray as an assault on open society (Gagyi 2017; Bárd 2020). What the literature clearly illustrates, in short, is that authoritarianism is a specter that continues to haunt open society in theory and practice.

Several contributors to this volume continue this line of argument and develop it further. Kenneth Ka-Lok Chan, for example, sheds light on the ongoing conflict between mainland China and Hong Kong's civil society through the lenses of "Liberal Universalism" and "Autocratic Functionalism." He argues that while Hong Kong's civil society organizations are in retreat under the pressure of Chinese autocratic rule, the normative appeal of open society as a custodian for the city's distinctive values and identity can be expected to grow against the backdrop of the moral and institutional decay of the official, "Orwellian," realm. However, the "uphill battle" against the oppressive government can only be successful if it is accompanied by "a generic identity that is both global and local, post-sovereign and post-national." Lyubomir Terziev shifts the geographical focus and analyzes the neologism "sorosoid," which has established itself as a buzzword with a strongly pejorative connotation in Bulgaria. A "sorosoid," according to this narrative, is someone who (allegedly) receives money from George Soros, for whom the West, the European Union, and NATO are "sacred cows" and for whom the establishment of liberal democracy with its "hollow mantras" is a primary goal. Terziev's central argument is that this neologism is not only an expression of tribalism but, more importantly, a linguistic ruse to dehumanize liberal-minded citizens. Not unlike the word "humanoid," "sorosoid" describes someone (or something?) who resembles—but is not quite—a human being. According to Terziev, these attempts to close Bulgarian society must be resisted, and he outlines two potential strategies to do so: the "rationalist approach" and the "affective strategy." Finally, Katalin Fábián turns to transnational alliances against feminism in Central and Eastern Europe. She argues that the reappearance of conservative, expressively masculine, and populist forces in post-communist politics has led to the embracing of anti-genderism in different national contexts. For Fábián, these movements resemble the proverbial canary in the coal mine: with the insistence on their monopoly to define sexual roles, these developments signal the instability of democracy and how much exclusionary nationalism has strengthened along with the normalization of anti-EU and anti-immigration sentiments and Islamophobia.

Feminism

Fábián's contribution also opens up a second important line of inquiry: it brings the literature on open society in conversation with feminism. This, it has to be noted, has been one of the blind spots of the open society literature. In fact, it is telling that the only engagement with open society from a feminist perspective until now has been Fábián's 2010 article, in which she analyzes the emergence of women's groups in post-Soviet countries as a response to globalization and democratization. The rise of these movements is, according to Fábián, inextricably linked to the fact that "the regime transitions have opened up a space where gender analysis, social movement activism, and domestic and international economic and political changes clash" (2010, 124). Fábián, in other words, demonstrates how the "new openness" (i.e., the pressure of international exposure) affected gender relations in this region and, thus, demonstrates the fruitfulness of a feminist perspective to open society in theory and practice. With the chapter in this volume, Fábián once again seeks to build a bridge between the literatures on feminism and open society.

Apart from Fábián's pioneering work, though, feminist engagements with the concept of open society have remained few and far between. It is to be hoped that future research will explore the complex relationship between these two traditions of thought in more detail.

Belonging and Identification in Open Society

The theme of feminism brings us up against the complex relationship between open society and what I would like to call "the problem of belonging and identification."[9] This problem has, in fact, three sides: The first is that rallying around collective identities such as gender, race, or the nation seems to throw us back to the "tribalism" that the original architects of open society sought to transcend. The second side of the problem, however, is that even open societies depend on common bonds and relationships that serve as a glue holding them together. Finally, open society's anti-authoritarian thrust, and its corresponding concern for the marginalized and oppressed, establishes a clear link to some forms of (so-called) identity politics.

The literature on open society finds it very difficult to get around this tripartite problem. With few exceptions, it has had precious little to say about (as noted) feminism or critical race theory. One of these exceptions is the aforementioned edited volume by Andrea Pitts and Mark Westmoreland, which brings Bergson into conversation with critical scholars of race and decolonial theory (2020). On the other side of the spectrum, we find Danny Frederick's scathing criticism in which he criticizes leftist identity politics through a Popperian lens as "the latest fashion for totalitarianism" (2019, 33).

In general, though, advocates of open society have paid more attention to nationalism. Particularly revealing in this context is a conversation (published in *Rethinking Open Society*) between Michael Ignatieff and Mark Lilla. Ignatieff admits that "an open society view of the world simply does not understand

---

9 The more common label, of course, is "identity politics." This term, however, suffers from several inconsistencies, which is why I prefer the terms "belonging" and "identification." What I mean here is that social and political relations are, for better or for worse, driven by the sentiment of belonging to, and identifying with, a specific group.

nationalism. For an open society credo, nationalism is almost exclusively negative" (2018, 21). For Lilla, this is a glaring blind spot of the open society ideal. Highly individualistic conceptions of open society simply turn a blind eye to the glue that holds societies together; thus, any conception of open society that neglects the fundamental human sentiments of belonging and identification is doomed to failure.[10] In his short essay "Popper's Return Engagement," Neil McInnes offers a similar, but perhaps even more radical, critique of Popper's conception of open society. In a passage worth quoting at length, McInnes eloquently expresses the gist of what might be called the communitarian critique of open society.

> A society as open and abstract as the one Popper sought sounds like a cold, draughty place to those of us who come still trailing clouds of partisan loyalty from the old closed society. Before every last one of us is divested of the attachments that made the old society cohesive and secure, we would have to undergo a moral transformation not far short of that mystical rebirth that Henri Bergson saw at the dawn of his open society. In the meantime, while sincerely preferring the open over the closed polity, most people would nevertheless shrink from a society as open, as abstract and as impersonal as Popper . . . conceived of. (2002, no pagination)

The problems of belonging and identification will not go away. Of course, advocates of open society can choose to neglect it, as they often have done. But this will only strengthen the hand of those who want to "forget open society." A more constructive strategy is to face the problem head on. In this volume, Rachid Boutayeb offers an original defense of an "open migration" based on the work of Helmut Plessner. A key concept in his narrative is, indeed, "coldness" as an anthropological condition that distinguishes society from community and its "suffocating warmth." Coldness, in other words, can serve as an antidote to the "community radicalism" that undergirds radical contemporary movements as well as nationalism. Gregory Lobo, too, takes on the problem of nationalism in his chapter. Based on a careful engagement with Karl Popper, who rejected nationalism as a "romantic utopian idea," Lobo portrays nationalism as a dangerous form of identity politics in which the individual is subjugated to the collective. But Lobo's argument "against identity" is also inspired by Popper's famous aversion to "essentialism" and the idea that "to claim an identity is,

---

10 To avoid misunderstandings, Lilla has long been a critic of "identity politics" (see Lilla 2018). Liberals, he argues, should focus on what unites them rather than on what separates them. In the conversation with Ignatieff, Lilla advocates the development of a "healthy nationalism," based on the idea that "if liberals do not present a view of national attachment and affirm it, someone else will. We, liberal democrats, need to be able to articulate why attachment matters" (2018, 21–22).

essentially, to essentialize oneself." As a consequence, he insists that there is no identity appropriate to open society.

Digital Technology and Public Emergencies

A burgeoning literature has evolved that brings the concept of open society together with digital technologies, big data, or surveillance. A considerable chunk of this literature is devoted to "transparency" as a fundamental ingredient of an open society (Holzner and Holzner 2006; Taylor and Kelsey 2016). One of the most fascinating pieces that brings open society together with the developing global surveillance regime is Ian Hosein's "Transforming Travel and Border Controls: Checkpoints in the Open Society" (2005). This article vividly describes the post-9/11 travel policies that have increased the collection of information and surveillance of individuals to an unprecedented level. Hosein's implicit argument is that 9/11 created a permanent state of exception in which measures implemented to combat terrorism are here to stay; and they do not target only terrorists but each and every one of us. It is important, though, not to miss the subtlety of Hosein's argument: it is not so much the existence of these measures, he argues, but the lack of public deliberation that challenges the open society. What characterizes an open society, according to Hosein, is not so much the result achieved through deliberation but the process itself:

> I am not calling for deliberation in the hope of coming to a consensus through some political process, I am calling for deliberation for the sake of deliberation. We need opposing views, not only because it may lead to better policy but also because it leads to public discourse. And the lack of public discourse was the first and greatest casualty in this new security environment. (2005, 620)

Hosein's article touches upon two—often intertwined—themes: digital technology and public emergencies. This volume features two discussions that at least touch upon the transformative role of technology in modern societies. In her contribution, Anna Eva Grutza asks how Karl Popper's criticism of certain social scientific methods relates to the work of intelligence services and, more broadly, the role of secrets in supposedly open societies. Bringing Popper's work into dialogue with the sociologies of Edward Shils, Grutza critically interrogates the unquestioned value of transparency that characterizes the relevant open society literature and brings to the fore the difficult balancing act of, on the one hand, acknowledging the importance of secrecy for the proper functioning of a state, and, on the other, taking into account the dangers this secrecy poses for an open society. Ultimately, then, Grutza's contribution seeks to demonstrate that reflecting upon and safeguarding the values of an open society points to important matters of futurity, which might help us to venture beyond secrecy and scientific prophecy.

The second theme can be dubbed "public emergencies." There is very little literature that asks the question if, and to what degree, societies can remain "open" during public emergency situations. Presumably, this blind spot of the literature has to do with the bad reputation of the state of emergency, which was most famously portrayed by Carl Schmitt as a tool in the repertoire of authoritarian sovereigns and later lambasted as such by thinkers like Giorgio Agamben. But Covid-19 has, of course, brought this question into sharper relief. One attempt to address this problem is Michael Esfeld's recent essay on open society and Covid-19. Drawing on Popper, Esfeld argues that the discourse around, and measures taken against, Covid-19 (as well as climate change) is incompatible with the idea of open society. Today's fear-mongering elites, in fact, have a lot in common with Popper's "enemies of the open society" because they "claim to possess knowledge of a common good" (2021, no pagination). Ultimately, the main point of Esfeld's essay is that "the totalitarianism of all-encompassing control, into which even liberally conceived states and societies can slide if one allows negative externalities to be defined so arbitrarily that in the end everyone with all their actions comes under general suspicion of harming others" (2021, no pagination). In this volume, Tarun Weeramanthri challenges this view. Drawing on the works of Karl Popper, Antonio Gramsci, and Jürgen Habermas, Weeramanthri rejects the idea that open society cannot acknowledge public emergencies. Weeramanthri, a public health expert, argues that in cases such as Covid-19, a delicate balancing act that takes into account both the necessity of governmental interaction and the importance of individual rights in counteracting the crisis is necessary. Against one-dimensional assessments, he insists that in public emergency situations both intervention and non-intervention come at a (heavy) price. The important task is to communicate the complexity of these cases more clearly and openly to avoid counterproductive and dangerous backlashes. Equally important, Covid-19—the "most modern of morality tales"—should be interpreted as an impetus to open up the discipline of Public Health beyond its roots in the biomedical establishment and toward an engagement with other disciplines, especially political philosophy and sociology.

The Organization of the Book

Following this introduction, the book consists of fourteen chapters, arranged in two major parts. Part I is entitled "Philosophical and Theoretical Perspectives on Open Society" and features Thom Scott-Phillips's "Human Nature and the Open Society," Rachid Boutayeb's "In Praise of Coldness," Gregory Lobo's "Against Identity," Gazela Pudar Draško and Predrag Krstić's "Empirical Embodiment of Critical Rationalism," Piers Turner's "Open Society as an Achievement," Avery White's "Nozick's Meta-Utopia as an Open Society," Andrea Timár's "Hannah Arendt in the Literature Classroom," and Jean-Louis Fabiani's "Can Bergson's Definition of Open Society Be Useful Today?"

Part II is entitled "National and Regional Perspectives on Open Society" and features Katalin Fábián's "The Gender of Illiberalism," Kenneth Ka-Lok Chan's "Open Society Contested," Lyubomir Terziev's "Sorosoids," Nwankwo Nwaeizeigwe's "An African Background to the Open Society," Anna Grutza's "Imagining the Future of Intelligence in Open Societies," and Tarun Weeramanthri's "Open Society in Crisis."

It is to be hoped that this structure helps to establish a certain coherence of the volume as a whole while, at the same time, reflecting the underlying vision of the book as a genuinely interdisciplinary and global effort to unlock the potential of the open society idea in theory and practice. As such, this structure should not be seen as a watertight demarcation. The reader will surely notice that chapters in the "philosophical and theoretical perspectives" part often venture into questions of practical relevance, and that contributions to the "national and regional perspectives" part strive for theoretical sophistication. Nonetheless, the structure of the volume and the arrangement of individual chapters will, I hope, bring to the fore the red thread that runs through the book and ensure its coherence and readability.

Conclusion: Challenges Ahead

The terrain of open society is—and will remain—contested. But the idea is not empty. A commitment to genuine human plurality and diversity, an aversion to all forms of authoritarian domination, a cosmopolitan conviction of the equal worth of individuals, a rejection of narrow ("tribal") attachments to collectives and uncritical groupthink—these beliefs lie at the heart of the open society concept. Advocates of open society also firmly believe in the value of open discussion and deliberation. Thom Scott-Phillips's chapter in this volume is a testament to this conviction. Bringing together evolutionary and cognitive perspectives with the social sciences, Phillips describes the human mind as a "fundamentally social mind," which allows him to defend the argument that "open discussion works." That is, relative to other forms of group decision-making, conclusions reached through open discussion are more likely to balance the interests of all parties and generate a number of features that defend against closed and populist ways of thinking. These include exposure to diverse perspectives, equality of deliberative opportunity, deliberative transparency, and the production of shared knowledge. Yet, the challenge, as he rightly emphasizes, is: How can we recreate these dynamics in the modern world, where large institutions and complex media can undermine these core features of open discussion? While Phillips proposes a model of randomly chosen citizens to deliberate on the laws and institutions that should govern them, this will remain a core challenge for advocates of open society. How do we build open society institutions?

A slightly different challenge is learning to live with and in an open society. One of the features that distinguishes Popper's conception of the open society from others is its resolute anti-utopianism. Open societies, Popper argues, are haunted by a "strain of civilization" that renders them insecure and uncomfortable. It is true that many commentators—including those who seek to advocate Popper's conception of open society—miss this point. Thus, Mark Notturno rightly admonishes that "many people who regard themselves as sympathetic to Popper's idea of open society seem to … regard open society as something warm, fuzzy, and comforting. But this … is not the way in which Popper thought about it … He certainly did not regard it as a utopia" (2014, 119–120). Advocates of open society would do well to pay heed to the "strain of civilization." Doing so raises the question: How can (and should) we deal with the uncertainties, inefficiencies, and imperfections of an open society?

The third challenge is drawing boundaries. For if it is true that open society is not merely a euphemism for relativism, and if it is true that open society stands for certain values, the question is how to defend these values against those who reject and violate them. An open society, as Piers Turner argues in this book, does not create and sustain itself—it is an "achievement." But this achievement rests on a delicate balancing act: being committed to the values of human freedom and plurality, on the one hand, and acknowledging that these values are not absolute, on the other. Advocates of open society must go beyond formulaic expressions and worn-out clichés and develop new ideas of how to strike this balance. This entails the critical skill to exercise judgment. Andrea Timár's chapter in this volume, in fact, develops some intriguing ideas on this human faculty. Drawing on Hannah Arendt's concepts of "enlarged mentality," "solidarity," and "representative thinking," Timár argues that the literature classroom "allows for students to experience the workings of an open society." It is this setting that produces (literary) judgment based on processes of persuasion, negotiation, compromise, and agreement, and that can serve as a source of inspiration for creating and sustaining open societies. Still, one of the central challenges ahead remains: How do we draw boundaries in, without sacrificing the values of, an open society?[11]

Finally, the previous point circles us back to the importance of avoiding complacency. True, drawing boundaries is important. Yet, open society and its underlying values must not be used as ideological to stigmatize "otherness." Openness must not become dogmatic. And a belief in the self-evidence of one's own values is not a hallmark of the open society idea—it is its enemy. This aversion to self-evidence and dogmatism also includes the question of the continuing relevance of the open society idea. Hence our emphasis on the unresolved nature of open society.

---

11 A related important insight on this question comes from Piers Turner who reminds us—pace Gaus—that "if the line is drawn precisely at the point of protecting diversity itself, then there seems to be good reason to draw it from the perspective of open society, even if it is to the detriment of some."

Bibliography

Ansell-Pearson, Keith. 2018. *Bergson: Thinking Beyond the Human Condition*. New York: Bloomsbury Academic.
Armbrüster, Thomas, and Diether Gebert. 2002. "Uncharted Territories of Organizational Research: The Case of Karl Popper's Open Society and Its Enemies." *Organization Studies* 23 (2): 169–88.
Bárd, Petra. 2020. "Defending the Open Society against its Enemies." *Verfassungsblog*. https://verfassungsblog.de/defending-the-open-society-against-its-enemies/.
Baugh, Bruce. 2016. "The Open Society and the Democracy to Come: Bergson, Deleuze and Guattari." *Deleuze Studies* 10 (1): 352–66.
Bergson, Henri. 1977. *The Two Sources of Morality and Religion*. Notre Dame, IN: University of Notre Dame Press.
Bovens, Mark. 2020. "The Open Society and Its Challenges." In *The Open Society and Its Future*, edited by Mark Bovens and Marcus Düwell, 1:5–11. Institutions for Open Society. https://www.uu.nl/en/research/institutions-for-open-societies/ios-think-paper-series.
Connolly, William E. 1993. *The Terms of Political Discourse*. Revised ed. Princeton, NJ: Princeton University Press.
Deleuze, Gilles. 1990. *Bergsonism*. Translated by Hugh Tomlinson and Barbara Habberjam. Reissue ed. New York: Zone Books.
Esfeld, Michael. 2021. "The Open Society and Its New Enemies." *European Scientist*, April 29. https://www.europeanscientist.com/en/uncategorized/the-open-society-and-its-new-enemies/.
Fábián, Katalin. 2010. "Open Societies? Connections between Women's Activism, Globalization and Democracy in Central and Eastern Europe." *The International Journal of Diversity in Organizations, Communities, and Nations*: Annual Review 9 (6): 119–30.
Frederick, Danny. 2019. "Identity Politics, Irrationalism, and Totalitarianism: The Relevance of Karl Popper's Open Society." *Cosmos + Taxis* 6 (6–7): 33–42.
Gagyi, Ágnes. 2017. "Cultures of History Forum: Hungary's 'Lex CEU' and the State of the Open Society: Looking Beyond the Story of Democratic Revolutions." *Cultures of History Forum*, September 12. https://www.cultures-ofhistory.uni-jena.de/focus/lex-ceu/hungarys-lex-ceu-and-the-state-of-the-open-society-looking-beyondthe-story-of-democratic-revolutions/.
Gaus, Gerald. 2017. "The Open Society and its Friends." *The Critique*. January 15. http://www.thecritique.com/articles/open-society-and-its-friends/.
Germino, Dante. 1982. *Political Philosophy and the Open Society*. Baton Rouge and London: LSU Press.
Gaus, Gerald. 2021. *The Open Society and its Complexities*. Oxford: Oxford University Press.
Götz, Norbert, and Carl Marklund. 2014. *The Paradox of Openness: Transparency and Participation in Nordic Cultures of Consensus*. Leiden, NL: Brill.
Hayek, Friedrich. 1978. *Law, Legislation and Liberty, Volume 2: The Mirage of Social Justice*. Chicago, IL: University of Chicago Press.
Hayes, Calvin. 2008. *Popper, Hayek and the Open Society*. London: Routledge.
Holzner, Burkart, and Leslie Holzner. 2006. *Transparency in Global Change: The Vanguard of the Open Society*. Pittsburgh, PA: University of Pittsburgh Press.

Hosein, Ian. 2005. "Transforming Travel and Border Controls: Checkpoints in the Open Society." *Government Information Quarterly* 22 (4): 594–625.

Ignatieff, Michael. 2018a. "Conclusions: The Future of the Open Society Ideal." In *Rethinking Open Society: New Adversaries and New Opportunities*, edited by Michael Ignatieff and Stefan Roch, 329–36. Budapest: Central European University Press.

Ignatieff, Michael. 2018b. "Introduction." In *Rethinking Open Society: New Adversaries and New Opportunities*, edited by Michael Ignatieff and Stefan Roch, 1–18. Budapest: Central European University Press.

Jacobs, Struan, and Ian Tregenza. 2013. "Rationalism and Tradition: The Popper-Oakeshott Conversation." *European Journal of Political Theory* 13 (1): 3–24.

Lilla, Mark. 2018. "Open Society as an Oxymoron: A Conversation between Mark Lilla and Michael Ignatieff." In *Rethinking Open Society: New Adversaries and New Opportunities*, edited by Michael Ignatieff and Stefan Roch, 19–30. Budapest: Central European University Press.

McInnes, Neil. 2002. "Popper's Return Engagement: The Open Society in an Era of Globalization." *The National Interest*. https://nationalinterest.org/article/poppers-return-engagement-614.

Mullarkey, John. 2012. "Equally Circular: Bergson and the Vague Inventions of Politics." In *Bergson, Politics, and Religion*, edited by Alexandre Lefebvre and Melanie White, 61–74. Durham, NC: Duke University Press Books.

Notturno, Mark. 2014. *Hayek and Popper: On Rationality, Economism, and Democracy*. London: Routledge.

Pitts, Andrea, and Mark Westmoreland. 2019. *Beyond Bergson: Examining Race and Colonialism through the Writings of Henri Bergson*. New York: SUNY Press.

Popper, Karl R. 2020. *The Open Society and Its Enemies*. Princeton, NJ: Princeton University Press.

Shklar, Judith N. 1998. *Political Thought and Political Thinkers*. Edited by Stanley Hoffmann. Chicago, IL: University of Chicago Press.

Taylor, Roger, and Tim Kelsey. 2016. *Transparency and the Open Society: Practical Lessons for Effective Policy*. Bristol: Policy Press.

Voegelin, Eric. 1967. *Order and History. Volume I: Israel and Revelation*. Columbia, MO: University of Missouri Press.

PART I
Philosophical and Theoretical Perspectives on Open Society

PART I

1

HUMAN NATURE AND THE OPEN SOCIETY[1]

Thom Scott-Phillips[2]

Developed in the specific historical context of two world wars, the Holocaust, and the rise of totalitarian regimes, the notion of open society is an attempt to answer the question of how we can most effectively live together in large and modern environments. Although hard to pin down precisely, open society can be fairly characterized by a commitment to the rule of law, freedom of association and debate, free and fair elections, and the protection of individuals and minority groups. Henri Bergson, who first coined the expression, and Karl Popper, who became its most influential proponent, together offered a mix of moral, political, psychological, epistemic, and normative arguments in favor of these ideals (Bergson, 1935; Popper, 1952). Like all political philosophy, these arguments necessarily depend on assumptions—sometimes hidden and unexamined—about "human nature" (admittedly an imperfect term). Popper, for instance, argued in favor of his model of open society based in part on his analysis of humans as problem solvers, which he justified with reference to the theory of natural selection and what he believed it implied for humanity (Stokes, 1995; 2016).

Here I present an updated model of the panhuman cognitive phenotype ("human nature") based on the findings of modern evolutionary, cognitive, and anthropological sciences; and I summarize what I believe these findings imply for how to think about collective governance. Here, "collective" can be understood at any scale from, say, a local housing organization to, at the other extreme, the resolution of truly global problems such as climate change and international tax avoidance. In short, I aim to address the question: What does our contemporary understanding of human nature suggest about how to most effectively live together in large and complex societies? I shall describe the human mind as a primarily social mind, far more finely tuned to the challenges of living together

---

[1] I presented an early version of this chapter at the online conference, "Forget Open Society? Critical Conversations on a Contested Concept," which helped me to develop the ideas. Several people provided me with useful comments on subsequent drafts: thank you in particular to Réka Blazsek, Stefaan Blancke, Daniel Nettle, Christof Royer, Dan Sperber, and the Behaviour Group at the Centre for Philosophy of Natural & Social Science, London School of Economics.

[2] The author was financially supported by the European Research Council, under the European Union's Seventh Framework Programme (FP7/2007-2013)/ERC grant agreement no. 609819 (Somics project).

than we understood even two decades ago; and I shall conclude that we should embrace far more overtly open approaches to governance. Standard liberal demands made in the name of open society do not go far enough.

Human Minds Are Social Minds

Governance and decision-making depend upon harnessing human capacities for reason and reasoning; yet there seem to be two contradictory views about the nature of human reason. On the one hand, the intuitive and historically influential idea is that reason functions to help each of us get closer to the truth and hence make better decisions. This is often called Cartesianism, following René Descartes's arguments for the privileged status of reason as a source of knowledge and hence for the distinctiveness of humans as a species. On the other hand, everybody knows that we're prone to biases and logical fallacies that are in fact formally quite simple. The most well-known example is confirmation bias: the tendency to search for, interpret, favor, and recall information in a way that confirms or supports your prior beliefs, rather than evaluating information on its own objective merits. As author and comedian Jon Ronson put it, "Ever since I first learned about confirmation bias I've been seeing it everywhere." There are dozens of logical fallacies like this, documented in many laboratory studies and with substantial real-world consequences. This raises the paradox—if the function of reason is epistemic and objective, then why are we often poor at it, including when it matters to be right? If reason is so basic to what makes us distinctive as a species, its recurrent bugs and flaws are hard to explain.

The apparent contradiction is resolved by dropping the assumption that the function of reason is epistemic and replacing it with an interactive perspective (Mercier & Sperber, 2017). Put simply, reason is not individual and objective; it is social and subjective. Reasoning with yourself is certainly possible and useful (as Descartes exemplified), but it is an acquired skill akin to, say, lifting heavy weights. Particular individuals can become highly competent but they also have off-days; they are prone to regress if the skill is not practiced. Strong institutional support—schooling—is necessary if the skill is to become widespread and stable in the population at large. Pushing this analogy further, reasoning with others is like walking. Like lifting weights, walking entails moving something heavy (your own body), but in this case the task is easy and natural because our bodies are built to do this. Correspondingly, just as the science of anatomy has revealed how our bodies have features specialized for the task of walking—muscles, bones, joints, and their particular designs—the science of thinking and reason has revealed how adept we are at reasoning when the target is other people, and how our minds have many features specialized for the tasks of arguing persuading and for critiquing what others say. This is why two heads are better than one.

Many experimental studies show the consequences of these cognitive dispositions and skills. Crowds are wise, collectives are intelligent, discussion augments utilitarian outcomes, and a diversity of perspectives enhances group decision-making (e.g., Page, 2008; Bahrami et al., 2010; 2012; Navajas et al., 2018; Shi et al., 2019; O'Malley et al., 2020; Keshmirian et al., 2022; Mercier & Claidière, 2022; inter alia). This happens, fundamentally, because interaction and discourse "go with the grain" of how panhuman capacities of reason and thinking actually work (Mercier & Landemore, 2012). The conclusions reached through interaction are more likely to balance the interests of all parties, relative to other modes of group decision-making, not just because all voices can be represented, important as that is, but because interaction ensures critique from people who are not already positively invested in an argument or point of view. This does not mean that everybody agrees, of course, but it does mean that to achieve their own goals in interaction, people have to develop and present good arguments and counter-arguments, and they have to be skeptically minded toward what others say. These demands help guide open discussion toward truths, equitable outcomes, and wise decisions. These collective goods are epistemic by-products of individuals acting in their own interests in communication.

Adversarial systems of legal decision-making provide a real-world example of these dynamics in action. Argumentation and deliberation occur at two distinct stages. First, legal teams each make their own best possible case, and they critique each other's. Their professional duty is not to present their own individually reasoned analysis, but rather the best possible case for their own side and the best possible critique of the other. Second, a randomly selected jury debates the relative merits of the two sides. These juries are large enough to have some diversity of perspectives, but small enough that genuine interaction and debate can take place. In short, both stages of legal decision-making are open and adversarial, and this in turn facilitates effective decision-making. This system is proof-of-concept for how institutional design can recapitulate conditions of openness and hence harness human reason for an important social purpose—criminal justice—with significant levels of success and common consent. The film *12 Angry Men* idealizes and simplifies this dynamic but nevertheless makes graphic this essential truth (Hans, 2007).

This interactive perspective aligns with a broader trend in the cognitive and evolutionary sciences, in which almost all the most distinctive features of human minds are explained as adaptations to the challenges of living together. Compare humans with, say, orangutans.[3] As great apes, orangutans share a great deal of DNA with humans, but unlike us they live rather solitary lives, not much and not often interacting with others (except for mating and, for females, raising offspring). From an evolutionary perspective, this lifestyle has both advantages and disadvantages. The costs of group living are avoided: no disease transmission, no conflict, no competition for food. (What bliss!) But there are benefits to group living too, such as collective foraging, win-win cooperation, and group protection against the risks of predation; and orangutans have none

---

3 Thank you to Coralie Chevalier for highlighting this contrast to me.

of this either. Middle-ground strategies are possible (chimpanzees, gorillas), but as species humans and orangutans have made, you can say, almost opposite ecological choices. Orangutans live somewhat solitary lives, and their bodies and minds have evolved to fit that mode of living. Humans, in very stark contrast, have evolved to live an intensely social existence, in groups that are long-lasting, loosely defined, and comprised of both kin and non-kin. To be clear, the point here is not the trite observation that humans are sociable, true as that is. The point is that, just as the human skeleton is specifically adapted for the possibilities and the demands of bipedal locomotion, the human mind is specifically adapted for the possibilities, and also the risks and the dangers, of an intensely social existence.

One important implication of this "social minds" perspective is what it suggests about human "rationality." For most of human evolutionary history, the likelihood of repeated interactions has been high: meeting once suggests you will meet again. Most interactions have a past and most are likely to have a future. This social ecology generates a delicate balance of both competition and cooperation, and substantial evolutionary pressure for capacities and behaviors that make the most of this mix (Humphrey, 1976; Frith, 2007; Barrett et al., 2010; Barclay, 2013; Krasnow et al., 2013; Tomasello, 2014; Baumard, 2016; Ho et al., 2017; Engelmann & Tomasello, 2019; McCullough, 2020; Pietraszewski, 2020; Williams, 2021; Heintz & Scott-Phillips, in press; inter alia). The capacities include many obviously social phenomena, such as moral dispositions, persistent self-monitoring, distinctive forms of communication, an awareness of potential opportunities to exploit others, a fine-grained concern for reputation, and so on; but also cognitive capacities that on first blush do not appear to serve social functions at all. Reasoning is one example (see above); our memories of past events, and maybe even consciousness, might be others (Graziano, 2013; Mahr & Csibra, 2018). Under conditions of ordinary social interaction, all these cognitive capacities perform in broadly optimal, or "rational," ways.

So humans are not rational in the mode of Popper or Descartes, geared toward logic, truth, and problem-solving. Humans can do these things but they are not the essential functions of mind. Nor are humans rational in the mode of *Homo economicus*, geared toward utility calculus. What the modern sciences of the mind have revealed is that humans are rational in the mode of, for instance, Jürgen Habermas (e.g., Habermas, 1984), geared toward effectiveness in repeated interpersonal engagement with other humans.

Minimal Conditions of Open Engagement

Here is a representative list of some "minimal" descriptive features of ordinary social interaction. Imagine, if you wish, a large-ish gathering of acquaintances or some other occasion where most people know who most others are, even if they don't necessarily know each other well. *Open access*. People can enter and leave conversations at will, subject to norms of politeness. *Free participation*.

People can start to speak to anybody else. At the same time, no one is forced to speak. *Listener's Choice.* People can choose to listen to anybody else, and they can change who they are listening to at any time. They cannot listen to multiple speakers at the same time. *Transparency.* People can see who talks to who and establish the relevant speaker-listener relations. They may not be privy to the details of what is said, but the existence and manner of conversations is visible. *Reputational effects.* Individuals can gain or lose reputations as worthwhile communicators. Reputations affect whether and how others engage. There are also second- and higher-order reputational effects: individuals can discuss others' reputations, and by doing so they can lose or gain reputations themselves.

Of course, all of these features are matters of more-or-less rather than yes-no. In different social settings, they can be more or less present, and some can be more present than others; but broadly speaking, in a social ecology of recurrent meetings with many of the same individuals, the above features tend to present to some substantial degree. People can come and go, they can talk and they can listen, they can see who is talking to who, and the reputational consequences of bad faith engagement are potentially serious. To a first approximation, these are the social conditions in which the human mind evolved.

These conditions have, in turn, several effects that facilitate good faith ("open") debate and engagement with others (Speikermann, 2020). These effects echo many of the demands and characteristics of open society and associated concepts, such as "civil society," "public sphere" and the "marketplace of ideas." First, the above listed features *expose individuals to a diversity of information and perspectives*. People are exposed to views they cannot choose in advance, and which include perspectives that differ from their own. Second, these features *facilitate expressive opportunity for all*. Everybody has the opportunity, in principle, to have their views heard. Third, they *provide transparency of deliberation and discussion*. Everybody is able to observe conversations between others, witnessing who talks to who. Fourth, ordinary social interaction *enables the creation of common knowledge*. Public announcement is possible; and, crucially, not only do all individuals hear public announcements, they observe each other hearing at the same time. Fifth, these features *ensure a degree of accountability*. So long as there is real probability of future interaction on similar terms, good faith engagement is incentivized. Sixth, interaction *provides some insurance against fallibility*. People will always make individual mistakes of reason and thought, but they will be exposed to counter-arguments. And of course, these features all support, reinforce, and to some extent depend on one another.

The prediction that follows is that if minimal features of ordinary social interaction are maintained to some sufficiently high degree, that will generate conditions of open engagement, and these which will, in turn, lead to the effective use of human reason and the accepted resolution of contested issues.

Above I gave the real-world example of juries in criminal trials. Online discourse provides another example and a revealing comparison. There are substantial potential upsides to social media—in particular, people are exposed to a far larger diversity of views than they otherwise would be—but also major downsides. In many domains, such as on Facebook and Twitter, all five of the minimal features summarized above are subject to dilution, one way or another. Users are often not free to enter and leave conversations at will. They are not able to communicate with all others at will. Users usually cannot see with full transparency who talks to who, because some conversations are private and because public conversations are simply too numerous. By virtue of large audience bases, some users have far greater influence and power over discourse than do others. And reputational effects can be inconsequential in a number of ways: because users can be anonymous, because many infractions are barely visible, and because interactions are often one-shot or likely to be so. These compromises are all understandable given the nature of the technology, but in any case there is a danger that self-interest can become less aligned with good faith engagement (Speikermann, 2020). Discourse ethics can become less incentivized, discourse can become toxic, and power dynamics can have outsized effects: all with the net effect that cognitive capacities of deliberation and reason are not put to effective use. The revealing comparison is Wikipedia. Here there are established, standard practices of discourse that govern the process by which articles are created and edited. Crucially, these practices adhere closely to the minimal features of open engagement I summarized above (Hansen et al., 2009; Firer-Blaess, 2011). I suggest it is not a coincidence that Wikipedia has a relatively good reputation for veracity and authority. To be fully explicit, I am suggesting a causality. The recapitulation of minimal features of ordinary interaction generates a discourse ethics within Wikipedia which, aside from being more pleasant in and of itself, also makes more effective use of reason and critique. This leads in turn to more accuracy and greater balance.

There are parallels here with the making and unmaking of egalitarian society. One of the most intriguing things learned in 150 years of anthropological fieldwork is that small and isolated communities tend to have levels and forms of egalitarianism that surprise modern eyes (e.g., Cashdan, 1980; Woodburn, 1982; Wiessner, 2002; Boehm, 2009; Borgerhoff Mulder et al., 2009). There is, commonly, collective decision-making; a relative absence of resource inequality; little coercive political authority; widespread intolerance of unkindness; a pervasive ethos of affiliation extending beyond immediate kin; and an absence of dominance based on strength and other physical characteristics. (The story is of course not quite as simple as this summary, but this is correct to a first approximation.) Why so? The fast and easy explanation is that humans are somehow "naturally" or "innately" egalitarian, and that large and modern societies have corrupted us (e.g., Bregman, 2019; see, e.g., Hallpike, 2020; Buckner, 2020, for critical reviews). The more nuanced and astute conclusion is that when groups are small and many people know your name, then the greatest individual rewards come from attending to local norms of how to behave, maintaining your reputation, and valuing group harmony above all (Singh et al., 2017; von Rueden, 2020, Hooper et al., 2021). Put simply, fairness and egalitarianism can overlap with self-interest, and when they do then the chances of social harmony are increased, sometimes dramatically so. What I am suggesting is that what is true of egalitarianism is also likely to be true of good faith in discourse. It can be incentivized and disincentivized, depending on the social ecology.

The challenge for large and complex societies is that minimal features of open engagement are very easily compromised. In fact, openness is compromised as soon as two people hold a conversation in private, and that is obviously only the thin end of the wedge. As soon as groups become large and decisions more complex, some dilution of the ideals of open discourse becomes both necessary and inevitable. In sizable groups, effective decision-making demands some form of group organization, making fully open discourse impossible in practice. It is no longer straightforward to enter and leave conversations at will; people no longer have fully free rein to speak to or listen to whoever they wish; people can no longer see who speaks to who; and so on. With these conditions comes the risk that good faith engagement is no longer incentivized. To put the point in paradoxical and challenging form, open engagement may be most effective when community is relatively closed. This is the essential challenge for large and complex societies.

Open Engagement within and between Institutions

What models of governance create the most effective epistemological and normative frame for large, complex, modern societies? Popper's answer mirrored his philosophy of science, according to which hypotheses that are falsified are let go, those that resist falsification remain, and in such ways does scientific knowledge progress. This is in effect a Cartesian approach to scientific rationality, and Popper argued that open society can do a similar job for power and governance. "The fundamental problem of a rational political theory ... can be formulated as follows: how is the state to be constituted so that bad rulers can be got rid of without bloodshed, without violence?" Popper's answer was, in effect, falsificationism in the domain of power: "Government can be dismissed by a majority vote" (Popper, 1988). Following this logic to its conclusion, he argued in favor of two-party systems over proportional representation, on the grounds that only two-party systems provide decisive rejections, just as only compelling experiments provide decisive falsifications (ibid.). Revealingly, Popper also coined the expression "conspiracy theory" (Runciman, 2018). Conspiracies are ancient, of course: Popper's novelty was to add the word *theory*, a clear indication of the link he saw between the domains of science and politics.

Yet while important, this focus on Cartesian rationality is not sufficient as a description how science and politics actually work. Many scientists and philosophers of science have pointed out that very little science is strictly falsificationist. In particular, when hypotheses appear to be falsified scientists often do not reject them outright, but instead explore and articulate further, ad hoc arguments and additional theories, in order to accommodate the discrepancy;

and they are often right to do so. The same basic dynamics operate in democracies: elected representatives adapt when their stated values and policy positions are challenged by events. They too respond with new arguments and assertions. So in both domains counterevidence is most commonly met not with supposed ideal of falsification, but with counter-counter-argument; and what keeps people in check is not the systematic application of any particular method, but rather the collective judgment of the relevant community (on the role of community in science, see, e.g., Ziman, 1968; Barnes et al., 1996; Longino, 2001; Pigliucci & Boudry, 2013).

To be fully clear, I'm not trying to suggest that scientists have the same motivations and ethics as politicians. What I'm pointing out is the similarity in praxis. There are clearly important differences between these two spheres of human activity (Weber, 2004), but one thing they share is that when ideas are challenged neither politicians nor scientists reason in a purely Socratic way. Rather, they reason argumentatively, as we should expect given the ultra-social nature of human cognition (see above). This is especially so in the human sciences, where predictions can rarely be made at a level of precision that would facilitate a strictly falsificationist approach (unlike, for instance, physics; see Meehl, 1967). So Popper's model for the open society misleads in the same way that his philosophy of science does: both are too much predicated on a model of the mind as a Cartesian tool of analytical logic and problem-solving. This is not the natural mode of human rationality.

The most effective epistemological and normative frames for governance will be those that harness the social rationality for which our minds are finely equipped. More specifically, we should endeavor to recapitulate *at the level of institutions* the conditions of open engagement that we already know generate good faith engagement in the resolution of contested issues at the level of individuals (see, e.g., Szegőfi & Heintz, 2022). If this is possible, it should in turn generate the positive social effects of good faith engagement. Contemporary advocates of open society, following Popper, sometimes place special emphasis on the importance of inculcating a critical frame of mind among the population at large. This is a desirable ideal and I certainly do not discourage it, but it is less aligned with the dispositions and distinctive capacities of the human mind than the more interactive perspective that I am advocating here.

The standard demands of open society can be read as demands for minimal conditions of open engagement *between* institutions of governance and power:

> Power checks power … Parliamentary democracy forces executive authority to justify its measures before the adversarial scrutiny of a parliament. Judges bring the critical epistemology of law to the review of administrative and legal decisions. A free media referees the battle over public choice with a complex epistemology of scrutiny, driven by skepticism, scandal mongering, and profit seeking. Universities play their role in subjecting public claims to peer-reviewed research. These

institutions ... [together] create the epistemological frame in which a free society struggles its way toward the knowledge it needs, or the closure on debate it must accept, in order to chart its collective course into the future. This is how an open society actually operates. (Ignatieff, 2018, p.7)

So open societies, as traditionally conceived, entail a degree of interaction between institutions that have the effect—so the theory goes—of recapitulating minimal conditions of repeated ordinary interactions, and hence facilitating the positive effects of debate, argument, and reputation.

Habermas's notion of the "public sphere," and its potential role in governance, can be read as an extended version of this between-institution approach. Building on the insight that humans are highly competent, or "rational," with respect to ordinary social interaction, and looking for ways to empower the demos, Habermas advocated in favor of deliberative approaches to governance. In particular he argued for the development of a public sphere on a level with, and in deliberative dialogue with, the public institutions of an open society (Habermas, 1989). One repeated criticism of this approach has been that, even with the best will and intent, the public sphere cannot perform this role in actuality (e.g., Tully, 2008; Landemore, 2020). Without any formal powerbase or institutional structure, the public sphere is not able to take part in genuinely reciprocal dialogue with the formal institutions of modern nation-states; and without that foundation, the collective benefits of sincere deliberation cannot accrue.

Another means by which to harness the epistemic, normative, and emancipatory benefits of deliberation may be to focus on interaction not only *between* institutions but also *within* them. One important source of inspiration here is Elenor Ostrom's Nobel Prize-winning empirical work on the principles that best guide governance of the commons, which include in particular defined space for open discussion (Ostrom, 1990). More recently, citizens' assemblies and other forms of deliberative mini-publics have been given an active role within institutions of lawmaking and policy, with substantial real-world impact. These are jury-like bodies of randomly selected citizens, sufficiently diverse to be representative of the demos at large but also small enough in number to enable careful, open, and sincere discussion (Bächtiger et al., 2018).

One well-known and successful example is the 2018 Irish referendum on the legalization of abortion. The referendum was made possible by a preceding citizens' assembly in which one hundred randomly chosen citizens (stratified for region, gender, and age) met over the course of successive weekends to hear from relevant experts and deliberate how the abortion issue should be addressed. Direct comparison between these deliberations and corresponding debates in more traditional domains of political discourse (parliament, media) reveals the citizens' assembly to have had the deeper and more sophisticated discussion, with better grasp of the subject matter (Suiter et al., 2021). This is akin to the other real-world examples mentioned above: juries in criminal trials, and the comparison between Facebook and Wikipedia. Each case shows how minimal conditions of genuine open engagement make it possible for deliberation and debate to take place in conditions of broadly good faith, and hence to make more effective use of human capacities for reason and argument. (That is not to say that all participants will agree on all issues, of course.) In the case of the Irish abortion referendum, the deliberative context allowed the vote to take place in conditions of broadly common consent, and for its result to be enacted without unnecessary tearing at the fabric of Irish society (Suiter, 2018).

This within-institutions approach can—and, in my view, should—be pushed much further. Taken to its logical conclusion, open engagement within institutions of governance would not *complement* representative democracy, but *replace* it. This is the essential idea of "open democracy": to use public deliberation at *all* levels of government and governance, via the systematic use of deliberative mini-publics, selected at random and frequently rotated (Landemore, 2013; 2020; van Reybrouck, 2016). This overtly and radically open approach to governance is in contrast to technocracy, epistocracy, and other forms of rule by expert, which are sometimes advanced as possible solutions to the shortcomings of representative democracy, but which are necessarily more closed and less democratic forms of decision-making (Brennan & Landemore, 2021).

There are many types of argument in favor of this overtly and radically open approach (Dryzek et al., 2019). One is emancipatory: if democracy is rule by the demos, then should the demos not have some entitlement to rule? A second type of argument is that it would circumvent the strategic incentives that impact, often in very substantial ways (and sometimes in fraudulent ways), on representatives planning to stand for election and re-election. There are no such incentives if there is both sortition and rotation in the appointment of lawmakers. A third type of argument is epistemic and normative. Put simply, open democracy may be simply a superior method of lawmaking. Empowering all members of the demos equally, giving them all equal right of access to the deliberations that shape law and policy, may be the most effective means by which to resolve shared problems.

What I am suggesting is that the findings of cognitive science, anthropology, and other fields studying "human nature" reinforce all these arguments, by describing the deep evolutionary and cognitive reasons *why* deliberative approaches are especially effective. These fields have revealed the depths and extent of human social competence and rationality, and the conditions in which that competence is best exploited for the common good.

I know it is not realistic to believe our present seats of power will vote themselves out of existence anytime soon. Nor do not believe that voters familiar with present modes of democracy would all be at ease with a shift from voting to deliberation, on the abstract grounds that this would be a supposedly *more* democratic system. However, I do think the in-principle argument for these actions is compelling: that this is a fairer and also just better way to achieve desirable features of decision-making bodies, such as legitimacy, accountability, and effectiveness. At the very least, deliberative mini-publics should be studied, discussed, advocated for, and indeed put to use far more commonly and in far more wide-reaching ways than at present (Dryzek et al., 2019). This would allow incremental progress, by enriching our understanding of when and how deliberation is especially effective and by advertising its potential to the public at large.

This far greater openness in governance might, furthermore, provide a compelling response to reasonable conservative concerns. The essential conservative worry is that advocates of open society mistake a rare historical achievement—social conditions in which freedom of association and opinion are secure—for the default nature of humanity (e.g., Scruton, 1980; Oakeshott, 1991; Fawcett, 2020). These freedoms are in fact dependent on secular law and, on conservative analyses, some shared identity provided by neighborhood, language, culture, and history. A society that loosens those ties too freely risks undermining itself, by unwittingly placing into danger the tacit forms of accountability and trust that bind people and hence secure good faith engagement in the resolution of contested issues. "Conservatism is not against openness and change; it is concerned with the conditions that must be kept in place if those things are to be possible" (Scruton, 2018, p.46). I suggest that in addition to its various epistemic and other decision-making benefits, deliberation and open democracy address this worry by proxy. In addition to its effectiveness as a means of collective governance, *open discussion can also renew and rejuvenate the fragile community relations that conservatives so value*. Citizens who have taken part in deliberative mini-publics often reflect that the human engagement factor allowed them to see and understand perspectives that they otherwise would not have, even with the best will and the full availability of relevant facts. Put simply, the social ties that bind people, which are inevitably loosened in large and complex societies, can be continually retightened by engagement with other members of the demos in the serious act of open governance.

Conclusion

A great deal of thinking and argument about possible links between human nature and the structure of society, from Plato's *Republic* onward, describes desired outcomes. What I am advocating for here is instead a type of process,[4] in which randomly chosen members of a community deliberate on what laws and social structures are most suitable for them. This process is more open even than traditional demands made in the name of open society: more open in terms of the process of lawmaking and more open in terms of who is granted power. I am suggesting, moreover, that this demand for greater openness should be valued not just on moral and emancipatory grounds, but on practical grounds too. Put simply, open discussion works. It facilitates the most effective use of distinctly

---

4 Thank you to Daniel Nettle for pointing out to me this contrast between outcome and process.

human cognitive skill. It should be harnessed at all levels of governance and collective decision-making.

Bibliography

Bächtiger, A., J. S. Dryzek, J. Mansbridge, and M. Warren, eds. 2018. *The Oxford Handbook of Deliberative Democracy*. Oxford University Press.
Bahrami, B., K. Olsen, P. E. Latham, A. Roepstorff, G. Rees, and C. D. Frith. 2010. "Optimally Interacting Minds." *Science* 329 (5995): 1081–85.
Bahrami, B., K. Olsen, D. Bang, A. Roepstorff, G. Rees, and C. Frith. 2012. "Together, Slowly but Surely: The Role of Social Interaction and Feedback on the Build-up of Benefit in Collective Decision-making." *Journal of Experimental Psychology: Human Perception and Performance* 38 (1): 3–8.
Barclay, P. 2013. "Strategies for Cooperation in Biological Markets, Especially for Humans." *Evolution & Human Behavior* 34 (3): 164–75.
Barnes, B., D. Bloor, and J. Henry. 1996. *Scientific Knowledge: A Sociological Analysis*. University of Chicago Press.
Barrett, H. C., L. Cosmides, and J. Tooby. 2010. "Coevolution of Cooperation, Causal Cognition and Mindreading." *Communicative & Integrative Biology* 3 (6): 522–24.
Baumard, N. 2016. *The Origins of Fairness: How Evolution Explains Our Moral Nature*. Oxford University Press.
Bergson, H. 1935. *The Two Sources of Morality & Religion*. Macmillan.
Boehm, C. 2009. *Hierarchy in the Forest: The Evolution of Egalitarian Behavior*. Harvard University Press.
Borgerhoff Mulder, M., et al. 2009. "Intergenerational Wealth Transmission and the Dynamics of Inequality in Small-scale Societies." *Science* 326: 682–88.
Bregman, R. 2019. *Humankind: A Hopeful History*. Bloomsbury.
Brennan, J., and H. Landemore. 2021. *Debating Democracy: Do We Need More Or Less?* Oxford University Press.
Buckner, W. 2020. Book review: *Humankind* by Rutger Bregman (blogpost).
Cashdan, E. A. 1980. "Egalitarianism Among Hunters and Gatherers." *American Anthropologist* 82(1): 116–20.
Dryzek, J. S., A. Bächtiger, S. Chambers, J. Cohen, J. N. Druckman, A. Felicetti, J. S. Fishkin, D. M. Farrell, A. Fung, A. Gutmann, H. Landemore, J. Mansbridge, S. Marien, M. A. Neblo, S. Niemeyer, M. Setälä, R. Slothuus, J. Suiter, D. Thompson, and M. E. Warren. 2019. "The Crisis of Democracy and the Science of Deliberation." *Science* 363 (6432): 1144–46.
Engelmann, J. M., and M. Tomasello. 2019. "Children's Sense of Fairness as Equal Respect." *Trends in Cognitive Sciences* 23 (6): 454–63.
Fawcett, E. 2020. *Conservatism: The Fight for a Tradition*. Princeton University Press.
Firer-Blaess, S. 2011. "Wikipedia: Example for a Future Electronic Democracy? Decision, Discipline and Discourse in the Collaborative Encyclopaedia." *Studies in Social & Political Thought* 19: 131–54.
Frith, C. D. 2007. "The Social Brain?" *Philosophical Transactions of the Royal Society, B* 362: 671–78.
Graziano, M. 2013. *Consciousness & The Social Brain*. Oxford University Press.
Habermas, J. 1984. *The Theory of Communicative Action, Volume I: Reason & the Rationalization of Society*. Translated by T. McCarthy. Beacon.

Habermas, J. 1989. *The Structural Transformation of the Public Sphere*. Translated by T. Burger and F. Lawrence. MIT Press.

Hallpike, C. R. 2020. "A Sceptical Review of Bregman's *Humankind: A Hopeful History*." *New English Review*.

Hans, V. P. 2007. "Deliberation and Dissent: *12 Angry Men* Versus the Empirical Reality of Juries." *Chicago-Kent Law Review* 82 (2): 579–89.

Hansen, S., N. Berente, and K. Lyytinen. 2009. "Wikipedia, Critical Social Theory, and the Possibility of Rational Discourse." *The Information Society* 25 (1): 38–59.

Heintz, C., and T. Scott-Phillips. accepted. "Expression Unleashed: The Evolutionary & Cognitive Foundations of Human Communication." *Behavioral & Brain Sciences*.

Ho, M. K., J. MacGlashan, M. L. Littman, and F. Cushman. 2017. "Social is Special: A Normative Framework for Teaching With and Learning From Evaluative Feedback." *Cognition* 167: 91–106.

Hooper, P. L., H. S. Kaplan, and A. V. Jaeggi. 2021. "Gains to Cooperation Drive the Evolution of Egalitarianism." *Nature Human Behaviour* 5: 847–56.

Humphrey, N. K. 1976. "The Social Function of Intellect." In *Growing Points in Ethology*, edited by P. P. G. Bateson and R. A. Hinde, 303–17. CUP.

Ignatieff, M. 2018. "Introduction." In *Rethinking Open Society: New Adversaries & New Opportunities*, edited by M. Ignatieff and S. Roch, 1–16. CEU Press.

Keshmirian, A., O. Deroy, and B. Bahrami. 2022. "Many Heads are More Utilitarian Than one." *Cognition* 220: 104965.

Krasnow, M. M., A. W. Delton, J. Tooby, and L. Cosmides. 2013. "Meeting now Suggests we Will Meet Again: Implications for Debates on the Evolution of Cooperation." *Scientific Reports* 3: 1–8.

Landemore, H. 2013. *Democratic Reason: Politics, Collective Intelligence, and the Rule of the Many*. Princeton University Press.

Landemore, H. 2020. *Open Democracy: Reinventing Popular Rule for the Twenty-First Century*. Princeton University Press.

Longino, H. E. 2001. *The Fate of Knowledge*. Princeton University Press.

Mahr, J., and G. Csibra. 2018. "Why do we Remember? The Communicative Function of Episodic Memory." *Behavioral & Brain Sciences* 41: e1.

McCullough, M. E. 2020. *The Kindness of Strangers: How a Selfish Ape Invented a New Moral Code*. Simon & Schuster.

Meehl, P. E. 1967. "Theory-testing in Psychology and Physics: A Methodological Paradox." *Philosophy of Science* 34 (2): 103–15.

Mercier, H., and N. Claidière. 2022. "Does Discussion Make Crowds any Wiser?" *Cognition*, 222, 104912.

Mercier, H., and H. Landemore. 2012. "Reasoning is for Arguing: Understanding the Successes and Failures of Deliberation." *Political Psychology* 33 (2): 243–58.

Mercier, H. and D. Sperber. 2017. *The Enigma of Reason*. Harvard University Press.

Navajas, J., T. Niella, G. Garbulsky, B. Bahrami, and M. Sigman. 2018. "Aggregated Knowledge from a Small Number of Debates Outperforms the Wisdom of Large Crowds." *Nature Human Behaviour* 2 (2): 126–32.

Oakeshott, M. 1991. *Rationalism in Politics & Other Essays*. Liberty Fund.

O'Malley, E., D. M. Farrell, and J. Suiter. 2020. "Does Talking Matter? A Quasi-Experiment Assessing the Impact of Deliberation and Information on Opinion Change." *International Political Science Review* 41 (3): 321–34.

Ostrom, E. 1990. *Governing The Commons: The Evolution of Institutions for Collective Action*. Cambridge University Press.
Page, S. 2008. *The Difference: How the Power of Diversity Creates Better Groups, Firms, Schools & Societies*. Princeton University Press.
Pietraszewski, D. 2020. "The Evolution of Leadership: Leadership and Followership as a Solution to the Problem of Creating and Executing Successful Coordination and Cooperation Enterprises." *The Leadership Quarterly* 31 (2): 101299.
Pigliucci, M., and M. Boudry, eds. 2013. *Philosophy of Pseudoscience: Reconsidering the Demarcation Problem*. University of Chicago Press.
Popper, K. 1952. *The Open Society & Its Enemies*. 2nd ed. Routledge.
Popper, K. 1988. "The Open Society and its Enemies Revisited." *The Economist* 23: 19–22.
Runciman, D. 2018. "Closed Minds: The Rise of Conspiracy Thinking." *Times Literary Supplement* 6041: 26–28.
Scruton, R. 1980. *The Meaning of Conservatism*. Penguin.
Scruton, R. 2018. "The Open Society From a Conservative Perspective." In *Rethinking Open Society: New Adversaries & New Opportunities*, edited by M. Ignatieff and S. Roch, 31–46. CEU Press.
Shi, F., M. Teplitskiy, E. Duede, and J. A. Evans. 2019. "The Wisdom of Polarized Crowds." *Nature Human Behaviour* 3 (4): 329–36.
Singh, M., and L. Glowacki. 2022. "Human Social Organization During the Late Pleistocene: Beyond the Nomadic-egalitarian Model." *Evolution & Human Behavior*, 43(5), 418–431.
Singh, M., R. Wrangham, and L. Glowacki. 2017. "Self-interest and the Design of Rules." *Human Nature* 28: 457–80.
Sperber, D., F. Clément, C. Heintz, O. Mascaro, H. Mercier, G. Origgi, and D. Wilson. 2010. "Epistemic Vigilance." *Mind & Language* 25(4): 359–93.
Spiekermann, K. 2020. "Why Populists do Well on Social Media." *Global Justice: Theory Practice Rhetoric* 12 (2): 50–71.
Stokes, G. 1995. "Politics, Epistemology and Method: Karl Popper's Conception of Human Nature." *Political Studies* 43 (1): 105–23.
Stokes, G. 2016. "Popper and Habermas: Convergent Arguments for a Postmetaphysical Universalism." In *The Cambridge Companion to Popper*, edited by J. Shearmur and G. Stokes, 318–51. Cambridge University Press.
Suiter, J. 2018. "Deliberation in Action: Ireland's Abortion Referendum." *Political Insight* 9(3): 30–32.
Suiter, J., D. M Farrell, C. Harris, and P. Murphy. 2021. "Measuring Epistemic Deliberation on Polarized Issues: The Case of Abortion Provision in Ireland." *Political Studies Review*. 14789299211020909.
Szegőfi, A., and C. Heintz. 2022. "Institutions of Epistemic Vigilance: The Case of the Press." *Social Epistemology*. 36(5): 613–628.
Tomasello, M. 2014. "The Ultra-social Animal." *European Journal of Social Psychology* 44(3): 187–94.
Tully, J. 2008. "To Think and act Differently: Comparing Critical Ethos and Critical Theory." In *Public Philosophy in a New Key, Volume 1: Democracy & Civic Freedom*, 71–132. Cambridge University Press.
van Reybrouck, D. 2016. *Against Elections: The Case For Democracy*. Bodley Head.
von Rueden, C. 2020. "Making and Unmaking Egalitarianism in Small-scale Human Societies." *Current Opinion in Psychology* 33: 167–71.

Weber, M. 2004. *The Vocation Lectures*. Hackett Publishing.
Wiessner, P. 2002. "The Vines of Complexity: Egalitarian Structures and the Institutionalization of Inequality among the Enga." *Current Anthropology* 43 (2): 233–69.
Williams, D. 2021. "Socially Adaptive Belief." *Mind & Language* 36 (3): 333–54.
Woodburn, J. 1982. "Egalitarian Societies." *Man* 17 (3): 431–51.
Ziman, J. M. 1968. *Public Knowledge: An Essay Concerning the Social Dimension of Science*. Cambridge University Press.

2

IN PRAISE OF COLDNESS: THE OPEN NEIGHBORHOOD AND ITS ENEMIES

Rachid Boutayeb

> Ever tried. Ever failed. No matter. Try again. Fail again. Fail better.
> —*Samuel Beckett*

The present chapter is a philosophical plea for an *open neighborhood*. By this, I mean a *neighborhood* that decides for the *ethos of society* and against the temptations of the *community*. Moreover, this plea is also to be thought of as an attempt to define the *political ethics* of *good neighborhood*, which today is met with great interest on a local as well as on a global level, and which I understand as a defense of *coldness* in Helmuth Plessner's (1892–1985) and Karl Popper's (1902–1994) view—but a *coldness* which is to be understood as a defense of, and not a critique of, modern society. It cannot be identified with the negative concept of *coldness* that Marx and Engels in *The Communist Manifesto* criticized, in which the two philosophers speak of the "icy water of egotistical calculation," or with Adorno's critique of "bourgeois coldness."[1]

How can *neighborhood* be thought of in a society that is characterized by the plurality of its cultures and memberships or by its *coldness*? This question leads directly to one of the most central themes of German sociology, social philosophy, and philosophical anthropology of the end of the nineteenth century and the beginning of the twentieth century, namely that of *community* and *society*. Certainly, an exploration of the classical approaches to the subject cannot be done here. Nevertheless, the social-philosophical work of the German philosopher Helmuth Plessner, namely his book *The Limits of Community* with his sharp criticism of *social radicalism*, shows an unexpected topicality and richness. Plessner uses in this book two times the notion "Coldness" and one time the adjective "cold." Concerning the coldness, he uses it against the "utopian avantgarde of his time," namely against the *community of blood* represented in nationalism and the *community of idea* incarned from communism; both struggle against the spirit of society, or, in Plessner's language, against "a certain Coldness in human relationships" (Plessner 1999, 74), and both are unable to understand it, because they still belong with their belief to the close logic of

---

1 Theodor W. Adorno, *Erziehung zur Mündigkeit: Vorträge und Gespräche mit Hellmut Becker 1959 bis 1969*, 1971, p. 101.

community. In another place, Plessner tries to draw the spirit of the politic in the modern time, which we cannot fellow "without the cold air of diplomacy and the logic of the public sphere, without these masks of the aura and of artificiality" (ibid., 160). And despite the fact that Plessner rarely uses the notion of coldness, he uses instead many other notions with the same meaning, such as "artificiality," "masks," "the spirit of play," "distance," "diplomacy," or "diplomatic game." All these notions express the end of a world and a world view; all of them describe the new development and transformations in the modern society.

Community and *Society*

Undoubtedly, *coldness* has nothing to do with the *community*, which represents a warm, familiar, and lasting coexistence from cradle to grave. Ferdinand Tönnies (1855–1936) describes the *community* in comparison with *society* as follows: "Community means genuine, enduring life together, whereas society is a transient and superficial thing. Thus, *Gemeinschaft* must be understood as a living organism, while *Gesellschaft* is a mechanical aggregate and artefact" (Tönnies 2001, 19). He talks about three forms of community—that of blood (kinship), that of place (neighborhood), and that of spirit (friendship). The three are interwoven. One notices that in this description of community, neighborhood is dependent on place, which makes its realization difficult, if not impossible, in the context of a decentered society. Yet the same is true for friendship as for kinship. They lose their traditional aspects and gain new ones, such as the relationship within the family between parents and children, or between man and woman. The relationship lives on beyond the community, but the rules of the game have changed. The same is true for the neighborhood, which today is more realized outside the local community, and which today is not to be understood in the mode of the traditional "oughtness," but rather as an open experiment that also brings unexpected things. The "oughtness" (*Das Sollen*), the Kantian one, which condemns man to divisiveness, at the same time blocks his way to reality; in its defense of a non-worldly morality, it borders on radicalism (Haucke 2016, 112). This is another reason why today it is necessary to understand the neighborhood beyond the "oughtness" and its zeal, by which I mean beyond an unworldly ethics or religiosity and to liberate us from a "desire for a meaning beyond the rules of the game" of society (ibid., 182).

The negative critique of society as a form of life based on the principle of purpose, as is the case with Tönnies, or the critique of the process of modernization and its dark sides, as is the case with Georg Simmel and Max Weber, cannot hide the fact that the individual will only discover his/her individuality within society, only when he/she has freed his flesh from the flesh of the community and ceased to be unconscious instruments in the hands of an overpowering fate, as Popper explains it in his critique of the totalitarian thinking and its determinist conception of history. This is also a reason why Plessner does not adopt the tragic image of classical German sociology. On the contrary, he sees in the community and its apologists the great danger that threatens modern society. Following his meditations on *The Limits of Community*, I try to rethink neighborhood's relationships in a multicultural society. Certainly, the neighborhood in its original sense is identified with spatial proximity. It is a social interaction that presupposes the commonality of the place of residence; it is discovered, following Ferdinand Tönnies, as a community of place (Tönnies 2001, 28). The members of this neighborhood share more than the common place—they remain trapped in a logic of the same and identity. No stranger belongs or can belong to this community, even if Tönnies does not say a word about it. It can be understood as an extended kinship. The destiny of today's neighborhood(s), however, in a modern society that has freed itself from the bonds of a homogeneous community, takes place beyond place and blood as well as from a common spirit. Nowadays, the neighborhood in the modern city requires a new definition. Certainly, it still depends on a place, but it is not the place of community, but a *secular, rhizomatic* place—a place *without identity*.

Are neighbors condemned to be similar? Or should we today, in view of the great, ongoing social changes, understand and learn to practice the neighborhood differently? The social conditions have changed massively, and the neighbors are no longer embedded in the same circumstances; they do not necessarily belong to the same social class or the same culture or worldview. Yet, does this mean that the neighborhood, which used to be an obligation in the village community, has become a choice today? We do not choose our neighbors, at least we who make up most of the urban population. The neighborhood living together resembles an adventure, even if it always remains a (social) fate!

The concept of place has now changed. Humans are no longer embedded in a single place. Through the communications revolution, they live in several places at the same time. The virtual has become part of our reality; it makes up a large part of it today. Perhaps we do not always live at the same time if we believe Paul Virilio's analyses (1977). Some of us already dream of a life in space and of other or no neighbors! Meanwhile, time and place threaten to become superfluous categories, which say little of today's reality and will perhaps disappear soon, in view of rapid technological developments. The divided humanity of capitalism is becoming more and more a single fate.

Open Neighborhood

What I understand by neighborhood today are the open relations that have arisen between the different cultures, religions, or worldviews in the context of migration. Therefore, it is no longer a local or communal neighborhood, but an *open neighborhood*—albeit one that demands more from us than that of community. So, by an *open neighborhood* I mean a coexistence that is no longer dependent on place and belonging. In a plural society, as Habermas points out, "the people" appears only in the plural (Habermas, 1994, 607), and the identity of the people, as Claude Lefort notes, is never a completed one. According to him, "Democracy inaugurates the experience of an ungraspable, uncontrollable society in which the people will be said to be sovereign, of course, but whose identity will constantly be open to question, whose identity will remain forever latent" (Lefort 1986, 303–4). Neighborhood today is to be understood in the plural, as an open process that brings with it the unexpected and the unknown. It is a matter here of a *free* and not a *total membership*, which only allows and propagates the path of total assimilation and, still, raves about an imagined *leading culture*, with foaming at the mouth and cold sweat.

Neighborhood means learning to live as a stranger, that is, beyond any *logic* of *fraternocracy*. Rightly, Helmuth Plessner pleads for a society based on distance and coldness. It is only in the distance implied by a cold spirit, free "from a supra-ordered source of being" (Plessner 1999, 87) that the individual can realize itself as an individual. The norm of distance, that is, of coldness, is a central aspect of modern social relations. It is what makes these relationships work. In other words: the concept of coldness is, in Plessner's sense, as an antidote to the communal and its conquering, advocating, and inauthentic warmth. Axel Honneth, in his lecture on Plessner's work, explains that the ideological attacks of the community on society, or what Plessner calls social radicalism, can be understood as social pathology (Honneth 1994, 35–37). Plessner defends the *public sphere*, which we can understand as a synonym for Popper's concept of *open society*, against the totalitarian social policy that destroys the individual: "The public sphere begins where love and blood-based obligations ends. It is the epitome of possible relationships between an indeterminate number and type of persons and exists as an eternally nontranscendent open horizon that surrounds the community" (Plessner 1999, 99).

One thing must be added here, namely that we do not freely choose our neighbors, but we do choose the neighborhood, yet always on the condition that we live in a democratic state. In totalitarianism, man has no neighbors or no neighborhood, but only a forced neighborhood (Evans and Schahadat 2012, 26). Hélène L'Heuillet, the French philosopher who has written extensively about neighborhood, is of the opinion that "the neighbor has replaced the relative," and at the same time she notes, based on the results of an empirical study, that 80 percent of French people do not want neighbors and prefer to live alone (2016, 8). This proves that the process of atomization has reached pathological dimensions. This is also why it is important today to learn and discover neighborhood again and differently, but, above all, not as L'Heuillet understands it, as a *"lien par le lieu"* (ibid., 19) but as a *social ethos*. The great enemy of *good neighborhood* today is what Edouard Glissant and Patrick Chamoiseau once called *The Temptation of the Wall* (*La Tentation du mur*) (2007). These are walls that betray the apartheid or identity politics of an unleashed capitalism inside and outside Europe. Let us not forget that the walls, as L'Heuillet rightly points out, are not only built on the periphery of Europe to protect the continent from the "misery of the world," but also within Europe! (L'Heuillet 2016, 115). This is also why I understand neighborhood as a daily education on democracy, not only because it is the radical opposite of the temptations of community but also because it works as an education against an excessive, narcissistic, and conquering individualism. Beyond that, it is also a solidarity that does not try to assimilate the other. However, it will be a mistake to make a social virtue, such as solidarity, dependent on a "we," on a belonging, on a collective feeling, as Mark Lilla does (Ignatieff and Roch 2018, 21). Political Islam in the Arab world, also known for its welfare activities, does nothing other than this, namely, to tie solidarity to an exclusive "we." In an open society, solidarity is *without identity*; it is to be sought beyond the close logic of belonging. Only as a democratic institution is solidarity still possible.

Social Radicalism

Apart from some unfortunate terms in Plessner's work that will seem, according to the gusto of postmodernism, inappropriate, Plessner's critique of social radicalism is very topical, and not only for the West but also to understand the impossible transition from *community* to *society* in the Islamic context. His analysis in *The Limits of Community* offers us a diagnosis of *social radicalism*, which is the great threat to modern liberal, open society, and which in its two variants, namely the *Blutgemeinschaft* (like nationalism yesterday or populism today) and the *Sachgemeinschaft* (like Marxism yesterday or religious fundamentalism today), will always accompany this society like its shadows.

Yet, what does Plessner mean by radicalism? Firstly, radicalism in all its forms is haunted by the *idea of return*. In most cases, it is an ideological return to an imaginary origin. Secondly, it represents a radical opposition to the present society, in other words, against society and its division, in the language of Claude Leforts, or against its ontological ambiguity, and fervor for a homogeneous community. For *social radicalism*, it is a question of a society that has lost its soul or a society that has been destroyed from within by external influences and internal enemies. This assertion is what makes the polemic of the radicals in large parts of the world. Plessner continues his definition of radicalism, one that has lost none of its relevance, and writes, "Its thesis is being without restraint, its perspective infinity, its pathos enthusiasm and its temperament passion; it is the innate world view of the impatient" (Plessner, 1999, 47).

Whatever the shade of meaning one affixes to the notion of social radicalism, there can be no doubt that it represents, with its "dialectic of the heart," a real threat for modern society and its central components, namely the political liberalism, the free-market economy, and the public sphere. To describe Islamic radicalism too, with its *intolerance of ambiguity*, we will not find a suitable language like that of Plessner. His criticism of Luther and his reform of the church "in the spirit of the ancient Christians" (ibid., 54) is undoubtedly true of the Islamist movements that, since Wahhabism in the eighteenth century, have sought to revive that imagined experience of the first Islamic community. A goal achieved by destroying the other Islamic traditions. Not even the Islamic monuments have survived this fanaticism. It is a *nihilism a l'envers*, that is, one that seeks to destroy the present in the name of the past, an imagined and idealized past. Popper, like Plessner, rightly remarks that this return to a closed society, that of the community, is impossible and can have fatal consequences: "For those who have eaten from the tree of knowledge, paradise is lost. The more we try to return to the heroic age of tribalism, the more surely, we arrive at the inquisition, at the secret Police, and at a romanticized gangsterism. Beginning with the suppression of reason and truth, we must end with the most brutal and violent destruction of all that is human. *There is no return to a harmonious state of nature. If we turn back, then we must go the whole way – we must return to the beasts*" (Popper 1966, 200–1).

If we approach the phenomenon of the Islamic *suicide bomber*, in the light of Popper's thought, we will find ourselves before an impatient man who seeks to anticipate the hereafter. He does not think, but, rather zealously, animated by a pathological enthusiasm, despises finite life and dreams of an infinity that borders on depravity. Moreover, as a false puritan, he fears and condemns his own body. He has no body, he has no joy, borne, as Plessner says, by an "insufficiency consciousness" (*Insuffizienzbewusstsein*), which is also why he knows only one law, namely "thoroughness," and "thoroughness is an expression of its prejudice against life" (Plessner 1999, 49).

Of course, these prejudices did not come out of nowhere, nor are they the result of his fantasies. They have much to do with the reality of radicalism and its concrete conditions. Perhaps this is what Plessner failed to say. That is also why we need to consider Plessner further today and, above all, to ask ourselves about the real conditions of these communalist or radical temptations that threaten to destroy the democratic ethos of society. This is precisely what Philip Manow does, for example, in his discussion of populism. According to him, we cannot talk about populism without talking about capitalism (Manow 2018, 9) and those who do end up in identity politics. We can say that they pose the problem of populism in a similar way to the populists themselves, who pose the problems of society falsely, for example, by seeing the great danger that Europe faces in migration or Islam.

In the context of migration, which is marked by a pluralism of cultures, any attempt to revive the communal is directed against this plurality, as against the divided structure of society. The attempt to organize this plurality under a *leading culture* also testifies to a monodemocratic policy that is incapable of encounter with the others, but only seeks to dominate them and to catch up with them in the totality of the same. The more a culture succumbs to communal temptations, the more it is prepared to make the other invisible. The apologists of the *leading culture* (*Leitkultur*) are community apologists, even if they do not necessarily defend a community of blood, place, or spirit, because they are talking about a politics that, in the final analysis, is trapped in the logic of belonging—one that is not capable of feeling a guilty conscience and no longer works as memory; I mean, as critique of the past, in the language of the constitutional patriots. Within a context like the German one, critique is only possible as memory, as *Eingedenken*. It is this critical remembrance that would remind us of the crimes of the politics of the heart, passion, and belonging, which confirm what Plessner defended in his definition of the public sphere, namely that the public sphere "begins where love and blood-based obligations ends" (ibid., 99).

Popper is of the same opinion in his conception of politics. Popper calls on politics to free itself from emotional-collective ties and to solve political problems rationally. However, Popper has been accused of defending an abstract, that is, a cold conception of politics, which does not consider real circumstances (Neil McInnes 2002, 80). In this criticism, one forgets that the political developments of the present prove Popper and his bloodless conception of the political. The pure, warm politics of the populists, their "moralistic imagination of politics" (Müller 2016, 19), their "claim to exclusive moral representation" (ibid., 38), and their "conspiracy theories," which are rooted in the logic of populism itself (ibid., 32), provide us with the proof that democratic politics cannot be conducted with unleashed emotions and anger. This coldness, which Plessner describes as the anthropological characteristic of society as opposed to community, is realized as a liberation of the individual from the suffocating warmth of the totality. Democracy today is only possible as a *Schulddemokratie*, that is, one that, as we have seen with Habermas, seeks to appropriate its national traditions and its warmth only critically and only in the mode of coldness, and not in the mode of an emotional belonging.

The claim that one can distinguish between a *healthy* and an *unhealthy* *nationalism* (Lilla 2018, 22), like Mark Lilla does, overlooks the fact that nationalism in all its forms, such as populism, neoliberalism, religious fundamentalism, is a threat to democracy today and that in its allegedly healthy as well as in its unhealthy variation strives for the same goal, namely what Jacques Derrida called "the political dictatorship of brotherhood" (Derrida 2003, 76).

Muslim Diaspora and Its Challenges

Migrants in the West must struggle with a double violence. On the one hand, they are heavily burdened with their own untimely culture; they are the children of a *neopatriarchy*, who constantly miss the connection to modernity if they do not work against it, as Hicham Sharabi explains (1988), and thus also miss the connection to tradition. In my opinion, a healthy relationship with tradition is only possible from a modern point of view and in the output of the scientific achievements of modernity. This is also why Abdelkebir Kathibi's emphasis that, in the Arab Islamic context, we are dealing with *traditionalism* rather than *tradition* is very apt, and "traditionalism – according to him – is forgetfulness of tradition" (Khatibi 1987, 25). This is another reason why we experience tradition in the Arab Islamic world as a social pathology, which is expressed in individual as well as collective action and thinking and which saps the transition from the *closed* to the *open society*. Mark Lilla is undoubtedly right when he combines the outbreak of *nostalgia* on the political scene of the present with a political disorientation. He writes that this maldevelopment allows demagogues different *couleurs* "to exploit this desire to return somewhere" (Lilla 2018, 30), and he does not exaggerate when he sees in jihadism "a good example of radical nostalgia. The idea that you are going to recreate the golden age of the first four righteously guided Califs and Mohammed and reapply Sharia law is the most obvious and extreme form of political nostalgia of our time" (ibid., 30).

To be radical means not only the radical rejection or condemnation of the "large city," of the "pathos of fatigue," or of "the incongruity of our will with the world" (Plessner 1999, 48), but also, and especially in the Arab Islamic context, the condemnation of the incongruity of our world with its roots or with its past, its closed and imagined past. It is a remark that Plessner already made masterfully in his discussion of *social radicalism*: "In general, by radicalism we understand the following: the conviction that genuine greatness and goodness arises only from a conscious return to the roots of existence; the belief in the healing power of the extreme; and the method of opposing all traditional values and compromises" (ibid., 47). This uncritical relationship to one's own past that we encounter among Western populists is expressed in the apologetics of the Islamic caliphate among Islamic populists. Neither of them is willing to learn from the mistakes of the past and neither of them is ready to elaborate a critical relationship with it, because they see themselves as morally superior. Here sits the embryo of the old and modern radicalism. It wants to own the past with the aim to determine the future, but the future, in an open society, as Popper expresses it, "is not fixed, it is open" (Popper 1966, 32), and it's also so, because open societies, "unlike dictatorships, they are exposed to critical debate and to constant review of the solutions adopted" (Corvi 1996 52). I think, not only the future in such a society is open but also the past. It will forever remain a "foreign country" that everyone invokes, or tries to manipulate it politically, without being able to own it. Karl Popper expresses this truth as follows: "To sum up, there can be no history of 'the past as it actually did happen'; there can only be historical interpretations, and none of them can be final; and every generation has a right to frame its own" (Popper 1971 267). On the other hand, *Muslim diaspora* is the victim of a paternalistic policy that still sees migrants to an end, thus preventing them from joining society. It condemns them to the communal, which in the end confirms the dominant policy with its monodemocratic discourse. So, their labor power is demanded, but not their social participation. The more invisible, the better!

Conclusion

To sum up, I have brought in this text two philosophers together, who come from different philosophical perspectives and proceed with different methodologies, Helmut Plessner and Karl Popper, in striving to explain what I mean with *open neighborhood*, or to rethink the neighborhood, that is, those forms of social relations and practices in a society governed by cultural pluralism, or to think about neighborhood and its realizations within society and away from community. The different references and approaches of both Plessner and Popper have not prevented them from emphasizing the centrality of the individual and individuality in contemporary society, defending the *abstractness* and *coldness* of this society and declaring its indeterminacy or what Plessner calls *groundlessness* (Pols 2014, 261).

Plessner found the problem of his time in the late 1920s in the turbulent, unclear, and unhealthy relationship between community and society, or what we might call the *temptation of community*, at a time, in Lukács's terms, of *transcendental homelessness* (*Transzendentale Obdachlosigkeit*) and as a desperate answer to it. Popper found this problem in the 1940s, when the Second World War was raging, in the struggle between an open society and its enemies, namely the protagonists of a closed or totalitarian society.

Today, the followers of communalist thinking—the followers of a closed society—return to threaten democracy, liberalism, and the open society under various names, including religion, identity, people, nation, and some of them even return to threaten freedom in the name of freedom itself, as Wolfgang Streeck explores in his analysis of the continuous divorce between democracy and capitalism since the 1970s (Streeck 2017).

The defense of coldness—or even an education to coldness, starting from Plessner and Popper—must be a part of democratic culture today, which is confronted with various forms of social radicalisms that can endanger the democratic order and work only for a *closed, adiaphoristic neighborhood*. This education in coldness means nothing else, to speak with Popper, then *bringing violence under the control of reason*.

Bibliography

Corvi, Roberta. 1996. *An Introduction to the Thought of Karl Popper*. London: Routledge.
Derrida, Jacques. 2003. *Voyous: Deux essais sur la raison*. Paris: Galilee.
Evans, Sandra, and Schamma Schahadat, eds. 2012. *Nachbarschaft Räume Emotionen. Interdisziplinäre Beiträge zu einer sozialen Lebensform*. Bielefeld: Transkript.
Glissant, Edouard, and Patrick Chamoiseau. 2007. *Quand les murs tombent – L'identité nationale hors la loi?* Paris: Editions Galaade.
Habermas, Jürgen. 1994. *Fraktizität und Geltung: Beitraege zur Diskurstheorie des Rechts und des demokratischen Rechtsstaats*. Frankfurt am Main: Suhrkamp.
Haucke, Kai. 2016. "Plessner's Kritik der radikalen Gemeinschaftsideologie und die Grenzen des deutschen Idealismus." In *Plessner's 'Grenzen der Gemeinschaft'. Eine Debatte*, edited by Wolfgang Essbach, Joachim Fischer and Helmut Lethen. Berlin: Suhrkamp, 103–130.
Honneth, Axel. 1994. *Pathologien des Sozialen. Die Aufgaben der Sozialphilosophie*. Frankfurt am Main: Fischer Verlag.

Ignatieff, Michael, and Stefan Roch, eds. 2018. *Rethinking Open Society. New Adversaries and New Opportunities*. Budapest and New York: Central European University Press.

Khatibi, Abdelkebir. 1987. *Maghreb Pluriel*. Paris: Denoel.

Lefort, Claude. 1986. *The Political Forms of Modern Society: Bureaucracy, Democracy, Totalitarianism*. Edited by John B. Thompson. Cambridge, MA: MIT Press.

L'Heuillet, Hélène. 2016. *Du voisinage: réflexions sur la coexistence humain*. Paris: Albin Michel.

Lilla, Mark, and Michael, Ignatieff. 2018. "Open Society as an Oxymoron." In *Rethinking Open Society. New Adversaries and new opportunities*, edited by Michael Ignatieff, and Stefan Roch. Budapest and New York: Central European University Press.

Manow, Philip. 2018. *Die Politische Oekonomie des Populismus*. Berlin: Suhrkamp.

McInnes, Neil. 2002. "Popper's Return Engagement: The Open Society in an Era of Globalization." *The National Interest*, 67 (Spring 2002): 72–80.

Müller, Jan-Werner. 2016. *What is Populism?* Pennsylvania: University of Pennsylvania Press.

Plessner, Helmuth. 1999. *The Limits of Community. A Critique of Social Radicalism*. Translated by Andrew Wallace. New York: Humanity Books.

Pols, Kirsten. 2014. "Strangely Familiar: The Debate on Multiculturalism and Plessner's Philosophical Anthropology". In *Jos de Mul, Plessner's Philosophical Anthropology: Perspectives and Prospects*. Amsterdam: Amsterdam University Press, 261–274.

Popper, Karl. 1966. *The Open Society and its Enemies I: The Spell of Plato*. Princeton, NJ: Princeton University Press.

Popper, Karl. 1971. *The Open Society and Its Enemies, Volume 2: The High Tide of Prophecy: Hegel, Marx, and the Aftermath*. Princeton, NJ: Princeton University Press.

Sharabi, Hisham. 1988. *Neopatriarchy: A Theory of distorted Change in Arab Society*. Oxford: Oxford University Press.

Streeck, Wolfgang. 2017. *Buying Time: The Delayed Crisis of Democratic Capitalism*. New York: Verso.

Tönnies, Ferdinand. 2001. *Community and Civil Society*. Translated by Jose Harris and Margaret Hollis. Cambridge: Cambridge University Press.

Virilio, Paul. 1977. *Vitesse et politique: essai de dromologie*. Paris: Editions Galilée.

3

AGAINST IDENTITY: INDIVIDUALITY AS THE FOUNDATION OF OPEN SOCIETY

Gregory Lobo

> The wise man belongs to all countries alike, for the home of a great soul is the whole world.
> —Democritus (quoted in Popper 1963, 593)

In the eponymous chapter 10 of his book, *The Open Society and Its Enemies*, Karl Popper considers what it means to move from "from tribalism to humanitarianism" (1945, 163). Without asserting that all tribal forms of life are similar, Popper highlights a common particular epistemological viewpoint: such forms do not distinguish "between the customary or conventional regularities of social life and the regularities found in 'nature'" (164). This being the case, no questioning or criticism exists; rather "taboos rigidly regulate and dominate all aspects of life" (164).[1] Taboo, then, dominates in closed society. As such, the member of it will "rarely find himself in the position of doubting how he ought to act," for the "right way is always determined" by such taboos (164). In other words, the "institutions" of closed society "leave no room for personal responsibility" (164).

That taboos dominate behavior in closed society does not mean that we are free of them today. Life is still beset with many different taboos, but in modern and at least to some degree open societies, we experience "an ever-widening field of personal decisions, with its problems and responsibilities" (165). Taboo is present but does not dominate us to the extent that it does in closed (or tribal) society. For us, then, the right way is not always determined. To the contrary, we must make decisions for which we are responsible. Indeed, this broadening field of individual responsibility constitutes the fundamental difference between closed and open society: the society where taboo rules—and rules out personal responsibility—will "be called the *closed society*" (165), Popper clarifies; whereas

---

[1] Whether Popper is historically correct here, or whether his understanding of so-called tribalism is informed by the Eurocentric prejudices, what Said (1978) identified in another context as orientalism, of his time is not important (I would argue). Though Popper is trying to situate his discussion of tribalism in time and space (i.e., with the historical ancient Greeks), here I am trying to grasp it conceptually, as closed society, as distinct from open society.

we will call "the society in which individuals are confronted with personal decisions, the *open society*" (165).

This difference may not, at first sight, strike the reader as much of one. But for Popper it is the central characteristic of "one of the deepest revolutions through which mankind has passed" (167). And in case such a formulation (in the past perfect tense) might lead the distracted reader to imagine that we are on the other side of this upheaval, that it has come to an irreversible conclusion, Popper quickly points out that, to the contrary, this "great revolution … is still in its beginning" (167). Which means its success, howsoever we might imagine it, is far from guaranteed.

The breakdown of closed society, of the uncontested regulation of human behavior by taboo, was prompted by, while also leading to, "that great spiritual revolution, the invention of critical discussion, and, in consequence, of thought that was free" (167–168). But this came—and indeed comes—at a cost. The cost is what Popper refers to early in and throughout the book as the "strain of our civilization" and its fundamental "demand for personal responsibility" (xlvii). He refers to this strain as a "deeply rooted unhappiness" (163) and admits that it is endemic to open society. For it is "created by the effort which life in an open … society continually demands from us—by the endeavor to be rational … to look after ourselves, and to accept responsibilities" (168). This strain, this unhappiness, according to Popper, "is the price we have to pay for being human" (168). For we are only truly human when we embrace our personal responsibility, which is the case only in open society. And thus we are only human in open society.

I want to leave aside the ambiguity of the word "human" for the moment. Popper is using human in a moral sense as opposed to the zoological sense, which we will unpack below. For now I want to acknowledge that clearly, not everyone wants to pay the price—the strain, the unhappiness—of being human (in the moral sense). And this can be taken as at least part of the explanation for why we find ourselves, since the ancient Greeks ("the first to make the step from tribalism to humanitarianism" (163), from closed to open society) onward, constantly invited by leaders, politicians, and activists to go back to the closed society. Popper characterizes this reactionary project throughout his book as the "perennial revolt against freedom and reason" (245), as the "revolt against civilization" (xlvi) itself. In this chapter, I want to explore the allure of this revolt, and the form it takes, drawing on the resources provided by *The Open Society* itself, but also on recent studies in the behavioral and neurosciences. Based on the latter, I argue that what drives the revolt are inescapable unconscious survival mechanisms that are part of our evolutionary baggage, and that the form it takes today is identity politics (absent such a term, Popper discussed tribalism, collectivism, and nationalism as the forms the revolt takes). In conclusion, I argue that if we want to defend and expand open society, we must take an implacable stand against identity politics—which is to say, against identity itself—while attempting to provide a social infrastructure which makes it a less compelling option than it has been to date.

Driving the Revolt: Individual Animals

Popper himself identifies the lure of closed society when he observes that with its "breakdown ... certainty disappears, and with it all feeling of security" (168). We become unmoored, overwhelmed by a "feeling of drift" (16). But if it is true that open society causes strain, if "deeply rooted unhappiness" is endemic to it, and if we follow Popper in supporting the slogan "Minimize suffering" (1945, 548),[2] why should we not revolt against open society and join the attempt to return to closed? Popper poses this question and answers it in his way. In short, we can't get (back) there from here. One reason is that "tribal paradise is, of course, a myth" (638). So there is no there *there*. Just because a deeply rooted unhappiness runs through open society, it does not mean that happiness ran through closed society. Furthermore, given where we are now, the "return to the *alleged* [emphasis added] innocence and beauty of the closed society" (189) is not possible without the "Inquisition," the "Secret Police," and "a romanticized gangsterism" (189). While it might begin "only" (I am using square quotes here, not quoting) with "the suppression of reason and truth" (189), it must "end with the most brutal and violent destruction of all that is human" (189), which is to say, of all our moral achievements, of the recognition of the universal dignity of the individual, of justice, of the difference between good and evil, and so on.

To be human, Popper argues, drawing on Socrates's moral understanding of human being, is to be more than "a piece of flesh," more than an animal body (180). I want to make clear an implicit and useful distinction here, between the animal body that would be a mere organism of the species homo sapiens and the human that is more than a mere animal of this sort. I would argue that when Foucault proclaimed that "one of the prime effects of power is that certain bodies, certain gestures, certain discourses, certain desires, come to be identified and constituted as individuals" (1980, 98), he was drawing implicitly on this distinction. And when Althusser formulated the idea that "all ideology ... interpellates concrete individuals as concrete subjects" (1971, 160), he was making a similar claim. Allowing that the authors are using the concept "individual" differently, they are both arguing that something concrete, a homo sapiens animal body, is given a new status, is made morally human, through something like cultural practice. This helps us understand what Popper means when he insists: "*If we turn back [towards the closed society], then we must go the whole way—we must return to the beasts*" (189). If we turn away from open society, that is, we must relinquish that which makes us human. In this sense, the revolt against freedom is a revolt against our humanity, that which makes us human, what Popper will call our "humaneness." But if, having discovered our humanity, "we wish to remain human, then there is only one way, the way into the open society. We must go on into the unknown, the uncertain and insecure, using what

---

2 In note 6 to chapter 5, Popper argues for the replacement of the "the utilitarian formula ... 'Maximize happiness', by the formula ... 'Minimize suffering'" (548).

reason we may have to plan as well as we can for both security *and* freedom" (Popper 189).

This is dramatic stuff, but nevertheless, as pointed out by Gray in his lucid reflection on Popper's liberalism, the "perennial revolt" shows no signs of abating. People may not understand their aversion to open society as a rejection of their own humanity (in the moral sense), nor as a preference for animality (or they may have some romantic [but mistaken] notion of what animality entails). But the fact that "various forms of neo-tribal barbarism [still] claim the allegiance of great masses of men" (Gray 1976, 355) in the second decade of the twenty-first century points to the fact that we have apparently not made much progress on the "programme of social and psychological research into the causes and character of this revolt" (355) suggested by Gray in the 1970s.

As part of my small contribution to that program, I want to remark on another fundamental characteristic of open society, as identified by Popper in his discussions of Socrates. According to Popper, the "greatest contribution" to open society was made by Socrates, "who died for it" (179). This contribution is "his creed of individualism, his belief in the human individual as an end in himself" (180); it is "the belief that there is nothing more important in our life than other individual men, [and consequently] the appeal to men to respect one another and themselves" (180).

I want us to foreground the individual because just as Socrates and Popper hold her to be open society's highest value, I argue that if we want to explain the revolt against freedom (open society) we must also value the individual. The difference is that while the individual of open society is a moral entity, the individual that drives the revolt against it is, rather, a zoological one, the animal individual of our species. Ironically, perhaps, I pursue a line of thought that approaches us as mere bodies rather than moral humans, drawing on studies from biology and evolution. For even though Popper gives his all to prevent a return to the beasts, the fact is that prior to our humaneness, beneath it all, we are indisputably animals.[3] And as animals—as, in ontological terms, individual animals or organisms—the first allegiance of each and every one of us is not to anything else but our individual survival.

The Evolutionary Nature of the Revolt

I believe our very nature drives the revolt against freedom. But what aspect of our nature drives it? It is not our collectivism, tribalism, or nationalism per se. These are rather the forms the revolt takes. What drives our flight from *humaneness*

---

3 Readers may be familiar with a philosophical subdiscipline called animalism. It is not at all clear, in my view, what the point of it is, since nobody of a scientific or philosophical bent would deny its *Ur* proposition, namely, that we are animals.

is, so to speak, our species-being,[4] our animality. In short, we are afraid. But, to be clear, we are not afraid for something like "us," whoever we are. We are each afraid for our individual, natural (noncultural) lives. And this is because while we are not merely pieces of flesh, bodies, or beasts, we are beasts much more fundamentally than we are humans. Precisely because we are beasts, we can be afraid even though we do not think we are afraid: we can engage in defensive behavior without being conscious or aware of the fact that we are doing so. The focus of neuroscientist LeDoux's recent work has been the neural "nonconscious processes that control defense responses elicited by threats" (2014, 2871). His work points to the notion that the brain "mechanisms that detect and respond to threats are not the same as those that give rise to conscious fear" (2871). It is not conscious fear that motivates us to engage in defensive behaviors. Consciousness—which is the modality through which we experience fear—is a late comer to biology and is ill-equipped to keep the individual organism alive long enough to shed its gametes.[5] Something else, something that has no necessary affinity for criticism, freedom, or truth, is keeping animals, in this case humanimals (to coin a term), alive.

The fMRI studies of Mobbs et al., for example, have shown two things of interest for our discussion. One is that the forebrain (the part of the brain activated when we engage in conscious thought) is involved in conscious thinking about our potential threats. On the other hand, "imminent danger results in fast, likely 'hard-wired,' defensive reactions mediated by the midbrain" (2009, 12236). The question for us, not treated by Mobbs et al., is what constitutes "imminent danger" for us? I argue that as a species, since time immemorial, the most imminent danger is other homo sapiens. Somewhat paradoxically, the best way to defend oneself against this danger, also since time immemorial, is by allying yourself with other homo sapiens. But this is further complicated by the fact that it is far from uncommon for those with whom we ally ourselves—given the wrong time, the wrong place, and the wrong circumstances—to turn on us, to hurt, and even kill us. Of course, we need to include here the fact that in homo

---

4 As an aside here addressed to readers familiar with Marx's notion of species-being, I want to acknowledge an extensive literature on this concept, attempting to understand how Marx understood and developed it (to some slight degree) based on Feuerbach's usage. The literature, in coming to the predictable conclusion that species-being refers to some kind of historical condition, misses the point entirely. In short, in so far as we are referring in any direct way to the species homo sapiens, we are referring, I would argue, to a species that emerges divided against itself, prone to (almost) wiping itself out again and again in fits of uncontrolled violent rage sparked by innate mimetic rivalry. I would further argue that culture is the response to this quite literal dead end. For culture does not extinguish such outbursts; rather it harnesses them, channels them, sublimates them to some degree, and even utilizes them, but in no way supersedes them. And indeed, since they are part of our nature, to do so would be impossible. These views are inspired by the work of Girard (1987).

5 De Loof (2018) makes the case that mammals (and especially humans) are not genetically driven to reproduce but to shed their gametes. That this frequently enough leads to reproduction is, one might say, pure luck.

sapiens, imagination is a form of perception: we can perceive threats, in other words, that might not be physically or temporally present. But our brains do not necessarily know the difference between what is empirically real or true and what is "merely" imagined. What is more, when under attack—which in homo sapiens need not refer to an actual empirical, physical attack; indeed, we today speak easily of being made to feel unsafe by words, questions, and even fictional representations of unconsciously raised eyebrows, involuntary double takes, and other sorts of "micro-aggressions"—the forebrain regions responsible for thinking about defensive strategies "are inhibited" (2009, 12241), which means we stop thinking clearly. Unconscious neural threat-perception systems are what biologists call "evolutionary conserved systems" (12242): we have them because we are evolved beasts, even if we are not merely such.

Work by Eilam, Izhar, and Mort allows us to develop this point. They distinguish between "perceptible threat," that is, threat that is empirically present, and "abstract potential threat" (2011, 999), which elicits "anxiety and vigilance" (999). They furthermore argue that anxiety, which as we have just seen, results from abstract potential threats, "frequently leads to rituals that confer a sense of controllability" (999). This, I argue, is akin to the rituals and taboos widely practiced in tribal societies, as mentioned by Popper, and no doubt undergirds their cohesion. The most important components of the brain that deal with danger "evolved before consciousness" (1004), and they are "biased towards perceiving threats *even when they do not exist* [emphasis added], under the principle that 'it is better to be safe than sorry'" (1004). But the authors point out that what leads to the belief that "I'm safe" is not well understood (1004): "Anxiety by its nature is a paramount response to an abstract potential threat, and … there is no external signal that might stop it" (1004). We should take a moment here to reflect on the fact that humans can work themselves into a frothing fear of others. We should consider also that the world is replete with difference, changes, novelty, and so on, always keeping us off-balance, always unsure. It is hardly surprising, then, that the primordial organization of our evolved brain which prompts it to be constantly on the lookout for possible danger and, as a result, for possible safety, clearly predisposes us to be ever weak-kneed before the seductive temptations of closed society, with its "natural" allies who will defend us from what were originally quite real threats. For our brains "tend to evaluate ambiguous situations as being dangerous rather than being safe" (1004). And let us not forget, they do this without our even being aware of it.

I want to discuss one further article which uses a language more closely aligned to the one we have been using in our reading of Popper. Woody and Szechtman (2011) discuss the "security motivation system." It is a "biologically ancient, 'hard-wired' neural system" (1020) which is "designed to detect subtle indicators of potential threat, to probe the environment for further information about these possible dangers, and to motivate engagement in precautionary behaviors, which also serves to terminate security motivation" (1019). Now, it is unfortunate that the biggest threat homo sapiens face is other homo sapiens; but this being the case, it is understandable that *other* other humans, so to speak, constitute our best defense against them. What I am going to say next is conjecture, but based on the studies cited from the neuro and behavioral sciences, I think it has solid foundations. Because of the sorts of animals we are—because we are capable of victimizing, or being victimized by, even those closest to us, even those, as one might say, "most like us," even those we love and who love us—it is clear that theories which suggest some sort of natural affinity based ultimately on genetics or blood or race or ethnicity have no real explanatory power when it comes to understanding group cohesiveness or "tribal unity." Rather, I argue, we are united—to the degree that we are so, in practical terms—by something like culture. What does this mean?

The Cultural Form of the Revolt

In *Wonder Woman* (2017), when the US pilot Steve Trevor somehow intrudes into the Amazons' island, he is pursued by German soldiers. The Amazons attack and vanquish them, incurring significant losses. They then turn on Trevor, whom they take to be the last enemy standing. Diana (Wonder Woman) puts herself between Trevor and her own mother, Hippolyta, insisting that he fought with the Amazons. Hippolyta asks, incredulously, "What man fights against his own people?" Here Trevor responds, "These aren't my people." "Then why do you wear their colors?" asks Diana's mother. The film thus reveals why he appears to Hippolyta to be on the side of those who had just killed many Amazons, including her sister: he is dressed like them, therefore he is one of them. My point, perhaps belabored, is that among other things, culture is the modality by which we identify friends and nonfriends, that is, unknown entities, potential threats, in the first instance. We do not do so via racial or ethnic markers.[6] So-called ethnic and racial conspecifics kill each other all the time. And in fact "in nature" there is nothing to signal naturally who is friend and who is foe, because by nature anyone might be friend or foe. Thus, humans have developed cultural codes to signal friend, and those who use different codes are obviously if not foe, then potentially so. They are, moreover, to be treated with suspicion up until the point their nonthreat status can be confirmed. Of course, people can engage in subterfuge, and do. But I think the model I have outlined captures best how ontologically individual humanimals have developed security—and indeed, become human—in an inherently insecure world.

The foregoing is first and foremost an attempt to really explain why people revolt against freedom: because they are afraid. But it is also an attempt to explain the form this revolt takes. In *The Open Society*, we can now resituate Popper's criticisms of tribalism, collectivism, and nationalism. These are the

---

6 As Brubaker (2004) has argued, race and ethnicity and national identity are not ontological givens. They result from symbolic practices attempting to present their referents as, precisely, not constructed but natural.

forms the revolt against civilization takes, as individual humans group themselves so as to simply preserve their lives. Let us look at what Popper says of these forms. "Tribalism," he writes, emphasizes "the supreme importance of the tribe without which the individual is nothing at all" (8). "Collectivism," similarly, "emphasize[s] the significance of some group or collective—for example, a class—without which the individual is nothing at all" (8). Popper uses these terms more or less seamlessly and interchangeably (see, e.g., 75–79, 102, 165–167). As for nationalism, Popper believes that "the principle of the national state … [is] … a principle which owes its popularity solely to the fact that it appeals to tribal instincts" (607). Now, based on this condensed review of what Popper says about tribalism, collectivism, and nationalism, he would be disinclined to truck in what today we would call identity politics. For the form of identity politics, like the aforementioned targets of Popper's criticism, brooks no individualism or individuality, but honors only the group. The individual is subservient to the group, not an end in her own right, and free only insofar as her actions contribute to the vitality of the group.

What Popper says of the morality of collectivism—"Good is what is in the interest of my group; or my tribe; or my state" (102)—can be said without modification of the morality of the identity group. Nor can it be otherwise. What I mean by this is that groups (not in themselves but for themselves) have a tendency to suppress dissension. This means that groups have a tendency to repress individual freedom. This happens because groups have an inescapable tendency to develop a "a rational unity that constrains their performance over time and that makes them distinct from their own members" (Pettit 2003, 187). This rational unity is the unity required by the group in order for it to exist as a group of members and not simply as an aggregate of bodies. The "rational unity" groups "display is one that they themselves police and implement in the fashion of creatures" who can be held "responsible": they are "creatures who count as persons" (187), and their survival counts infinitely more than the survival of any individual constituent member.

The group as person is entitled to monitor, police, and in the end suppress dissent among its membership. This means that collective identification, identification with the group—tribalism, collectivism, nationalism, in Popper's lexicon—must always result in at least some degree of what Scott Atran (2016) calls identity fusion. In identity fusion, one's own agency disappears; it becomes merely an expression of group agency, which is to say, one's own capacity to think and act is at most and at best merely derivative of the group's thinking and acting. One loses one's individuality; one becomes an organ of the group, directed wholly and entirely by the group and its purpose.

We have said that one joins and adheres to a group because of a primordial evolved bodily disposition to stay alive. In an unsecure world, we turn—and we have emphasized that we turn unconsciously—to others who will, we hope, defend us, secure us (perhaps die/be killed in our place?). We must now emphasize that such behavior is not restricted to those we might describe as pathological: the white supremacist, anti-immigrant, Q anon, Islamist, other. Nonetheless, scholars who discuss the phenomenon, such as Hobfoll (2018), and even Popper himself in his discussions of collectivism, focus on extremist examples of group belonging, like Atran, who sees identity fusion as a pathological form of identification which characterizes radical actors. But I would argue that we are all susceptible to it—to identity fusion, to seeking protection among those we take to be like us—to some degree. Liberal elites fall prey to identity fusion; antiracists and critics of white supremacy do; members of the Republican and Democratic Parties do. As they must, given the logic of group existence. Pettit is attempting to explain how "entities [i.e., groups] that individuals compose can assume a life of their own" (191). And I think Pettit's explanation is correct. But if he is correct then we must almost always be on guard against such entities doing that. They are indeed a sort of form of artificial intelligence that, as we observe with evermore frequency today, are almost predisposed to run amok at the expense of the individual freedom of members and nonmembers alike.

Conclusion: Against the Politics of Identity

Though Popper uses the word "identity" occasionally in *The Open Society*, it is never used there in the way we use it today. Since the cult of identity and the concept of identity politics only really emerged after the 1960s, they were unavailable to him in the 1940s. But there is a more interesting reason. Our modern usages of identity and identity politics depend on notions of essence. To claim an identity is, essentially, to essentialize oneself. It is to restrict oneself. It is to contain oneself, to make oneself static, unmoving. It is in short to define oneself. And Popper, readers of *The Open Society* well know, had no sympathy for essentialist definitions (see 30–33). He believed these lead directly to error, confusion, and stagnation, whether we are trying to understand society or the people whose relations make it up. Thus it is to be expected that instead of defining tribalism, collectivism, and nationalism,[7] Popper, as we have seen, describes what he would call their behaviors or regularities: in each case, the group itself is placed over and above the individual, who has no inherent value or dignity otherwise.

With this insight, we can proceed to our conclusion. There is no identity appropriate to open society. To really participate in open society, as Popper understands it, one cannot be bound—which is to say, tied up and unfree—by being subject to an identity. Rather one's relationship to identity must be negative in some sense. To be able to engage in what Popper calls "free criticism" and "friendly-hostile" (424) debate, one must be free of what Pettit identifies as the constraints of group rationality and far from fusing into the third-person plural examined by Atran. The authority of the group must be null, which is to say that it must be nullified. And thus the benefits of belonging in identitarian fashion to the group must be nullified too.

---

7 In chapter 10, Popper is clear: There is "no uniformity in tribalism. There is no standardized 'tribal way of life'" (164). There is no essential way of being a tribe.

What this means is that insofar as the group counts as a refuge in open society, it does so not because of who you are but because of how each member adheres to the value or virtue of honoring the humanity of her conspecifics, which amounts to "fundamentally an attitude of admitting that '*I may be wrong and you may be right, and by an effort, we may get nearer to the truth*'" (431). I admit this not because of who or what I am, but because of what I value: how I value you but also how I value myself, because of how I understand myself in relation to others, not because of how I understand them in relation to me. The burden is, first and foremost, mine. But to be clear, I can only consistently hold these values and live up to them in a situation in which my existence is not constantly threatened.

Open society, in other words, must be society wherein ontological insecurity, which is to say, existential precarity is extinguished.[8] Somehow. We need "stable social conditions in which conventional expectations are not continually frustrated and conventional ideas not radically incompetent" (Geertz 1973, 232–233) if we are to deliberate over contentious matters without extremism. Without such security the lure of identification with a group, and all the perils for freedom thereby entailed, is inescapable. But insecurity rules—the last fifty years of global economic policy have constituted nothing if not an assault on people's security. This is the main obstacle to developing and extending open society. For if individuals feel insecure, they will tend not to care too much about the niceties and the benefits of open society and will indeed prefer to submit to the dictums of the group that they perceive to be their best source of protection; and insofar as they take it to be the best source of their protection, they will identify with it.

How to rebuild security, with freedom, is the question. But in the meantime, if we want open society to flourish, we must commit not to open society as such but to the values that subtend it. We must engage in free criticism and expose ourselves to free criticism. We must, in so far as is possible, refuse to be bound by any identitarian sentiments and civilly but tenaciously refuse to defer to the identarian pieties of others. Put another way, we need identity without identification. Or, identification may cease to be with a group and become an individual matter. For it is the "uniqueness of our experiences which … makes our lives worth living" (Popper 449). And as Arendt argues, in "acting and speaking, men show who they are, reveal their unique personal identities" (1958, 179); they do not perform predetermined collective ones. Indeed, "it is more than likely that the 'who,' which appears so clearly and unmistakably to others, remains hidden from the person himself" (179): we do not even know who we are. Such "knowledge" could only ever really amount to a conjecture; and anyone with the slightest bit of lived experience knows the refutations will be ceaseless.

Which is to say that in a way still to be worked out, we must somehow abandon identity if we care about the future of the open society. In the penultimate chapter to his book, Popper once more sets out the stakes: "The choice with

---

8 This is how I think tenure and academic freedom should be understood. Whether they are understood in this way is not clear to me.

which we are confronted is between a faith in reason and in *human individuals* [emphasis added] and a faith in the mystical faculties of man by which he is united into a collective; … a choice between an attitude that recognizes the unity of mankind and an attitude that divides men into friends and foes, into masters and slaves" (449–450), them and us. The former option in each choice is one which privileges not identity but simply being humane. It is the right choice, even if not everyone agrees.

Bibliography

Althusser, Louis. 1971. *Lenin and Philosophy and Other Essays*. New York: Monthly Review Press.
Arendt, Hannah. 1958. *The Human Condition*. Chicago, IL: University of Chicago Press.
Atran, Scott. 2016. "The Devoted Actor." *Current Anthropogy* 57 (17): 192–203.
Brubaker, Roger. 2004. *Ethnicity Without Groups*. Cambridge, MA: Harvard University Press.
De Loof, Arnold. 2018. "Only Two Sex Forms but Multiple Gender Variants: How to Explain?" *Communicative & Integrative Biology* 11 (1). https://doi.org/10.1080/19420889.2018.1427399.
Eilam D., R. Izhar, and J. Mort. 2011. "Threat Detection: Behavioral Practices in Animals and Humans." *Neuroscience and Biobehavioral Reviews* 35 (4): 999–1006. https://doi.org/10.1016/j.neubiorev.2010.08.002.
Foucault, Michel. 1980. *Power/Knowledge: Selected Interviews and Other Writings, 1972–1977*. New York: Pantheon Books.
Geertz, Clifford. 1973. *The Interpretation of Cultures*. New York: Basic Books.
Girard, René. 1987. *Things Hidden since the Foundation of the World*. Palo Alto, CA: Stanford University Press.
Gray, John N. 1976. "The Liberalism of Karl Popper." *Government and Opposition* 11 (3): 337–55. http://www.jstor.org/stable/44482132.
Hobfoll, Stevan E. 2018. *Tribalism: The Evolutionary Origins of Fear Politics*. New York: Palgrave/Springer.
LeDoux Jospeh, E. 2014. "Coming to Terms with Fear." *Proceedings of the National Academy of Sciences of the United States of America* 111 (8): 2871–78. https://doi.org/10.1073/pnas.1400335111.
Mobbs, D., J. L. Marchant, D. Hassabis, B. Seymour, G. Tan, M. Gray, P. Petrovic, R. J. Dolan, and C. D. Frith. 2009. "From Threat to Fear: The Neural Organization of Defensive Fear Systems in Humans." *The Journal of Neuroscience* 29 (39): 12236–43. https://doi.org/10.1523/JNEUROSCI.2378-09.2009.
Pettit, Philip. 2003. "Groups with Minds of Their Own." In *Socializing Metaphysics*, edited by Frederick F. Schmitt, 167–93. Lanham, MD: Rowman & Littlefield.
Popper, Karl R. [1945] 2013. *The Open Society and its Enemies*. Kindle ed. Princeton, NJ: Princeton University Press.
Said, Edward. [1978] 2003. *Orientalism*. London: Penguin Books.
Woody, E. Z., and H. Szechtman. 2011. "Adaptation to Potential Threat: The Evolution, Neurobiology, and Psychopathology of the Security Motivation System." *Neuroscience and Biobehavioral Reviews* 35 (4): 1019–33. https://doi.org/10.1016/j.neubiorev.2010.08.003.

4

EMPIRICAL EMBODIMENT OF CRITICAL RATIONALISM: DELIBERATIVE THEORY AND OPEN SOCIETY

Gazela Pudar Draško and Predrag Krstić

> Your responsibility and mine is to uncover errors, correct them and do whatever is in our power to help one another to gradually build a better world. I say "gradually" because, as we are fallible, we are certainly going to make mistakes: let us be wary of false prophets who have a solution for everything! Especially when they have cannons to support their propositions.
>
> —*Popper (1993: 17)*

Cognitivist approaches to politics and political action underlie both Karl Popper's and deliberative political theory. In this article, we claim that deliberative theory inherits—or in parallel develops—Popper's call for reason in political decision-making. Starting from its first clear articulation in 1980 by Joseph M. Bessette, and then further elaboration in (a book with the evincive title of) *The Mild Voice of Reason* (1994), deliberative theory prompted many innovations and social experiments whose core aim was to improve decision-making and governance through greater or better scaled participation. Habermas was one of the pioneers of deliberative democratic theory, when advocating for *discursive democracy* or a deliberative approach to governance (Habermas, 1989). His attempt to establish deliberative dialogue between a developed, powerful public sphere and public institutions had a huge impact in the theory of democracy, especially in advocacy for the right and benefits of consenting to disagree. However, it has also been criticized as non-implementable, without a support structure for the public sphere (Scott-Phillips 2023; Landemore 2020).

In seeking an alternative that would allow critical reasoning (and deliberation), focus has shifted from dialogue *between* institutions—dialogue between, in fact, society and the state, as implied in Habermas's approach, was difficult to grasp—to a dialogue *within* institutions. Different deliberative democratic innovations evolved to fulfill the need for informed discussion for the sake of better decision-making, mostly based on deliberative mini-publics (Goodin and Dryzek 2006; Fung 2003; Gastil et al. 2008; Smith 2009; Warren 2009; Smith and Ryan 2012). This proliferation was so remarkable that it has been named the *deliberative turn* in democratic theory (Dryzek 2000). The deliberative turn and significant development of the deliberative theory is supported by cognitive science, anthropology and other fields studying "human nature," grounded in deep evolutionary and cognitive reasons why deliberative approaches are especially effective in complex societies (Scott-Phillips 2023).

The power of group reasoning has been evidenced in more recent studies, emphasizing the epistemic value of deliberative democracy and proving that it yields epistemically superior outcomes—more informed and more coherent opinions and decisions (Landemore 2007; Wu 2011; Mercier and Landemore 2012; Fiket 2019).

For our argument, we are particularly interested in the systemic approach to deliberative democracy, as it develops the criteria of deliberative quality of social practices (Parkinson and Mansbridge 2012). These criteria are epistemic, ethical, and democratic functions.[1] The *epistemic* function of deliberative social actions is to form preferences, opinions, and decisions that are based on the *weighing of all relevant information and arguments*. This function strongly relies on the deliberative ideal of *inclusiveness*, which guarantees the inclusion of "all" discourses and exposure to different views (Thompson 2008; Habermas 1984). Also, it relies on the *communication of justified arguments* (reason giving), given that in a heterogeneous environment an argument has to be justified in terms of common good, to be accepted and considered for deliberation (Habermas 1984; Cohen 1989; Gutmann and Thompson 2004; Mendelberg 2002; Thompson 2008). In fact, this function enables us to thoroughly investigate the issue at stake in the similar way that scientific argument is exposed to the investigation. *Fallibility* of the justified arguments is tested in the mutual communication of deliberative arenas. Finally, justifications must be both procedurally and substantively "accessible," conferring a certain amount of legitimacy upon the decision-making process (Sen 2013).

A systemic approach strongly indicates that different social practices are deliberative arenas. It implies that its deliberative quality could be improved and society benefit from what Popper called *piecemeal engineering approach*—experts work on populating the social space with deliberative mini-publics in various forms, contributing, thus, to better governance. Such an idea was

---

1 The other two functions are concerned with the procedural aspects that contribute to the success of the process and final good decisions—or in Popper's spirit—the least bad decisions. The *ethical* function of the deliberative system is concerned with *mutual respect* among citizens. It is strongly related to the previous function, since the fulfillment of the epistemic function allows for the development of mutual respect. Exposure to different arguments and views, in fact, makes us think respectfully about the reasons and interests of others involved in the public discussion (Cooke 2000). Recently, studies evolved around *empathetic* function of the deliberation, speaking for the empathetic understanding as a product of the deliberative discussions (Hannon 2019). The *democratic* function of deliberative systems is related to the deliberative requirement of the equality of participation and is intrinsically connected to the other two functions. It posits that all those that could be affected by a decision should have the possibility to participate in the public discussion about that decision.

further advanced by Landemore's concept of open democracy, conceived as a system that sets standards for public deliberation on all political levels, becoming *a new model of democracy* (Landemore 2013; 2020). It is an open question whether Popper would appreciate the concept of *open democracy*, as his model of *open society* was more technocratic and envisaged as epistocracy.

We believe, however, that Popper's political philosophy is not incompatible with theories of deliberative democracy. What's more, we can situate Popper at the core of deliberative theory, where a carefully designed top-down approach has been dominant so far. The experimental models have been lauded as enabling the emergence of new political styles and administrative practices. We will try to show how these practices coincide with basic postulates of Popper's political theory of critical rationalism. By showing that Popper's theory is valuable for deliberative theory, we try to bridge these two traditions that have not been communicating to each other before. In fact, we try to show that Popper is not less important to be included in a corpus of deliberative theoretical foundation and when stripped from his elitist view of the policymaking, he could very well communicate own principles as basic postulates of the first wave of deliberative theory.

Popper's Critical Rationalism and Negative Utilitarianism as Foundations of Open Society

When introducing the concept of *open society*, Popper says that "our Western civilization" made an eastern breakthrough, that is, that the Ancient Greeks made a step from "tribalism towards humanitarianism" (Popper 1947a: 151). Tribalism is founded on a collective tribal tradition that leaves no space for personal responsibility. This is what constitutes the original *closed* society, as magical or tribal or collectivist. Open society, on the other hand, lets its members face personal decisions and their consequences. Popper admits that the division between closed or magic and open or rational/critical society is not straightforward but based on ideal models, and that (elements of) both can be identified in contemporary societies. The transition between traditional closed societies to open societies happened when institutions were recognized as a human creation that institutes action toward people-oriented goals or human purposes (Popper 1947a: 247). The *discovery of critical discussion* makes a crucial, revolutionary turn in human (and social) development. Following this path is not without challenges, as this requires human and social beings to behave rationally, take care of themselves, and take on a huge responsibility. Yet, this is the price of being human (Popper 1947a: 154, 176). Popper also reinforces that it is not possible to bring back the glorious past of the innocent and beautiful closed society, as all these attempts lead to destruction and totalitarian projects with millions of victims. Once the rational path has been taken, we need to find methods to improve things, without appealing to a "philosopher's stone, or a formula that will convert our somewhat corrupt human society into pure, lasting gold"

(Popper 1947b: 316–317). "But if we wish to remain human, then there is only one way, the way into the open society. We must go on into the unknown, courageously, using what reason we have, to plan for security and freedom" (Popper 1947a: 177). Popper's bold proposal of open society is at once its strongest open advocacy. There is a clear antinomy between openness and closeness that is, in fact, inhuman behavior, which is anticivilizing as it is unscientific.

Civilization and science go hand in hand for Popper. Interpreters agree that Popper's approach to the social and political philosophy is specific precisely in that it begins with the understanding of the scientific method and strives to implement it in society, beyond science. Contrary to, for example, Foucault (2018), Popper is persistent in seeing science as a privileged field of interaction (Popper 1978) and wholeheartedly advocates applying a methodology of *critical rationalism* (Popper 1962: 52, 216, 312–313; Popper 1947b: 213, 224–225; cf. Miller 1994). It is already affirmed in the natural sciences and it should be embedded in the social sciences and (real) politics. Popper talks about the lack of rationality that enables the realization of Hitler—"The 'world' is not rational, but it is the task of science to rationalize it. 'Society' is not rational, but it is the task of the social engineer to rationalize it. Ordinary language is not rational, but it is our task to rationalize it, or at least to keep up its standards of clarity" (Popper 1947b: 337). In one unified vision of the science and politics, openness to constant questioning ought to permeate institutions and enable not only scientific but also general progress. Through uncompromisingly thorough questioning, a given political course may be modified or abandoned, following the falsification model of scientific theories.

The advantage of open society institutions in modern liberal democracies, "the world of Western democracies" that "may not be the best of all conceivable or logically possible political worlds, but it is the best of all political worlds of whose existence we have any historical knowledge" (Popper 2002a: 90), except for individual freedom, lies in the capacity for peaceful autocorrection. Open societies nurture freedom and social progress through embedding and stimulating the critical rationalist approach, as all knowledge, including social, is hypothetical and dependent on the same scientific method (translated into an institutionalized trial and error process, Popper 1962: 5; Popper 2002a: 81–92; cf. Corvi 1997; Notturno 2000; Currie and Musgrave 1985; Jarvie and Pralong 1999). It is almost as if he is saying that their democratic character and prosperity are a collateral benefit of critical rationalism as a pervasive scientific/social method.

Popper, thus, argues for open society, but not by using the moral defense of liberalism (cf. Jacobs 1991); rather, he does so proving that its totalitarian rival is not fallible (Popper 1962: 336–338; cf. Simkin 1993; Stokes 1998). It is *fallibilism* that actually connects Popper's theory of knowledge and philosophy of society: as we progress in science, deliberately submitting theories to uncompromising questioning, rejecting those that are wrong, so the critical spirit can and should operate in society. Instead of historical determinism, falsely imagining that the future is predictable, historical indeterminism is the only philosophy of history that matches the correctly understood nature of the scientific knowledge (Popper 1982). The *piecemeal engineering approach* that leads us to accomplish specific goals one by one is the only antidote to the fatal frenzy of holistic social planning (Popper 1957: 64–71; Popper 1947a: 139–144, 224, 245–246; Popper 1994: 76, 104, 201, 228; Popper 2000: 40–48; cf. James 1980).

Popper's political vision is specific and difficult to situate in established ideological fields. Perhaps the easiest label is liberal—reason, tolerance, nonviolence, and individual freedom are values that he openly advocates for, while modern liberal democracy is the best historic form of open society. However, Popper himself stated that the idea of "liberal," "liberalism, etc." does not designate a follower of any political party, but "simply a man who values individual freedom and who is alive to the dangers inherent in all forms of power and authority" (Popper 1962: viii). Liberalism understood so widely is the reason behind appropriating Popper not only to liberal but also sometimes to conservative and socialist segments of the ideological spectrum.

His political theory resonates with some of the prominent scholars who established the grounds for the deliberative turn in democratic theory. In his interesting article on the liberal community, Dworkin emphasizes that "political communities have a communal life, and the success or failure of a community's communal life is part of what determines whether its members lives are good or bad" (Dworkin 1989: 492). The communal life of one society—embodied in the acts of government, meaning its legislative, executive, and judicial institutions—is the collective framework that sets the ethical standards for individual success or failure. The actor—Dworkin designates them an integrated liberal—clearly understands that they cannot live the good life in a community that does not treat everyone with equal concern (ibid.: 501).

Popper's thinking also has parallels with Dworkin's understanding of the communal life principles. When injustice is substantial and pervasive in a political community, says Dworkin, "someone with a vivid sense of his own critical interests is inevitably thwarted when his community fails in its responsibilities of justice" (1989: 504). Discussion that revolves around disagreement is essential for serving the common interest of all in securing the *just* solution. Healthy disagreement is necessary, since citizens are members of a community who know (or should know) that they can only win or lose together. In fact, citizens need *critical rationalism* when they coordinately act within their own political community to overcome disagreement and gradually eliminate injustice. This principle of securing the just solution lies within a broad and universally acceptable idea that we should, whenever possible, minimize suffering (through solidarity). "Whatever else our exact ethical commitments and specific positive goals are, we can and should certainly all agree that, in principle, and whenever possible, the overall amount of conscious suffering in all beings capable of conscious suffering should be minimized" (Metzinger 2003: 622). It originates from what Smart (1958) saw as Popper's moral doctrine: *the principle of negative utilitarianism*.

The capacity to suffer, whether the exclusive domain of humans or extended to all animate beings, as well as the aversion to suffering from those who only might experience it or who sympathize with the suffering of others—allows it to be the basis of practical, moral, and/or political action. It is undeniable that suffering should provoke moral considerations, but also present us with further ethical questions: first of all, the question of the nature, scope, or measure of our obligations toward those who suffer; but also the question of necessary affective capacities and moral virtues for an appropriate or responsible response to suffering (Mayerfeld 2002). The issue becomes still more complicated when suffering is not only something that elicits response from moral beings, but when it is itself entailed by certain actions. Every ethical school of thought, without exception, contains some prohibition on causing suffering; however, all too often, the prohibition comes with an addendum—"unnecessary" suffering. This inevitably leads to a new point of contention: when is it "necessary"—that is, justified—to cause suffering? In other words, who has the power to judge its necessity and then inflict suffering? Regardless of the different answers to these questions, what has become well established, thanks in large part to Popper's commitment, is that "if there's one ethical principle that most people agree on, it's the importance of reducing suffering. It seems to be a widespread intuition that there's something particularly morally urgent about suffering" (Gorton 2015). This is the *lowest common denominator*, at which calculation ends and the character of justified action is preserved.

From Epistocracy to Deliberative Democracy

In spite of the technocratic character of Popper's vision of the open society, there are elements that allow greater participation of the citizens if carefully observed. When he says, "the liberal does not dream of a perfect consensus of opinions; he only hopes for the mutual fertilization of opinions, and the consequent growth of ideas" (Popper 1962: 352), he is very much in line with deliberative argumentation that seeks not consensus but better understanding and decision-making based on (acknowledging) the interest of others. His description of the necessary precondition for practicing critical rationalism clearly resonates with the definition of the deliberative arenas: "All that is needed is a readiness to learn from one's partner in the discussion, which includes a genuine wish to understand what he intends to say" (ibid.).

Additionally, Popper advocated a certain and limited degree of state interventionism, allowing the development of practices that could enable state-guided enhancement of good governance, as long as it was aimed at reducing suffering in society. This interventionism is not to be equated with utopian efforts to create social and economic equality (cf. Danaher 2018, Kadlec 2008); rather, they are attempts of the state to diminish the worst consequences of capitalism step by step.[2] Popper suggested applying nonmarket-oriented, gradual *social engineering* precisely to solve the problems of poverty, unemployment, health care, and vast class inequalities. It is clear that Popper's vision of politics is mostly technocratic and directed top to bottom. However, although unclear from his writing how this social engineering would work practically, it nevertheless allows us to "upgrade" his theory with deliberative arenas. Indeed, as piecemeal engineering, they could precisely be that social practice whose operationalization is lacking in Popper. Rational action for Popper implies experiments on or with institutions, which would be performed step by step, on a small scale, enabling timely detection of errors and continuous correction.

Suspicion toward direct state intervention as a way of solving social problems is not contradictory to what we are advocating here. Popper acknowledges the longstanding tension between the principles of freedom and justice: intervention inevitably strengthens the state, potentially endangering individual freedom; yet, it is also (often) the only way to make society fairer and more stable. The fear that giving necessary and always potentially dangerous power to the state could mean the loss of freedom and end of planning leads Popper to a request for a balanced state engagement: "State intervention should be limited to what is really necessary for the protection of freedom. We must intervene, but knowing this to be a necessary evil, we should intervene as little as possible" (Popper 1947b: 122). If instruments of citizens' will, such as deliberative arenas, are embedded in state power, it allows for decisions to not only be freer and more just but also transform them from individual to collective.

Still, we cannot claim that Popper's vision of the political order and policymaking gave a significant role to the citizens. He thought that exemplary "public policy" would not be driven by the wisdom or character of a superior leader—as in Plato—nor by the people, who are *not there to pursue policies but to judge their (un)successes* (Popper 2000: 72). Popper based his whole system on epistocracy[3]—socially committed devotees of the scientific method who would guarantee gradual changes and their responsible correction step by step.

2 Popper's abhorrence of extensive central planning definitely fits into the libertarian tradition. The same may be said of the unreserved privileging of individual freedom as the most important political value and deprecation of (imposed) equality because it is the road to tyranny (cf. Popper 2002b: 36; Shearmur 1996). However, while admitting the extensive benefit from the mechanism of the free market, Popper persisted in warning against unbridled capitalism. He fully acknowledged the injustice and inhumanity of the laissez-faire system depicted by Marx and considered the state a counterpower to the economic monopoly. He advocated for abandoning the politics of unlimited economic freedom and its replacement with economic interventionism that would protect the economically weak (Popper 1947b: 116–117).

3 Popper's open society was technocratic rather than aristocratic. However, there is a very specific *aristocracy* not foreign to Popper's vision—an aristocratic liberalism (Kahan 1992). We believe that Popper would not mind being in the company of Jacob Burckhardt, John Stuart Mill, or Alexis de Tocqueville. His open society is also *pancritic*, a society of *all* open issues, a *debate club* whose members are committed to "truths" or better solutions to problems (see also Kendel 1989 or Jarvie 1972).

We dare claim here, based on the works of Dworkin, Gutmann, Thompson, Cohen, Cook, etc., that deliberation is a normative ideal that not only yields better laws but also induces a positive transformation in its participants—making them more epistemically and empathetically equipped. In addition to epistemic, we emphasize also empathetic quality, whose main function is to accommodate polarization and antagonism in society that lead not to critical rationalism but judgmentalism (Hannon 2019; Grimm 2018).[4] People need to be persuaded that deliberation is in their best interest for it to be successful and yield better decisions: "When people are motivated to reason, they do a better job at accepting only sound arguments, which is quite generally to their advantage" (Mercier and Sperber 2011: 96; see also Petty et al. 1981). Even if we factor in confirmation bias, as it is impossible to eliminate at the individual level, deliberation leads to better decisions at the collective level (Mercier and Landemore 2012). This argument speaks against criticism of Popper made by critical theorists, that is, Adorno, who claims that "positivist cognitive ideals of harmonious and consistent, logically flawless models" are unsustainable (Adorno 1997: 308–309, our translation). If we do not aim at logically flawless models but on ones that allow collective reasoning on diverse arguments, regardless of how logically flawed, and without *predetermined correct answers*, this will bring us closer to contextually specific, less flawed decisions and policies.

Reason can flourish only if we provide the appropriate environment.[5] In this "we," we see a place for making peace with the role of socially committed scientists or experts, so important to Popper. It is difficult to project deliberative democracy and its development as a replacement of representative democracy (or at least a substantive complement to it), without socially committed actors that devote their expertise to building social norms and practices that will be the skeleton of such deliberative democracy. This "we" would be a community of deliberative theorists and practitioners who invest their expertise to find better models of deliberative innovations that would further involve more citizens and secure better decisions. These socially committed experts may be various social actors and come from different layers of society.[6]

In a recent study of deliberative process through a citizens' assembly in Serbia (Fiket and Đorđević 2022), and a study of trust-building through social movements (Fiket et al. forthcoming), the role of experts was widened to include all those who gained knowledge through practice and engagement. They are considered as equal to, if not more important, than mere academics and intellectuals possessing theoretical expertise. Deliberative mini-publics (DMPs), namely,

---

4 There is also opposing evidence, where beneficial epistemic effects were recorded in a not so favorable atmosphere characterized by deep polarization, i.e., Catholics and Protestants in Northern Ireland (Luskin et al. 2014).
5 "Once we come to understand the perspectives of people on the other side of the ideological spectrum, we can begin to have a sensible discussion about what divides us" (Hannon 2019: 10).
6 The emergence of citizens' science and its promotion fully aligns with this view of, at first glance, contradictory notion of lay experts.

were organized in Serbia in the contexts of the highly discouraging institutional environment of captured institutions of hybrid state. They still offered us a positive example of the ability of the—generally apathic—citizens to make an effort to come to the rational solutions for the two communal problems in focus (air pollution and expanding pedestrian zone). Serbian DMPs urged us to understand that this kind of experimentation is valuable and is able to produce considerable effects in rationalization of the decision-making process, but only if they are institutionally backed up. Without political will to utilize and institutionalize this instrument in order to bring its results directly into the policymaking process, the effect will be non-existing on a long-term basis. When Popper talks about piecemeal social engineering, we hold that he thinks that this should be political strategy, and institutionalization is the *conditio sine qua non* deliberative innovations can succeed.

When we look back in time, the deliberative turn in theory at the beginning of the twenty-first century was initially focused on introducing citizens into representative democratic politics in a limited and circumscribed way (Parvin 2020; Dryzek 2012; Mansbridge et al. 2012). After the severe crisis of representative democracy (approximately 2008), there was a rise in participatory democracy and proliferation of democratic innovations that sought not merely to complement but even completely replace representative democracy. With the loss of public trust in expert decision-making, the efforts to introduce more lay citizens and trust them to be capable of making decisions have been substantially deepened. Parvin openly opposes full participatory democracy, claiming, rather, that reforms aimed at incorporating citizens in elite-level debates would in general be more resilient to the current issues in liberal societies of low and unequal rates of citizen participation (Parvin 2020). Deliberative theory remains, thus, a significant and potent field of investigation of how to *institutionalize critical rationalism*, with the aim of achieving better decisions. Studies show that knowing or not knowing the mere facts is not the same as citizens' competence to solve political problems once that information and knowledge are presented to them (Janković 2022). If deliberative institutions are carefully designed, able to compensate for well-known cognitive and emotional biases, with "scientifically constructed conditions, supportive institutional features, such as balanced information materials, experts on multiple sides available for questioning, facilitation, and sessions with different actors, as well as necessary deliberative norms" (ibid.: 33), then we can indeed speak of realization or even *materialization* of Popper's ideals of critical rationalism and piecemeal social engineering.

Concluding Remarks

An open society is, among other things, a loud and well-founded protest against expectations, demands, and, especially, against prescriptions of paths to social happiness. It is intended as a necessary and, in all likelihood, sufficient check against tyranny, authoritarianism, bias, lack of freedom, irresponsibility, and intolerance (cf. Popper 1947b: 225–226). Thanks to its negativism, the binary opposition actually dissolves into a basis for rational disagreement. Thanks to deliberative arenas, we can think of paths toward better decisions that are sound, rational, but also widely accepted and legitimate. It may be seen as a shell, a skeleton of an open society, without ideological substance, established to invite various arguments and conciliate the majoritarian principle with the inclusive character of open society.

In other words, we could say that the critical rationalism of open society provides the conditions of possibility for what deliberative democracy puts into practice. Indeed, epistemic, moral, and democratic unity does not reside only in the functions of a desirable society, but, if we may reconstruct Popper's response to the challenge of deliberation, in its establishment. Namely, what Popper calls the "rationalist attitude" or "the attitude of reasonableness," always quite similar to the "scientific attitude," implies, among other things, the "idea of impartiality," the idea that no one should be his or her own judge: faith in reason is not only faith in one's own reason but also in the reason of others. Thus, the "rationalist" rejects any request for authority, including the affirmation of his own, aware that they are "capable of learning from criticism as well as from his own and other people's mistakes, and that one can learn in this sense only if one takes others and their arguments seriously" (Popper 1947b: 213, 224–225). Popper further specifically connects rationalism with the right to be heard and to defend one's own arguments. He concludes that this implies "the recognition of the claim to tolerance, at least of those who are not intolerant themselves" (Popper 1947b: 225). From the ideas of impartiality and tolerance then derives the idea of responsibility—"we have not only to listen to arguments, but we have a duty to respond, to answer, where our actions affect others"—along with rationalism's association with "the recognition of the necessity of social institutions to protect freedom of criticism, freedom of thought, and thus the freedom of men" (Popper 1947b: 225–226). The adoption of so critically understood rationalism, Popper points out, at last implies the recognition that there is a unity of human reason: that there undoubtedly exists a "common medium of communication, a common language of reason," which imposes something like a "moral obligation … to keep up its standards of clarity and to use it in such a way that it can retain its function as the vehicle of argument" (Popper 1947b: 345). If there should be something like qualified deliberation, we dare suggest, there should also be its underlying postulations.

Bibliography

Adorno, Theodor W. 1997. *Negative Dialektik / Jargon der Eigentlichkeit, Theodor W. Adorno: Gesammelte Schriften, Band 6*. Frankfurt am Main: Suhrkamp.
Bessette, Joseph M. 1980. "Deliberative Democracy: The Majority Principle in Republican Government." In *How Democratic is the Constitution?* edited by Robert A. Goldwin

and William A. Schambra, 102–16. Washington: American Enterprise Institute for Public Policy Research.
Bessette, Joseph M. 1994. *The Mild Voice of Reason: Deliberative Democracy and American National Government*. Chicago, IL: The University of Chicago Press.
Cohen, Joshua. 1989. "Deliberation and Democratic Legitimacy." In *The Good Polity. Normative Analysis of the State*, edited by A. Hamlin and P. Pettit, 17–34. Oxford: Basil Blackwell.
Cooke, Maeve. 2000. "Five Arguments for Deliberative Democracy." *Political Studies* 48 (5): 947–69.
Corvi, Roberta. 1997. *An Introduction to the Thought of Karl Popper*. London: Routledge.
Currie, Gregory and Alan Musgrave, eds. 1985.*Popper and the Human Sciences*. Dordrecht: Martinus Nijhoff.
Danaher, John. 2018. "Popper's Critique of Utopianism and Defence of Negative Utilitarianism." *Philosophical Disquisitions*. http://philosophicaldisquisitions.blogspot.com/2018/01/poppers-critique-of-utopianism-and.html.
Dryzek, John S. 2000. *Deliberative Democracy and Beyond: Liberals, Critics, Contestations*. Oxford: Oxford University Press.
Dryzek, John S. 2012. *Foundations and Frontiers of Deliberative Governance*. Oxford: Oxford University Press.
Dworkin, Ronald. 1989. "Liberal Community." *California Law Review* 77 (3): 479–504.
Fiket, Irena. 2019. *Deliberativno građanstvo* [Deliberative Citizenship]. Belgrade: Akademska knjiga, Institut za filozofiju i društvenu teoriju.
Fiket, Irena, and Biljana Đorđević. 2022. "Promises and Challenges of Deliberative and Participatory Innovations in Hybrid Regimes: The Case of Two Citizens' Assemblies in Serbia." *Philosophy and Society* 33 (1): 3-25.
Fiket, Irena, Ilić Vujo, and Gazela Pudar Draško. forthcoming. "The Pandemic in Illiberal Democracies: Challenges and Opportunities for Social Movements in Serbia." *Southeast European and Black Sea Studies*.
Foucault, Michel. 2018. "Šta je kritika? [Kritika i Aufklärung]" [What is Critique?] In *Šta je Kritika?* edited by Adriana Zaharijević and Predrag Krstić, 35–91. Novi Sad: Akademska knjiga; Belgrade: Institut za filozofiju i društvenu teoriju.
Fung, Archon. 2003. "Recipes for Public Spheres: Eight Institutional Design Choices and Their Consequences." *Journal of Political Philosophy* 11 (3): 338–67.
Gastil, John, Black Laura, and Kara Moscovitz. 2008. "Ideology, Attitude Change, and Deliberation in Small Face-to-Face Group." *Political Communication* 25 (1): 23–46.
Goodin, Robert, and John S. Dryzek. 2006. "Deliberative Impacts: The Macro-Political Uptake of Mini-Publics." *Politics & Society* 34 (2): 219–44.
Gorton, William. 2015. "Negative Utilitarianism FAQ." *Internet Encyclopedia of Philosophy and its Authors*. https://www.utilitarianism.com/nu/nufaq.html.
Grimm, Stephen. 2018. "Understanding as an Intellectual Virtue." In *The Routledge Handbook of Virtue Epistemology*, edited by Heather Battaly. London: Routledge, 340–351.
Gutmann, Amy, and Dennis F. Thompson. 2004. *Why Deliberative Democracy*. Princeton, NJ and Oxford: Princeton University Press.
Habermas, Jürgen. 1984. *The Theory of Communicative Action, Vol. 1: Reason and the Rationalization of Society*. Boston: Beacon Press.
Habermas, Jürgen. 1989. *The Structural Transformation of The Public Sphere: An Inquiry into a Category of Bourgeois Society*. Cambridge, MA: MIT Press.

Hannon, Michael. 2019. "Empathetic Understanding and Deliberative Democracy." *Philosophy and Phenomenological Research* 101 (3): 591–611.
Jacobs, Struan. 1991. *Science and British Liberalism: Locke, Bentham, Mill and Popper*. Aldershot: Avebury.
James, Roger. 1980. *Return to Reason: Popper's Thought in Public Life*. Shepton Mallet: Open Books.
Janković, Ivana. 2022. "Deliberative Democracy – Theory and Practice: The Case of the Belgrade Citizens' Assembly". *Philosophy and Society* 33(1): 26–49.
Jarvie, Ian C. 1972. *Concepts and Society*. London: Routledge.
Jarvie, Ian C., and Sandra Pralong, eds. 1999. *Popper's Open Society after 50 Years*. London: Routledge.
Kadlec, Erich. 2008. "Popper's 'Negative Utilitarianism': From Utopia to Reality." In *Karl Popper's Response to 1938*, edited by Peter Markl and Erich Kadlec, 107–21. Frankfurt am Main: Peter Lang.
Kahan, Alan S. 1992. *Aristocratic Liberalism: The Social and Political Thought of Jacob Burckhardt, John Stuart Mill, and Alexis de Tocqueville*. Oxford: Oxford University Press.
Kendel, Vilmor. 1989. "'Otvoreno društvo' i njegove zablude" [Open Society and Its Illusions]. In *O toleranciji. Rasprave o demokratskoj kulturi*, edited by Igor Primorac, 161–80. Belgrade: "Filip Višnjić".
Landemore, Helene. 2007. *Democratic Reason: Politics, Collective Intelligence, and the Rule of the Many*. Cambridge, MA: Harvard University Press.
Landemore, Helene. 2013. *Democractic Reason: Politics, Collective Intelligence, and the Rule of the Many*. Princeton, NJ: Princeton University Press.
Landemore, Helene. 2020. *Open Democracy: Reinventing Popular Rule for the Twenty-First Century*. Princeton, NJ: Princeton University Press.
Luskin, Robert C., Ian O'Flynn, James S. Fishkin, and David Russell. 2014. "Deliberating across Deep Divides." *Political Studies* 62 (1): 116–35.
Mansbridge, Jane et al. 2012. "A Systemic Approach to Deliberative Democracy." In *Deliberative Systems: Deliberative Democracy at the Large Scale*, edited by John Parkinson and Jane Mansbridge, 1–26. Cambridge: Cambridge University Press.
Mayerfeld, Jamie. 2002. *Suffering and Moral Responsibility*. Oxford: Oxford University Press.
Mendelberg, T. 2002. "The Deliberative Citizen: Theory and Evidence." In *Political Decision Making, Deliberation and Participation: Research in Micropolitics*, vol. 6, edited by M. X. Delli Carpini, L. Huddy, and R. Y. Shapiro, 151–93. Greenwich, CT: JAI Press.
Mercier, Hugo, and Helene Landemore. 2012. "Reasoning Is for Arguing: Understanding the Successes and Failures of Deliberation." *Political Psychology* 33 (2): 243–58.
Mercier, Hugo, and Dan Sperber. 2011. "Why do Humans Reason? Arguments for an Argumentative Theory." *Behavioral and Brain Sciences* 34: 57–111.
Metzinger, Thomas. 2003. *Being No One: The Self-Model Theory of Subjectivity*. Cambridge, MA: MIT Press.
Miller, David. 1994. *Critical Rationalism: A Restatement and Defence*. Chicago: Open Court.
Notturno, Mark. 2000. *Science and Open Society*. New York: Central European University Press.
Parkinson, John, and Jane Mansbridge. 2012. *Deliberative Systems: Deliberative Democracy at the Large Scale*. Cambridge: Cambridge University Press.

Parvin, Phil. 2020. "The Participatory Paradox: An Egalitarian Critique of Participatory Democracy." *Representation* 57 (2): 263–85.
Petty, Richard, John Cacioppo, and Rachel Goldman. 1981. "Personal Involvement as a Determinant of Argument-Based Persuasion." *Journal of Personality and Social Psychology* 41 (5): 847–55.
Poper, Karl R. 1993. *Otvoreno društvo i njegovi neprijatelji I: Čar Platona*. Belgrade: BIGZ.
Popper, Karl R. 1947a. *The Open Society and its Enemies I: The Spell of Plato*. London: George Routledge & Sons. / Poper, Karl R. 1993. Otvoreno društvo i njegovi neprijatelji I: Čar Platona. Belgrade: BIGZ.
Popper, Karl R. 1947b. *The Open Society and its Enemies II: The High Tide of Prophecy: Hegel, Marx, and the Aftermath*. London: George Routledge & Sons.
Popper, Karl R. 1957. *The Poverty of Historicism*. Boston: The Beacon Press.
Popper, Karl R. 1962. *Conjectures and Refutations: The Growth of Scientific Knowledge*. New York: Basic Books.
Popper, Karl R. 1978. "Three Worlds." *The Tanner Lecture on Human Values* 7. April. http://tannerlectures.utah.edu/_documents/ a-to-z/p/popper80.pdf.
Popper, Karl R. 1982. *The Open Universe: An Argument for Indeterminism*. London: Hutchinson.
Popper, Karl R. 1994. *In Search of a Better World: Lectures and Essays from Thirty Years*. London: Routledge.
Popper, Karl R. 2000. *The Lessons of This Century: With Two Talks on Freedom and the Democratic State*. London: Routledge.
Popper, Karl R. 2002a. *All Life Is Problem Solving*. London: Routledge.
Popper, Karl R. 2002b. *Unended Quest: An Intellectual Autobiography*. London: Routledge.
Scott-Phillips, Thom. 2023. "Human Nature and the Open Society." In *Open Society Unresolved: The Contemporary Relevance of a Contested Idea*, edited by Christof Royer and Liviu Matei. Budapest, Vienna and New York: CEU Press. doi:10.31234/osf.io/k3cx9
Sen, Maya. 2013."Courting Deliberation: An Essay on Deliberative Democracy in the American Judicial System." *Notre Dame Journal of Law, Ethics and Public Policy* 27: 303–31.
Shearmur, Jeremey. 1996. *The Political Thought of Karl Popper*. London: Routledge.
Simkin, Colin G. F. 1993. *Popper's Views on Natural and Social Science*. Leiden: Brill.
Smart, R. N. 1958. "Negative Utilitarianism." *Mind* 67 (268): 542–43.
Smith, Graham. 2009. *Democratic Innovations – Designing Institutions for Citizen Participation*. Cambridge: Cambridge University Press.
Smith, Graham, and Matt Ryan. 2012. "Defining Mini-Public: Making Sense of Existing Conceptions." Paper presented at the PSA Annual Conference, Belfast, April 3–5.
Stokes, Geoffrey. 1998. *Popper: Philosophy, Politics and Scientific Method*. Cambridge: Polity Press.
Thompson, Dennis F. 2008. "Deliberative Democratic Theory and Empirical Political Science." *Annual Review of Political Science* 11: 497–520.
Warren, Mark E. 2009. "Two Trust-Based Uses of Mini-Publics in Democracy." APSA 2009 Toronto Meeting Paper.
Wu, Kevin. 2011. "Deliberative Democracy and Epistemic Humility." *Behavioral and Brain Sciences* 34 (2): 93–94.

5

OPEN SOCIETY AS AN ACHIEVEMENT: POPPER, GAUS, AND THE LIBERAL TRADITION

Piers Norris Turner

The idea of "open society" has experienced a small revival within academic political philosophy in the United States since the publication of Gerald Gaus's *The Tyranny of the Ideal* (2016).[1] Of course, "open society" has been an influential theme in public discourse since Karl Popper published *The Open Society and Its Enemies* in 1945 (1966a, 1966b), and it has continued to engage thinkers across the political spectrum through the work of the Open Society Foundations, related academic organizations like the Open Society University Network, and think tanks like the Niskanen Center (Niskanen 2022).[2] But within American analytic philosophy departments, the idea of open society has largely ceased to frame debates about the nature of a sustainable liberal political order. This is unfortunate at a time when broad church liberalism needs a robust defense against authoritarian threats, dogmatic partisans, and the decline of liberal democratic norms in many countries. The attention Gaus and others have paid to the idea of open society is, therefore, a welcome development, but I worry that some leading ideas in that revival fail to meet our political moment.

In *The Tyranny of the Ideal*, Gaus reminds us of important core elements of Popper's account of open society: that being committed to justice is not necessarily the same as being committed to one's own current conception of justice, that we should always remain open to critical discussion and social diversity, that this has implications for the way we organize ourselves socially and politically, and that such openness suggests a piecemeal approach to solving social and political problems. Gaus extends this line of thought to contemporary debates within political philosophy, arguing that it should limit the role that ideals of justice play in our current collective decision-making about how to organize ourselves.

I regard Gaus's *The Tyranny of the Ideal*, and his magnum opus *The Order of Public Reason* (2011), as among the most important works in political philosophy

---

1 Besides Gaus (2016, 2017, 2018, 2021), see, for example, Landemore (2020, 17), Muldoon (2018), Muldoon, ed. (2018), Thrasher (2020), Thrasher and Vallier (2018), and Vallier (2019).
2 Some leading discussions of Popper and open society over the years include Gray (1976), Hacohen (2000), Jarvie (2001), Magee (1985 [1974]), Notturno (2000), Ryan (1985), Shearmur (1996), Soros (2000), Stokes (1998), and Wolin (2004, 495–503).

in the last generation. Nevertheless, in this chapter I will resist a shift Gaus makes in his final, posthumous book, *The Open Society and Its Complexities* (2021). In that work, and in some writing leading up to it, Gaus moves away from his Popper-friendly position toward a Hayekian vision of open society that instead casts Popper as a false friend of open society. I think this shift in his final works is a mistake that can be instructive about the demands of maintaining open society and the continuing relevance of Popper's work.

Following Hayek, Gaus comes to identify open society as a diverse market society with a minimal legal framework focused on protecting individuals' jurisdictional rights (such as private property rights), within which social morality—our widely shared normative expectations of each other—may spontaneously evolve. On this view, open society is threatened by any attempt to rationally manage or mitigate the results of market processes, because doing so inevitably invokes controversial concrete ends that are imposed on others.[3] The transgressions in doing so are both moral and epistemic. What is striking is that, in his later work, Gaus seems equally suspicious of attempts like Popper's to articulate a broad tradition of fallibilism, tolerance of diversity, and critical exchange as a crucial component of social morality for any open society. As we shall see, Gaus argues that even this relatively thin commitment is objectionably "sectarian" and hubristic because it places conditions on how people hold their beliefs or values, and so is incompatible with a truly diverse open society. By contrast, for Popper, such a tradition is practically necessary to preserve a diverse open society over time.

I will argue that Gaus makes two key mistakes in his later engagement with Popper. First, he comes to associate Popper's fallibilistic problem-solving and piecemeal social engineering with the hyper-rationalism and hubristic forms of ideal theory that he rightly argues are incompatible with open society. In doing so, he presents a false dichotomy between the Hayekian vision and authoritarian or totalitarian alternatives, when in fact Popper is sensitive to many of the same concerns as Hayek.[4] Second, I believe Popper is right that open society depends on developing and protecting a widely shared tradition of fallibilism, tolerance of diversity, and support for critical exchange—what Popper calls "critical rationalism"—to mitigate the threat of devolving into factional and violent states of affairs. As we shall see, for Popper, such a tradition is grounded partly in an attitude of "reasonableness" capable of being adopted by individuals from a wide variety of perspectives. This attitude will challenge some perspectives, drawing a line between the reasonable and unreasonable. But not all line-drawing is equally susceptible to Hayek-style critiques. In Popper's case, the line is drawn to preserve the benefits of diverse open society itself.

---

3 For a succinct introduction to Hayek's approach to these issues, which also provides something of a guide to Gaus's final book, see Hayek (1966).
4 This false dichotomy is a dominant feature of Hayek's own writing.

The need for a liberal tradition such as Popper describes is what I mean by saying that open society is an *achievement*.[5] To obtain the benefits of diversity and to avoid its pitfalls, we must cultivate certain norms within our social morality, and protect them once established. In this chapter, I can only begin that argument by showing that Gaus's concerns about Popper's "sectarian" defense of open society largely miss their mark.

Gaus's Criticism of Popper

As mentioned already, the main argument of *The Tyranny of the Ideal* is self-consciously an update of Popper's broadly epistemic argument against fascism, communism, and other authoritarian or totalitarian schemes. In that book, Gaus is on the side of Popper against anyone who might believe that they can know with confidence the concrete blueprint of ideal society and thereby reverse engineer answers for our nonideal circumstances. Instead, Popper and Gaus argue that to find what is better, we must admit that we do not know what is best. Moreover, because we will never be in a position to assert confidently that we have arrived at the ideal, we must commit *indefinitely* to an open society allowing for perspectival diversity, critical exchange, and piecemeal reforms. While we might approach the ideal over time, we must always remain committed to open society—even if (in principle) the ideal might in some ways conflict with open society. Like Gaus, I think this is an extremely important argument in the history of liberalism, due not only to Popper but also to Mill (1977) and Dewey (1993a, 1993b).[6]

Gaus seems initially to accept Popper's position that our epistemic limitations still allow for rational efforts to make piecemeal improvements in policy and law—within what he calls the "neighborhood" of our current social world (Gaus 2016, 81)—subject to critical re-evaluation. But in an essay entitled "The Open Society and Its Friends" (2017), he comes to regard Popper as a defender of an objectionably "sectarian" model of open society that fails to respect and include some of the populist elements in American society today. Gaus's critical fire in that article is aimed less at the populists or reactionaries than it is at other defenders of open society. Why?

Gaus argues that in Popper's view the open society is "defined by opposition to 'superstition,'" rejection of religion, and "devotion to reason" such that those who "reject secularism, follow traditional rules ... and are skeptical of our ability to rationally understand our society, are essentially classified among the enemies

---

5 For further discussion of open society as an achievement, see Shearmur (1996, 151–3). Shearmur argues ultimately that Popper should have embraced a more Hayekian vision.
6 For elaboration of Mill's commitment in *On Liberty* to ongoing free discussion and social experimentation, see Turner (2013). Much of Dewey's expression of similar ideas is in the context of democracy as "a way of life." He writes: "Democracy is the faith that the process of experience is more important than any special result attained ..." (1993b, 244).

of open society" (Gaus 2017, 3). This view is "arrogant" and "condescending" and "encourage[es] a retreat to the very reactionary tribalism it opposes" (Gaus 2017, 3). The sectarian defenders of open society themselves become enemies of open society because their conception of open society involves "dismissing religion as superstition, traditional norms as bigoted and oppressive" (Gaus 2017, 16). The sectarian defense, Gaus writes, "begins by supposing a correct perspective on justice" rather than appreciating the "foundational insight" that "the admissible perspectives are many and varied" and trying to understand how many diverse perspectives "can share a moral and political framework" that participants can see as consistent with their deepest convictions, which "all can see as beneficial" (Gaus 2017, 16).

One way this arrogance manifests itself is in the willingness to impose changes on an unwilling public through the courts. Gaus's main example of self-righteous, sectarian overreach on behalf of open society is the Warren Court—the period of the US Supreme Court in the 1950s and 1960s that reinforced the civil rights movement in the United States. Although Gaus supports some of the Court's decisions (even some of the most controversial ones it seems), he also claims that the Warren Court created a rights revolution that went well beyond what could be accommodated by social morality, and so invited backlash.[7]

The basic problem—which Gaus says is "fueled by left-leaning professional philosophy" (Gaus 2017, 14)—is a failure to recognize sufficiently the way that social morality is a publicly supported set of shared expectations and rules that provide social stability and coordination by upholding practices of holding each other accountable. In an open society, he argues, this social morality is constructed out of the evaluative perspectives of all of us (more or less). We threaten social morality when we claim to have grasped the one true morality and impose it on others; doing so is inconsistent with the essential coordinating, practice-sustaining role of social morality.

In place of what he sees as the sectarian defense of open society, Gaus proposes a nonsectarian, Hayekian defense: "One that seeks basic rules for social and political life that not only can be endorsed given the widely diverse perspectives in our society, but understands how this diversity might be harnessed to promote mutual benefit" (Gaus 2017, 16). In *The Open Society and Its Complexities*, he then argues that only market processes can sustain social morality in an open society, precisely because they do not involve us in imposing our views on others and they respect the limits on what any individual can know concerning the appropriateness of any social morality for a complex society like ours. Each of us has our own purposes. The political and legal structure exists merely to help reconcile those different purposes for mutual benefit by facilitating spontaneous

---

7 This struck me as a surprising example. Much of the civil rights legislation was justified not by appeal to some concrete ideal of social or distributive justice, but rather by appeal to basic fairness or impartiality at the level of the abstract rules of society that I might have thought both Hayek and Gaus would accept.

social evolution, and should not introduce some other social purpose or concrete ideal in the process. Gaus is also optimistic that the more egalitarian and rule-following elements of human nature will help to preserve a diverse open society against the introduction of dominance hierarchies.

What Gaus offers in place of Popper's "sectarian" defense, then, is a Hayekian view, according to which "the open society is an evolving moral, legal, and economic framework that encourages toleration, trust, mutually advantageous interactions, and the flow of information … [and] the core of the open society is free and willing cooperation of strangers on the basis of rules that allow each space to effectively pursue her aims and values" (Gaus 2017, 2–3).

There is a great deal more one might say about both Gaus's and Hayek's views. Much of that will have to wait for another time. In the remainder of this piece, I will push back on the representation of Popper's view as objectionably sectarian, to challenge what Gaus sees as the available conceptions of open society. Popper's account is not sectarian in the ways Gaus claims. But he does believe that the establishment of norms of toleration and trust—which Gaus acknowledges are essential to the open society—are a precarious achievement. If that is correct, then we cannot rely on the nonsectarian, Hayekian vision.

Resisting Gaus's Criticism

Let us begin by noting that Popper is not "devoted to reason" in the way Gaus suggests. Popper's entire career was devoted to rejecting the same overconfident rationalism that Gaus rejects, and to articulating a critical rationalism that embraced intellectual modesty but allowed us to make intellectual progress through careful, fallible, intersubjective criticism. It was Popper who rejected "utopian engineering" in favor of "piecemeal engineering" in *The Open Society and Its Enemies* (Popper 1966a, 158).

It is true that the urgency Popper felt in articulating critical rationalism was not just to reject utopianism or overconfident rationalism, but also to avoid irrationalism or antirationalism.[8] For example, in response to the political realist Hans Morgenthau's denying the possibility of bringing power under the control of reason and suppressing war, Popper writes: "But clearly, he proves too much. Civil peace has been established in many societies, in spite of that essential lust for power which, according to Morgenthau's theory, should prevent it. He admits the fact, of course, but does not see that it destroys the theoretical basis of his romantic contentions" (Popper 1996a, 260). I believe a similar point applies also to Hayek and Gaus: in rejecting overconfident rationalism we needn't give up on rationalism or the social sciences altogether. Gaus writes, "Critical to Hayek's analysis of complex social systems … is our inherent inability to predict specific states of the system and, so, to plan or control them with any degree of precision" (Gaus 2021, 11). But it is not clear why the limits of reason should rule out the

---

8 For a useful discussion, see Birner (2014).

sort of careful, piecemeal intervention that Gaus himself had seemed to allow in *The Tyranny of the Ideal*. As Václav Havel once wrote:

> I am opposed to holistic social engineering. I refuse, however, to throw out the baby with the bathwater … I believe, as Popper does, that neither politicians, nor scientists, nor entrepreneurs, nor anyone else should fall for the vain belief that they can grasp the world as a whole and change it as a whole by one single action. Seeking to improve it, people should proceed with utmost caution and sensitivity, on a step-by-step basis, always paying attention to what each change actually brings about. (Havel 1997, 205, 206)

For Popper, critical rationalism that respects our epistemic limits means committing only provisionally to piecemeal reform in light of our best available social science. He proposes that we experiment with "blueprints for single institutions": "health or unemployment insurance … arbitration courts, or anti-depression budgeting or educational reform" (Popper 2008, 56); "institutions for securing civil peace" and prevention of international aggression (Popper 2008, 58); new kinds of life insurance, new kinds of taxation, a new penal reform (Popper 2008, 59). These might have broad repercussions, but "without re-modelling society as a whole" (Popper 2008, 59). With piecemeal reforms, he argues, we are able to make continual adjustments as we go, fitting things together. Moreover, "if they go wrong, the damage is not very great, and a re-adjustment not very difficult" (Popper 2008, 56).

Popper is also not antireligious. In a 1969 interview, he says "I do think that all men, including myself, are religious. We all believe in something more important and more – it is difficult to find the right words – than ourselves" (Popper 2008, 49). He further states that "some forms of atheism are arrogant and ignorant" (Popper 2008, 49). But, in line with his critical rationalism, he also argues that *everyone*—atheists, agnostics, and religious alike—must work not to turn "ignorance into anything like positive knowledge" (Popper 2008, 49). Popper does not care much about where our ideas come from, but he cares a great deal about what we do with them once we have them. What he rejects is dogmatism that would interfere with openness to criticism, learning, and peaceful resolution of differences. Irrationality for Popper is not located in the source of one's ideas, or in the failure to have the "correct" ideas, but in one's unwillingness to subject those ideas, whatever their sources, to serious critical examination. But that is no objection to religion in and of itself. Many religious people are willing to engage others' ideas with an open mind. With Samuel Butler, one can imagine Popper saying, "It is in the uncompromisingness with which dogma is held and not in the dogma or want of dogma that the danger lies" (Butler 1998 [1903], 318).

Moreover, Popper is not antitradition. In his "Towards a Rational Theory of Tradition," he argues that "all social criticism, and all social betterment, must refer to a framework of social traditions" (Popper 1989, 132) and that the "long-term 'proper' functioning of institutions depends ... [on] traditions" (Popper 1989, 134). He recognizes that "institutions are never sufficient if not tempered by traditions," and that when we consider changing traditions, we should "never forget ... the merit which lies in the fact that they are established traditions" (Popper 1989, 132). These are hardly the words of someone who fails to recognize the importance of starting from where we are, and of respecting existing practices. But it is entirely consistent with such a view to argue that open society may require new traditions. Because of our tendencies toward dogmatism and close-minded "tribalism," he says we should introduce a "new tradition—the tradition of tolerance" and an "attitude ... that considers existing traditions critically" even as we respect them (Popper 1989, 132).

Popper further recognizes the significance of what Gaus calls "social morality" for social stability and coordination. In his "Public Opinion and Liberal Principles," he argues:

> Among the traditions we must count as the most important is what we may call the "moral framework" (corresponding to the institutional "legal framework") of a society. This incorporates the society's traditional sense of justice or fairness ... This moral framework serves as the basis which makes it possible to reach a fair or equitable compromise between conflicting interests. (Popper 1994, 157)

It is true that Popper argues that everyone should be open to the improvement of our shared traditions and moral framework. But his recognition of the limits of reason as well as his sensitivity to religious belief, tradition, and social morality bears little resemblance to the sectarian arrogance of Gaus's description. This poses a problem for the Hayekian vision insofar as it presents itself as the only alternative to authoritarianism or totalitarianism.

Conclusion: Popper on Reasonableness

What makes Popper's view sectarian (if at all) is not that it expresses an arrogant rationalism, invokes a concrete ideal, or rejects religion and tradition. Rather what makes Popper's view sectarian (if at all) is that, in order to sustain a diverse open society, he argues for the protection of a tradition of fallibilism, tolerance of diversity, and critical exchange in addition to the active cultivation of an "attitude of reasonableness" (Popper 1989, 355ff).

Popper's account of reasonableness—laid out most succinctly in his 1948 essay "Utopia and Violence," and in *The Open Society and Its Enemies*—is almost never discussed, but it anticipates Rawls's more famous account in broad strokes. On Popper's account, the attitude of reasonableness has two main elements: first, a willingness to commit to argument rather than violence and, second, intellectual humility and an openness to learning from others (Popper 1989, 356). On

Rawls's account, reasonableness is constituted by two similar elements: a commitment to offering and abiding by "fair terms of social cooperation between equals" and an epistemic component characterized as the recognition of the "burdens of judgment, which leads to the idea of a reasonable toleration in a democratic society" (Rawls 2005, 488). (Rawls also follows Popper in distinguishing reasonableness from a more instrumental notion of rationality.)

Despite the similarities, however, there are also key differences. In particular, Popper's account of reasonableness is thinner because it does not appeal to "fairness" or "equals." It is more thoroughly epistemic than Rawls's account, and so avoids some standard worries about the moral commitments being smuggled into Rawls's political liberalism via his account of reasonableness.

For Popper, the cultivation of a widespread attitude of reasonableness is important not only to support the processes of discovering compromise and learning from others in a diverse society, but more specifically to ameliorate the "strain of civilization" that can lead individuals to reject living in a diverse, pluralistic society altogether and return to the psychological safety of tribalism or factionalism (Popper 1966a, 176). The sustainability of open society depends on reasonableness becoming a central part of our social morality itself:

> I believe that we can avoid violence only in so far as we practice this attitude of reasonableness when dealing with one another in social life; and that any other attitude is likely to produce violence … We all remember how many religious wars were fought for a religion of love and gentleness; how many bodies were burned alive with the genuinely kind intention of saving souls from the eternal fire of hell. Only if we give up our authoritarian attitude in the realm of opinion, only if we establish the attitude of give and take, of readiness to learn from other people, can we hope to control acts of violence inspired by piety and duty. (Popper 1989, 356–7)

The effect of this argument is not to impose a concrete ideal on others, but to show that a diverse open society can be sustained only if it takes a stand for the value of diversity itself and creates identity around the very idea of being open to others.

The argument articulated here reflects, of course, Popper's well-known discussion of the "paradox of tolerance":

> Unlimited tolerance must lead to the disappearance of tolerance. If we extend unlimited tolerance even to those who are intolerant, if we are not prepared to defend a tolerant society against the onslaught of the intolerant, then the tolerant will be destroyed, and tolerance with them.—In this formulation, I do not imply, for instance, that we should always suppress the utterance of intolerant philosophies; as long as we can counter them by rational argument and keep them in check by

public opinion, suppression would certainly be most unwise. But we should claim the right to suppress them if necessary even by force; for it may easily turn out that they are not prepared to meet us on the level of rational argument, but begin by denouncing all argument. (Popper 1966a, 265)

Just as preserving a tolerant society requires not always tolerating the intolerant, so preserving a diverse society requires cultivating an attitude of reasonableness and protecting a tradition of fallibilism, tolerance of diversity, and critical engagement.

Perhaps this is wrong on empirical grounds. But at least we can see that not every way of drawing a limit to diversity is equally sectarian. In particular, if the line is drawn precisely at the point of protecting diversity itself, then there seems to be good reason to draw it from the perspective of open society, even if it is to the detriment of some individuals.[9] Gaus's conflation of Popper's argument with truly sectarian political philosophies should be reconsidered. In thinking about how open society is to be maintained in the context of real-world politics, then, we should ask again whether we can do without reinforcing and protecting liberal traditions and attitudes of the sort Popper prescribes.[10]

Bibliography

Birner, Jacobus. 2014. "Popper and Hayek on Reason and Tradition." *Philosophy of the Social Sciences* 44 (3): 263–81.

Butler, Samuel. [1903] 1998. *The Way of All Flesh*. New York: The Modern Library.

Dewey, John. [1930] 1993a. "Individuality in Our Day." In *The Political Writings*, edited by Debra Morris and Ian Shapiro, 81–88. Indianapolis: Hackett Publishing.

Dewey, John. [1939] 1993b. "Creative Democracy—The Task Before Us." In *The Political Writings*. edited by Debra Morris, and Ian Shapiro, 240–245. Indianapolis: Hackett Publishing.

Gaus, Gerald. 2011. *The Order of Public Reason: A Theory of Freedom and Morality in a Diverse and Bounded World*. Cambridge, MA: Cambridge University Press.

Gaus, Gerald. 2016. *The Tyranny of the Ideal: Justice in a Diverse Society*. Princeton, NJ: Princeton University Press.

---

9 A further question, not taken up here, concerns the value of diversity itself as a commitment to individual choice or autonomy versus the value of diversity as an engine of intellectual and social progress. Hayek and Gaus differ from Popper (and Mill and Dewey) in the emphasis they place on these considerations. For a criticism of Millian and Popperian open society along these lines, see Gaus (2021, 95ff).

10 I wish to express my thanks to Christof Royer, John Thrasher, and Ryan Muldoon for discussion of general themes related to this paper, and to the participants at the October 2021 conference on "Forget Open Society?" organized by the Open Society Research Platform at Central European University, where an earlier version of this paper was presented.

Gaus, Gerald. 2017. "The Open Society and Its Friends: With Friends Like These, Who Needs Enemies?" *The Critique*, January 15. Accessed April 30, 2022. http://www.thecritique.com/articles/open-society-and-its-friends/.

Gaus, Gerald. 2018. "The Complexity of a Diverse Moral Order." *Georgetown Journal of Law & Public Policy* 16 (S). Accessed April 30, 2022. https://www.law.georgetown.edu/public-policy-journal/in-print/volume-16-special-issue-2018/the-complexity-of-a-diverse-moral-order/.

Gaus, Gerald. 2021. *The Open Society and Its Complexities*. New York: Oxford University Press.

Gray, John. 1976. "The Liberalism of Karl Popper." *Government and Opposition* 11 (3): 337–55.

Hacohen, Malachi H. 2000. *Karl Popper: The Formative Years, 1902–1945*. Cambridge: Cambridge University Press.

Havel, Václav. 1997. *The Art of the Impossible: Politics as Morality in Practice*. New York: Knopf.

Hayek, F. A. 1966. "The Principles of a Liberal Social Order." *Il Politico* 31 (4): 601–18.

Jarvie, Ian C. 2001. *The Republic of Science: The Emergence of Popper's Social View of Science 1935–1945*. Amsterdam: Rodopi Publishing.

Landemore, Hélène. 2020. *Open Democracy: Reinventing Popular Rule for the Twenty-First Century*. Princeton, NJ: Princeton University Press.

Magee, Bryan. 1985. *Philosophy and the Real World: An Introduction to Karl Popper*. La Salle, IL: Open Court Publishing.

Mill, John Stuart. [1859] 1977. "On Liberty." In *Collected Works of John Stuart Mill, Vol. 18*, edited by J. M. Robson and others, 33 vols. Toronto: University of Toronto Press.

Muldoon, Ryan. 2016. *Social Contract Theory for a Diverse World: Beyond Tolerance*. New York: Routledge.

Muldoon, Ryan. 2018. "The Paradox of Diversity." *Georgetown Journal of Law & Public Policy* 16 (S). Accessed April 30, 2022. https://www.law.georgetown.edu/public-policy-journal/in-print/volume-16-special-issue-2018/the-paradox-of-diversity/.

Muldoon, Ryan, ed. 2018. "Symposium on Gerald Gaus's *The Tyranny of the Ideal*." *Cosmos + Taxis: Studies in Emergent Order and Organization* 5 (2). Accessed May 2, 2022. https://cosmosandtaxis.org/back-issues/ct-52/.

Niskanen Center. 2022. "Open Society." Accessed April 30, 2022. https://www.niskanencenter.org/policy/open-society/.

Notturno, Mark A. 2000. *Science and the Open Society: The Future of Karl Popper's Philosophy*. Budapest: Central European University Press.

Popper, Karl R. [1945] 1966a. *The Open Society and Its Enemies. Volume I. The Spell of Plato*. Revised 5th ed. Princeton, NJ: Princeton University Press.

Popper, Karl R. [1945] 1966b. *The Open Society and Its Enemies. Volume II. The High Tide of Prophecy: Hegel, Marx and the Aftermath*. Revised 5th ed. Princeton, NJ: Princeton University Press.

Popper, Karl R. [1963] 1989. *Conjectures and Refutations: The Growth of Scientific Knowledge*. Revised 5th ed. London: Routledge.

Popper, Karl R. 1994. *In Search of a Better World: Lectures and Essays from Thirty Years*. London: Routledge.

Popper, Karl R. 2008. *After The Open Society: Selected Social and Political Writings*. Edited by Jeremy Shearmur and Piers Norris Turner. London: Routledge.

Rawls, John. 2005. *Political Liberalism*. Expanded ed. New York: Columbia University Press.

Ryan, Alan. 1985. "Popper and Liberalism." In *Popper and the Human Sciences*, edited by Gregory Currie and Alan Musgrave, 89–104. Dordrecht: Martinus Nijhoff.

Shearmur, Jeremy. 1996. *The Political Thought of Karl Popper*. London: Routledge Press.

Soros, George. 2000. *Open Society: Reforming Global Capitalism*. New York: Public Affairs.

Stokes, Geoffrey. 1998. *Popper: Philosophy, Politics and Scientific Method*. Malden, MA: Polity Press.

Thrasher, John. 2020. "Agreeing to Disagree: Diversity, Political Contractualism, and the Open Society." *The Journal of Politics* 82 (3): 1142–55.

Thrasher, John, and Kevin Vallier. 2018. "Political Stability in the Open Society." *American Journal of Political Science* 62 (2): 398–409.

Turner, Piers Norris. 2013. "Authority, Progress, and the 'Assumption of Infallibility' in On Liberty." *Journal of the History of Philosophy*. 51(1): 93–117.

Vallier, Kevin. 2019. *Must Politics Be War? Restoring Our Trust in Open Society*. New York: Oxford University Press.

Wolin, Sheldon. 2004. *Politics and Vision*. Expanded ed. Princeton, NJ: Princeton University Press.

6

NOZICK'S META-UTOPIA AS AN OPEN SOCIETY

Avery Fox White

Introduction

Is an open society not only "good" or "right" but also *desirable*? That is, why should people *want* to live in an open society, given that many people are frankly little motivated by normative argument alone? By way of answering this question, I suggest that we turn to the utopian writing of Robert Nozick from the last chapter of *Anarchy, State, and Utopia*.[1] While Nozick is not usually thought of as a member of the broader open society tradition, I will argue that we can interpret his version of utopia as "meta-utopia" as an open society without much difficulty. Furthermore, if we take this step, Nozick offers us the resources to articulate why an open society might be desirable, at least to reasonable and informed individuals. The essay proceeds in five parts. First, I briefly discuss the concept of an open society, in order to establish what precisely I mean when I say that Nozick's utopia is a version of such a society. Second, I will offer an exegesis of the substance of Nozick's notion of utopia as a meta-utopia, with the goal of demonstrating that it is a form of open society, and ought to be incorporated into the open society tradition. Third, I discuss how Nozick responds to various challenges faced by his utopia. Fourth, I show how Nozick's utopia presents the open society as a desirable form of political organization. Fifth and finally, I provide some suggestive comments on the concrete application of Nozick's utopia.

What Is an Open Society?

Because Nozick neither uses the term "open society" nor cites established open society thinkers like Popper, my argument that Nozick's utopia offers a version of an open society rests upon certain conceptual similarities between the two approaches. To establish such similarity, however, requires that we be

---

1 This portion of Nozick is less well read than the prior chapters. Indeed, it is essentially possible to list the entire corpus of analysis of Nozick's utopian arguments: Bader (2010); Bader (2011); Hailwood (1996); Hunt (2015); Kukathas (2011); Lacey (2001); Lomasky (2002); Singer (1981); Wolff (1991).

conceptually clear about what is meant by the open society, or at the very least, clear about what I mean by the term in this chapter.[2]

While controversy may be unavoidable, there is still room for evaluating definitions of the open society as better or worse depending upon whether or not they capture what is distinct about the open society tradition. That is to say, if we conceive of an open society as simply another term for liberal democracy, it is not clear why we ought to pick out certain authors (Mill [2002], Dewey [1954], Popper [2013], Gaus [2016]) rather than others in the liberal tradition (Rawls, for example, especially in *A Theory of Justice* [1999]).[3] A useful characterization of the open society will therefore be one that explains what is unique to an open society versus any other kind of liberal society. What, then, ties together the open society tradition and also distinguishes it from other liberal theories?

I would like to suggest that the distinguishing feature of the open society is its particular relationship to knowledge of how we (as both individuals and in groups) ought to lead our lives.[4] In particular, the open society takes the view that how to live is (at least regarding *social* life) an open question, and furthermore, a question that we can only begin to answer via something like Mill's notion of "experiments in living" (Mill 2002). Furthermore, the open society tends to place such experimental efforts into a larger framework of *progress*. This is not to suggest that an open society is subject to some Whiggish notion of inevitable and linear moral progress. Instead, the idea is more akin to scientific progress; at best, we learn *how to solve problems better*. The goal is cumulative progress in knowledge of how we might live, individually and collectively, via "trying things out" over time and disseminating the results of those attempts throughout society, but such progress is nonetheless a goal, not a fact about the nature of humanity. Progress, in other words, is something that we achieve, not something that happens to us as a form of natural law. This progressive experimentalism, combined with more general liberal notions of reasonable pluralism regarding ways of life and the primacy of liberty as a political good, leads us to the open society.[5]

---

2 Of course, as the title of this volume suggests, the nature of the open society is itself a contested topic; such contestation means that any usefully precise definition of the open society is likely to also be a controversial one.
3 This is one reason to be leery of turning over the open society entirely to Hayek, as Gaus seems close to doing in *The Open Society and Its Complexities* (2021). If the open society is more or less identical to Hayekian neoliberalism, it is not clear what work the term "open society" is doing, or whether it defines anything particularly unique above and beyond neoliberalism.
4 I mean ought here in the sense of practical reason, rather than moral duty.
5 One can, of course, imagine an experimentalist society that is *not* liberal in nature; the open society differs, for instance, from the kind of experimentalism advocated by someone like Roberto Unger (1997). However, by understanding the open society explicitly as experimentalist, we might thereby open up new resources to support the project by engaging with nonliberal experimentalist work.

Nozick's Meta-Utopia as Open Society

Now that we have a better sense of what an open society consists of, the question becomes whether or not Nozick's utopia qualifies as such a society. It is simple enough to see that Nozick argues in favor of the primacy of liberty—this is the subject of the first nine chapters of *Anarchy, State, and Utopia*, beginning from the very first line, "Individuals have rights, and there are things no person or group may do to them (without violating their rights)" (1974, xix). But what of the notions of reasonable pluralism and experimental progress? By briefly describing Nozick's utopia, we will come to see that these further two components of the open society are indeed not only present, but also the central pillars of Nozick's utopia.

First, a brief overview: Nozick's version of utopia is in fact what he calls a "meta-utopia," or a framework in which various substantive utopian projects can be simultaneously carried out by citizens as per their preferences (1974, 312).[6] Nozick describes such a meta-utopia as

> a wide and diverse range of communities which people can enter if they are admitted, leave if they wish to, shape according to their wishes; a society in which utopian experimentation can be tried, different styles of life can be lived, and alternative visions of the good can be individually or jointly pursued. (1974, 307)

In its ideal form, Nozick's utopia bears a productive resemblance to a market—individual citizens can choose which association within the framework they would like to join (depending upon which provides them with the most benefits, broadly construed), as long as they are accepted by said association (which depends upon the benefits the would-be member brings to the association, broadly construed). Such associations, Nozick notes, might not themselves look much like the minimal state that the rest of *Anarchy, State, and Utopia* is concerned with; indeed, such associations might not even be liberal, as long as they respect the overarching framework provided by the minimal state.[7] This overarching framework has few requirements beyond foregoing the use of violence

---

[6] These "associations," as Nozick calls them, seem to consist of something like nonsovereign territorial political units that are subordinate to the sovereign minimal state; however, Nozick never engages fully with this issue, though he does seem to think that relations between associations can be characterized as something like "foreign relations" (1974, 307).

[7] I am unconvinced that Nozick's meta-utopia actually *does* provide an independent argument in favor of the minimal state, as he seems to think it does (1974, 333). In particular, it is not at all clear to me that rights of exit and founding will be able to overcome the practical challenges involved in actually exercising said rights without some support from the state. Indeed, I would go so far as to argue, though I lack the space to do so here, that Nozick's meta-utopia points us toward some form of left-libertarianism, in which the state provides something along the lines of a universal basic income in order to enable individual citizens to exit their current associations or found brand new associations (see Vallentyne and Stiener 2004).

in order to expand an association. Furthermore, each association must respect the rights of its members to leave the association and found new communities that provide greater benefits.[8] In this manner, one association might resemble a Marxist utopia, while another might be nearly anarchic, and yet another a version of liberal social democracy, all within the same meta-utopian framework.

It should be clear from this brief description that Nozick's utopia is characterized by something much like reasonable pluralism. This relationship is made even more explicit in Nozick's arguments in favor of his conception of utopia as meta-utopia. Nozick makes two plausible assertions regarding the nature of the citizens who might inhabit his meta-utopia. First, Nozick suggests that it is simply a "fact that people are different" for Nozick: "They differ in temperament, interests, intellectual ability, aspirations, natural bent, spiritual quests, and the kind of life they wish to lead. They diverge in the values they have and have different weightings for the values they share" (1974, 309–10). Given this fact, "there is no reason to think that there is *one* community which will serve as ideal for all people and much reason to think that there is not" (1974, 310). Furthermore, Nozick also notes that even if there is only one objective good for all people, it is likely the case that individuals will differ in the way that they weigh the components of that good (or if there are multiple objective goods, how we weigh each of them). That being the case, "different communities, each with a slightly different mix, will provide a range from which each individual can choose that community which best approximates *his* balance among competing values" (1974, 312). Taken together, these two arguments suggest that Nozick shares a concern for something not substantially different from reasonable pluralism, much like the open society has favored at least since Mill offered his liberal paean to individuality in *On Liberty* (2002). Pluralism with regard to the nature of the good life is the justification for, and is characteristic of, Nozick's meta-utopia.

So much, then, for whether Nozick's version of utopia involves the kind of reasonable pluralism that the open society entails; what of experimentalism? This feature is present as well in Nozick's meta-utopia, in particular in the form of his ideas of a "design device" versus a "filter device" (1974, 314).[9] A design device "constructs something (or its description) by some procedure which does not essentially involve constructing descriptions of others of its type" (1974, 313). In other words, when we use a design device, we do not need to consider other kinds of things than the one we are designing. If we are designing a car,

---

8 The addition of a right of founding, in addition to a right of exit, is notable; Nozick makes a useful addition here to Gaus's notion of communities of inquiry by describing where such communities come from—in Gaus, the existence of such communities is more or less taken for granted (Gaus 2016, 147–148).

9 Nozick uses the term "experimental" explicitly at least once, but it is in the context of suggesting that "[n]ot *everyone* will be joining special experimental communities, and many who abstain at first will join the communities later, after it is clear how they actually are working out" (1974, 312). This is similar to Mill's notion that experiments in living will only be conducted by a few individuals of genius, rather than the public at large (2002).

for example, we can do so without reference to all the other designs for cars that exist. This might produce a *poor* design, but it will be a car nonetheless as long as it has the essential features of a car. We design the car from a set of principles.[10]

By contrast, "filter devices involve a process which eliminates (filters out) many from a large set of alternatives" (1974, 314). One can also design the filter to become more judicious over time, as the products of the filter improve with regard to the filtering mechanisms; when this is the case, "then one legitimately may expect that the merits of what will remain after long and continued operation of the process will be very high indeed" (1974, 314). Consider the same issue of car design. The process of car design in the real world is largely the product of consumer's choosing which designs they find appealing and buying accordingly. Furthermore, there is some objective progress regarding car quality over time with regard to things like fuel economy or safety features, again generated to a large extent by individual consumer behavior.[11] Actual practices of car design are not *purely* a filter device—there are still people who literally sit in chairs and try to think of new designs for cars, which exemplifies a design device.

Nozick himself acknowledges that we are unlikely to find pure design or filter devices in the real world, but that when it comes to the rules of society at the most general level, we should *design* the rules to *enable* a relatively pure filtering process (1974, 315). This is what the meta-utopia is meant to enable with regard to modes of living. As Hunt notes, the framework itself is not a filtering device, but an enabling condition that allows individuals to behave as a filtering device via making their own choices about what sort of community they would most like to live in (2015). Communities that people choose to leave are then filtered out, and communities that people join or remain members of stay in.

The operation of the filter device via movement between associations in the meta-utopia can be properly described as not only experimental (both at the level of citizens who join or found new associations as individual experiments in living, and at the level of society at large where different associations come and go), but also progressive in precisely the way that an open society is meant to operate.[12]

---

10 As applied to ways of life, Nozick asks us to imagine (in words that could have come from Gaus) "cavemen sitting together to imagine up what, for all time, will be the best possible society and then setting out to institute it. Do none of the reasons that make you smile at this apply to us?" (1974, 313–14).
11 Of course, contra Nozick, the car example also shows how government regulation can sometimes outpace consumer demand in a positive manner—see the government requirement for seat belts, for instance, in the United States, which preceded mass consumer demand.
12 Notably for other open society theorists, Nozick provides for the possibility that previously rejected ways of life might have greater appeal in the future (1974, 317).

Utopian Challenges

Nozick's utopia is a form of open society, despite his lack of use of the actual term itself and his lack of engagement with other figures within the tradition. However, despite conceptual similarities, there is another potential source of resistance to declaring Nozick part of the open society tradition, namely, that much of that canon is precisely *anti*-utopian in nature. This concern is some allayed regarding Nozick, at least on conceptual grounds; as the previous section demonstrated, Nozick's meta-utopia involves both reasonable pluralism regarding the nature of the good life or good society (see Nozick's arguments against a "one size fits all" approach to utopia) and epistemic humility (see the use of filter devices as opposed to design devices). As a matter of ideal theory, Nozick is not engaged in the same kind of utopian project as someone like Plato in the *Republic* (1997) or Rawls in *A Theory of Justice* (1999).

It is also worth noting Nozick's response to another standard criticism of utopias, namely that they are unrealistic. Nozick's arguments here ought to be of interest to any theorist of the open society, given that if Nozick's meta-utopia is unrealistic, it is hard to imagine that other versions of an open society will not be subject to a similar accusation, regardless of whether or not they use the term "utopia." This will be so because any version of the open society, in order to be progressive, must somehow enable the dissemination of the results of experiments throughout society; otherwise, it is unclear how such a society will enable the kind of progress toward better ways of life (relative to current needs) that is core to the concept and appeal of an open society.

What is Nozick's response to concerns about the operation of the meta-utopia in the real world?[13] He provides three answers. The first is the typical response of the ideal theorist to an accusation of being unrealistic, which is to note that we must know something about the ideal situation in order to evaluate our satisfaction with our present, actual situation. Nozick goes on, however, to make two further arguments that might have more appeal to nonideal theorists and other critics of utopia. Nozick's second response to the challenges of the real world is to note that the divergence between reality and utopia is not merely the basis for philosophical evaluation of the ways in which reality could be improved; it also plays an empirical role in human psychology, as without understanding individuals' "fantasies," we will be unable to understand their behavior when it comes to "expanding the range of their currently feasible alternatives" (1974, 308). In other words, it is an empirical fact that at least some of the time, individuals behave as though they are in pursuit of something like a utopia, despite all of the various challenges that they face; it therefore is worthwhile to think about the framework in which this sort of behavior can produce fruitful results.

---

13 Nozick helpfully lists a multitude of such challenges himself in the chapter, though the specifics are not germane to my argument here (1974, 307).

We might raise yet another concern regarding Nozick's meta-utopia, which is that in avoiding the faults of a standard utopia, it is actually *too permissive*. But although Nozick's meta-utopia may seem at first to enable literally any sort of utopian project, he quite clearly argues that this will not be the case. To do so, Nozick describes three different types of "utopian": (1) "existential" utopians, who aim at a particular substantive utopia but have little interest in whether others follow their lead; (2) "missionary" utopians, who use persuasion but not force in their attempts to spread their particular utopian vision across the broader meta-utopia; and finally (3) "imperialistic" utopians, who are willing to use force to spread their version of the best of all possible worlds (1974, 319–20).[14] Both existential and missionary utopians will find the meta-utopia amenable to their ends, as the former do not care if their utopia spreads, and the latter will believe that the filtering device of the meta-utopia will lead others to see the light voluntarily over time. However, imperialistic utopians, who are willing to use force in order to spread their utopia, will find the meta-utopia unacceptable, as one of the few duties of the minimal state is to prevent such individuals and groups from employing force against fellow citizens.[15]

Desiring an Open Society

One of the productive features of interpreting Nozick's utopia as an open society is that it shows why such a society is not just good or right, but also *desirable*. That is, individuals ought to *want to live in an open society*, if in fact it is utopian in character. This is not a normative point, but an empirical one; it is, at least in Nozick's estimation, factually the case that individuals will find his meta-utopia attractive. Regarding the meta-utopia in particular, I mentioned above that there are two types of utopians who will not need to be transformed in order to find the meta-utopia attractive, namely those of the existential and missionary varieties; another way to put it is that any (reasonable and informed) person who is not interested in spreading their vision of the good life by force should, as a matter of fact rather than as a matter of moral duty, want to live in Nozick's meta-utopia.

---

14 Note that insofar as Nozick refers to a person or group as utopian, it does not necessarily mean that they possess what we would usually recognize as a utopian theory; it simply means that they have some notion of what their best possible world is, which might simply amount to finding their current association "good enough" that they are uninterested in leaving. In other words, while not everyone or every group has a utopian theory at hand, they will generally have some idea of whether or not they are satisfied with their current association. The different kinds of utopian are then merely descriptions of how an individual or group relates to other individuals or groups that have different preferences. Thus, Nozick is describing all individuals and groups in society as one of the three types of utopian.
15 On this role of the minimal state, see chapter 3 of *Anarchy, State, and Utopia* on "Moral Constraints and the State" (1974, 26).

It is helpful here to introduce Nozick's concepts of "stable" and "unstable" associations. A stable association is, in an important sense, "the best of all possible worlds" for its members (1974, 298). This is not to say that such a stable association is *perfect* for any of its members. Especially in the real world, stable associations depend upon their ability to attract members, and given the fact of reasonable pluralism with regard to the good life, it is unlikely that any individual person's vision of a perfect world will be shared by enough other people to make that possibility a reality. Instead, the emphasis is on a stable association as the best *possible* world for its members—and further, this will be true for *all* of a stable association's members, *all at the same time*. In Nozick's words, we can give stable associations "one very desirable description ... namely, *none* of the inhabitants can *imagine* an alternative world they would rather live in, which (they believe) would continue to exist if all its rational inhabitants had the same rights of imagining and emigrating" (1974, 299). This is because, if there were some other extant or realistically imaginable association that any member of a given association would prefer, they can leave their current association for the preferable one at any time, as discussed above regarding the operation of the meta-utopia's filtering device.

What, then, will such a stable association be like? After all, it is in stable associations that we would spend most of our time, and therefore in such associations that we should try and find what is appealing about Nozick's utopia. Nozick writes that stable associations are likely to

> contain a diversity of persons, with a diversity of excellences and talents, each benefiting from living with the others, each being of great use or delight to the others, complementing them. And each person prefers being surrounded by a galaxy of persons of diverse excellence and talent equal to his own to the alternative of being the only shining light in a pool of relative mediocrity. All admire each other's individuality, basking in the full development in others of aspects and potentialities of themselves left relatively undeveloped. (Nozick 1974, 306)

At the very least, this description ought to appeal to theorists of the open society, who presumably already have in mind a similar kind of society, albeit often expressed in a less poetic fashion. But will others find such an association appealing, given the reasonable pluralism of utopian yearnings that Nozick himself acknowledges?

Nozick's view is that any and all nonimperialist utopians ought to view the meta-utopia's compatibility with the widest possible range of utopian visions (in addition to their own) "as an enormous virtue; for their particular view would not fare as well under utopian schemes other than their own" (1974, 320). That is, unless we are imperialist utopians, we are certainly *no worse off* within the meta-utopia than we would be in *any other utopian framework*. This is because any association within the meta-utopia is free to attempt to persuade others to join them, while being protected from coercion from both the state and other associations. In any other sort of utopia, there would be at least some potentially appealing associations that would be precluded from existing via the coercive power of the state; indeed, in most utopian theories, there would only be *one* kind of association, which would be identical with the state.

The only utopians who will not find Nozick's meta-utopia appealing, then, are imperialists, but even this is not quite correct—this will only be true, I would argue, of delusional imperialists, not sane ones. After all, even for imperialist utopians, the meta-utopia is only unappealing if the imperialists in question think they can actually bring their preferred utopia into being across an entire society now and forever, despite that society being characterized by pluralism with regard to the good life. That no such utopia can be achieved coercively would seem to be well supported by various twentieth-century attempts to do just that. There was neither thousand-year Reich, nor a permanent achievement of communism in its pure form. Even liberalism is under attack for failing in many people's minds to deliver on its notion of the best society. Any enduring society, in other words, would seem to need to have enough appeal to its members that they voluntarily remain, at least over a long enough time horizon.

Conclusion

By way of conclusion, I would like to offer some thoughts on the concrete application of Nozick's utopian argument. In particular, I would note that Nozick's meta-utopia draws our attention to a tension between freedom of association and democratic governance. In more practical terms, while we *can* pursue our vision of the best possible world via utopian association in Nozick's meta-utopia, we *cannot* do much when it comes to making decisions as a society via democratic means. This is because the state, although perhaps not identical with Nozick's minimal state that is only concerned with regulating coercion and defending the society from aggressors, will have very little that is legitimately within its purview relative to a modern liberal democracy. In other words, in Nozick's meta-utopia, the will of the majority of citizens is more or less irrelevant.

Unless an association is engaged in the outright murder or enslavement it its members, or is preventing its members from exercising their right of exit should they so choose, the state has no legitimate policymaking role to play.

Many current hot button issues—immigration, public religious practices, the power of big tech companies—would be taken out of the state's hands entirely in Nozick's meta-utopia. The state's *welfare* function might be preserved to some degree, should we take the view that it is important to not only protect but also actively enable the rights of exit and founding that undergird the operation of the meta-utopia, but the same cannot be said of the modern state's *regulatory* function. In other words, the state might still *help* its citizens do things, but it could almost never *tell its citizens what to do*, unless what they are doing is coercive toward other citizens. There would be no national immigration policy in Nozick's meta-utopia, but many association-level immigration *policies*, just as there would be no state level rules regarding the practice of religion, or state wide antitrust laws. It is not that Nozick is against democracy, as there is just not much to *do* via the state, as so much of what we think of as state functions will be transferred to the level of associations.

Does this implication of Nozick's meta-utopia render its appealing qualities moot? If that is the case, it would be a problem not only for Nozick but for the open society tradition as a whole, given the tendency within that tradition to emphasize the primacy of freedom of association. While this question requires a more satisfying answer than I can provide here, I would at least suggest that democracy at the level of a modern state is perhaps worth giving up, even if we value democratic governance, precisely because the quality of such democratic governance may well be higher within substate associations. Take the example of the United States, for instance—is it better to fight at the state level over issues like immigration, or would it in fact be better for everyone involved to simply have the possibility of a statewide immigration policy taken off the table? Such an idea is radical but not ridiculous, and Nozick does us the service of bringing such a possibility to the forefront of the open society tradition.

Bibliography

Bader, Ralf M. 2010. *Robert Nozick*. New York: Continuum.
Bader, Ralf M. 2011. "The Framework for Utopia." In *The Cambridge Companion to Nozick's Anarchy, State and Utopia*, edited by Ralf M. Bader and John Meadowcraft, 255–88. Cambridge: Cambridge University Press.
Dewey, John. 1954. *The Public and its Problems*. Athens, OH: Swallow Press.
Gaus, Gerald. 2016. *The Tyranny of the Ideal: Justice in a Diverse Society*. Princeton, NJ: Princeton University Press.
Gaus, Gerald. 2021. *The Open Society and its Complexities*. Oxford: Oxford University Press.
Hailwood, Simon A. 1996. *Exploring Nozick: Beyond Anarchy, State and Utopia*. Aldershot: Ashgate.
Hunt, Lester H. 2015. *Anarchy, State, and Utopia: An Advanced Guide*. Malden: Wiley Blackwell.
Kukathas, Chandran. 2011. "*E Pluribus Unum*, or, How to Fail to Get to Utopia in Spite of Really Trying." In *The Cambridge Companion to Nozick's Anarchy, State and Utopia*, edited by Ralf M. Bader and John Meadowcraft, 289–302. Cambridge: Cambridge University Press.
Lacey, A. R. 2001. *Robert Nozick*. Princeton, NJ: Princeton University Press.
Lomasky, Loren E. 2002. "Nozick's Libertarian Utopianism." In *Robert Nozick*, edited by David Schmidtz, 59–82. Cambridge: Cambridge University Press.
Mill, John Stuart. 2002. *The Basic Writings: On Liberty, The Subjection of Women & Utilitarianism*. New York: Modern Library.
Nozick, Robert. 1974. *Anarchy, State and Utopia*. New York: Basic Books.
Plato. 1997. *Collected Works*, edited by John M. Cooper. Indianapolis, IN: Hackett Publishing Company.

Popper, Karl. 2013. *The Open Society and its Enemies*. Princeton, NJ: Princeton University Press.
Rawls, John. 1999. *A Theory of Justice*. Revised ed. Cambridge: Belknap Press.
Singer, Peter. 1981. "The Right to be Rich or Poor." In *Reading Nozick: Essays on Anarchy, State, and Utopia*, edited by Jeffrey Paul, 37–53. Totowa, NJ: Rowman & Allanheld.
Unger, Roberto Mangabeira. 1997. *Politics The Central Texts*. edited by Zhiyuan Cui. London: Verso.
Vallentyne, Peter and Hillel Steiner, eds. *Left-Libertarianism and Its Critics: The Contemporary Debate*. New York: Palgrave: 345–62.
Wolff, Jonathan. 1991. *Robert Nozick: Property, Justice and the Minimal State*. Stanford, CA: Stanford University Press.

7

HANNAH ARENDT AND LITERARY PEDAGOGY

Andrea Timár

The university is a "public thing," a necessary condition of democratic life. Public things, as Bonnie Honig argues, "are part of the 'holding environment' of democratic citizenship; they furnish the world of democratic life" (Honig 2017, 5). Public things are the things we build, use, and maintain collectively, that interpellate, constitute, and affect us, and without which there would be nothing to debate, constellate around, or agonistically contest. Public things also "press us into relations with others. They are sites of attachment and meaning" (Honig 2017, 6). The significance of the public university as a public thing is especially relevant in societies where only a few universities remain truly "public," in the sense understood by Honig.

I will suggest that the university, and most eminently, the literature classroom itself, understood as a "public thing" can serve as a model for open society, the core values of which are "free minds, free politics, and free institutions" (Ignatieff 2018, 1). I shall primarily draw on Hannah Arendt's discussions of the public realm and the place of art in it. Although it is customary to draw parallels between Karl Popper's arguments in *Open Society and Its Enemies* and Arendt's *The Origins of Totalitarianism* (Ignatieff 2018, 4), this chapter will show how Arendt's use of Immanuel Kant's *The Critique of Judgment* in her essays "The Crisis in Culture" and "Truth and Politics," and particularly her argument that political judgments should be modeled on aesthetic judgments, can be related to an idea of open society modeled in and by the literature classroom. In my understanding, the literature classroom is a public thing, both removed from and deeply engaged with the common world in which multiple perspectives can be imagined. It makes it possible to engage with uncertainty, while the plurality of unique voices can yield discussion, agonist contest as well as, perhaps, compromise. Although this model of open society offered by the small community of the classroom is not necessarily transferable to the practical world, it can certainly influence it. In fact, it is precisely by operating as an "inoperative community" (cf. Nancy 1990) that the literature classroom can become an impetus to critical and free thinking, to the initiation of new beginnings, and, therefore, a place of resistance to all kinds of authoritarian coercion.

Hannah Arendt, Literature, and the Classroom

By public, Hannah Arendt means the world common to all of us, where we appear, speaking and acting in a way relevant to the community. In *The Human Condition* (2018, 176), she writes: "Speech and action reveal [man's] unique distinctness. Through them, men distinguish themselves … *qua* men. … A life without speech and without action … is literally dead to the world; it has ceased to be a human life." By distinctively human life, Arendt means political life, the plurality of human uniqueness forming the public. Discussing the public, she uses the image of the "table" that both separates and connects us. "To live together in the world means essentially that a world of things is between those who have it in common, as a table is located between those who sit around it; the world, like every in-between, relates and separates men at the same time" (2018, 52). Men heaped together without a table to both separate and connect them either are too close (like the de-individualized members of mass society) or have nothing to do with each other at all; they do not share a common world. The notion of in-betweenness, which will be of utmost significance in Arendt's later writings, emerges here via the image of the table: the distance between the people around prevents them from having one perspective only. For the public realm, as Arendt further argues, "relies on the simultaneous presence of innumerable perspectives and aspects in which the common world presents itself and for which no common measurement or denominator can ever be devised. … Being seen and being heard by others derive their significance from the fact that everybody sees and hears from a different position" (2018, 57). In other words, in this common world shared by a plurality of unique human beings, everybody speaks about the same object from different, often contesting, perspectives. This free and open debate voiced from a plurality of points of view is what Dana Villa calls the *agonistic* quality of the public realm (Villa 2021, 43).

What makes the literature classroom particularly apt to model this ideal of the public is that the shared object participants talk about is neither the present and contingent public world nor the separate, private world of each, but a common world represented in and by pieces of verbal art. Meanwhile, literature is also special because it singularly allows for the appearance of the private and the intimate (which would otherwise be hidden) to appear in the public realm of visibility.

> For us, appearance—something that is being seen and heard by others as well as by ourselves—constitutes reality. Compared with the reality which comes from being seen and heard, even the greatest forces of intimate life—the passions of the heart, the thoughts of the mind, the delights of the senses—lead an uncertain, shadowy kind of existence unless and until they are transformed, deprivatized and deindividualized, as it were, into a shape to fit them for public appearance. The most

current of such transformations occurs in storytelling and generally in artistic transposition of individual experiences. (Arendt 2018, 50)

Normally, according to Arendt, the passions of the heart have no place in the public[1] ("the qualities of the heart need darkness and protection against the light of the public"; they are not "for public display"; Arendt 1963, 96). Indeed, literature and the arts are the only way in which emotions and passions can be brought into the light of the public, and the passions of the heart can make an appearance.[2] In other words, art makes it possible for the forces of intimate life (which belong to the private, nonpolitical domain) to make public appearance.

At the same time, as Arendt argues, in order to be able to properly appreciate artworks, that is, artistic transpositions of individual experiences, we must possess a certain freedom to contemplate them, that is, neither should we be bound to our own world by everyday necessities, nor should we approach the artwork too closely (becoming prone to a personal interest, or emotional investment in it). In other words, "the distance," which separates the person who appreciates the artwork and the artwork itself, "cannot arise unless we are in a position to forget ourselves, the cares and urges of our lives"; 1977, 210). What makes this possible is, on the one hand, the artist's own distance from the world, and the dependence of the artwork itself on memory, which, making present what is absent, also bridges the distance between present and past.

On the other hand, it is difficult to forget our cares among the goings-on of our everyday lives. The appreciation of art therefore also requires a safe space, removed from the everyday: either a separate communal space such as the theater or a museum, or some inner silence, a separation from the world around; for instance, while we are reading a book. However, as has been mentioned, private experience, according to Arendt, does not count as political experience; that is, in itself, it is not an experience relevant for the community. So that something can have political relevance, so that it can form part of our specifically human life, which, according to Arendt, is lived in a "web of human relationships" (2018, 183), it needs to appear, to be seen and to be spoken about, discussed in the light of the public. The literature classroom can thus offer a model for the public sphere where one can discuss art in a disinterested way, free from the surrounding world of historical and political contingency: it is spatially separated from the general goings-on of our everyday life and cares while also being deeply

---

1 For the various reasons passions should remain private, according to Arendt, see Timár (2022).
2 Otherwise, in case emotions themselves become politicized and appear directly in the public realm, we witness the kind of totalitarian control that appeared first during the French Revolutionary Terror, when Robespierre wanted to tear away "the mask of hypocrisy" to get to the "heart" of the people and check the purity of their intentions. Then, it appeared in various totalitarian regimes, wishing to squeeze out, using torture, the "true emotions" driving the political person, thereby totally destroying not only personal integrity but the human person as well (the best literary example being George Orwell's *1984*). On the other hand, and perhaps in the same vein, Arendt also rejected Freudian psychoanalysis.

engaged with it. And, as will be argued in the following sections, it equally offers opportunity for the practices of persuasion, negotiation, and compromise, which would otherwise be characteristic of the processes of law and politics.

Art and Taste: Bridging the Gap between Philosophy and Politics

The artist has no place in politics understood as the public realm of speech and action formed by and in the web of human relationship; the artists work in solitude and withdraw themselves from the public world. In this sense, the artist is different from the political activist, whose acting and speaking cannot be performed without the public (1977, 217). However, artworks, the products of the artist are different: they are public and are not only entangled with but can also act upon the web of human relationships; just like words and deeds, they are phenomena of the public world. Indeed, only works of art are made for the sole purpose of appearance, so that their appearance can be contemplated. What's more, their value may surpass that of politics because, as opposed to the transitoriness of events, deeds, and speeches, artworks are durable, and, therefore, at least from the viewpoint of durability, clearly superior. Artworks also differ from consumer goods and objects: they do not have any function and are removed from the sphere of human life necessities; they are meant to outlast mortals and the coming and going of generations. Most importantly, without artworks, we would also lose the holding environment that makes this world human, that makes this world our own: "This earthly home becomes a world … only when the totality of fabricated things is so organized that it can resist the consuming life processes of the people dwelling in it, and thus outlast them" (1977, 210).

As we have seen, both the work of art and the person appreciating it are removed from life necessities and individual interests; that is, both are *free*. In this sense, both artworks and the appreciation of art share with philosophy their contemplative and disinterested character. At the same time, as we will see in what follows, both the work of art and the person appreciating it are deeply engaged in and with the world, and their performance is thus also eminently political. Whereas philosophy, "the love of knowledge," is inactive, approaching the world as a "mere spectator," the appreciation of art as "the love of beauty" is always active: it delivers judgments. Arendt thus (rhetorically) asks, "Could it be that philosophy … – which begins in wonder and ends … in the speechless beholding of some unveiled truth – is more likely to lead to inactivity than love of beauty?" Yes, it does. Whereas philosophy may yield inactivity, the love of beauty is always active. This active love of beauty, contrasting philosophy, is called by Arendt, via Kant's *Critique of Aesthetic Judgment*, "taste." As she goes on to say:

> Could it be … that love of beauty remains barbarous [i.e. inactive] unless it is accompanied by … the faculty to take aim in judgment,

discernment, and discrimination, in brief, that ... capacity we commonly call taste? And finally, could it be that this right love of beauty ... has something to do with politics? Could it be that *taste belongs among the political abilities*? (1977, 214–215, emphasis added)

Taste as "the discriminating, discerning, judging elements of an active love of beauty" (1977, 219) thus shares something with politics too. Indeed, taste can actually serve as the missing link between philosophy and politics: taste is both disinterested, like philosophy, and active, like politics. Meanwhile, taste shares not only the active, but also the public character of politics: judgments of taste require agreement from everyone else.

Indeed, when we make a judgment, we have to "woo" the consent of others, in the hope of coming to an agreement. This means that taste judgments also share with political judgment their persuasive character: both political judgments and esthetic judgments *demand* the agreement of everyone present. To use Austin's formulation, philosophic, scientific, or factual truth claims are constative, which can be falsified or verified; as a contrast, judgment as an act of persuasion is performative: it is rooted in an opinion *not* presenting itself as the only truth. "Taste judgments ... share with political opinions that they are persuasive. ... Persuasion ruled the intercourse of the citizens of the polis because it excluded physical violence; but the philosophers knew that it was also distinguished from another non-violent form of coercion, the coercion by truth" (1977, 222–23). Speech and opinion as persuasion thus not only exclude physical violence but also what Arendt calls "coercion by truth," the violence of truth claims.[3] Truth claims cannot be contested; there is no dispute about them, and they close down the situation by a statement. According to Arendt, only opinions can change the world, because they change the state of things and preform something new into existence.[4]

Arendt raises the example of one of the most famous performatives of European history—"All men are created equal"—to claim that this statement, being a matter of opinion and not of truth, stands in need of agreement and consent so that it can become politically relevant (1977, 246).[5] According to Arendt, while truths are beyond "agreement, dispute, opinion, or consent" (240), and are therefore coercive, "in matters of opinion ... our thinking is truly discursive, running ... through all kinds of conflicting views" (1977, 242). Consequently, culture and politics "belong together," because what is at stake in both "is not

---

3 What we may just as well call, after Derrida, a performative camouflaging itself as constative (cf. Derrida 1986).
4 One could also evoke here Arendt's key concept of "natality": "The new beginning inherent in birth can make itself felt in the world only because the newcomer possesses the capacity of beginning something anew, that is, of acting" (1998, 9).
5 This is also Derrida's example of the performative camouflaging itself as constative in "Declarations of Independence."

knowledge or truth," but rather "judgment and decision, the judicious exchange of opinion about the sphere of public life and the common world" (1977, 223).

Political Judgments Modeled on Aesthetic Judgments

It is in this essay too that Arendt makes the startling but now famous claim that "'Critique of Esthetic Judgment,' contains perhaps the greatest and most original aspect of Kant's political philosophy" (1977, 219). That is, she suddenly reverses the analogy she has so far established between artworks and the appreciation of art, that is, taste. Now it is not art and/or taste that is presented as being similar to politics, but political judgment and politics itself become modeled on Kant's aesthetic judgment. Of course, we cannot speak about the aestheticization of politics. That is, it is not the object of politics, the network of human relationships, that Arendt presents as the object of an aesthetic judgment, but, instead, she finds an analogy between two kinds of judgments: political judgments and aesthetic judgments.[6] So how can one apply the characteristics of aesthetic judgment, that is, taste, to political judgment? Where does Arendt find the analogy?

During the exercise of practical reason, that is, when man makes a moral judgment, he has to agree only with himself, with his own conscience. But aesthetic judgments require a whole different way of thinking. When we judge aesthetically, we seek the agreement of everyone, which not only means that judgments are performative but also that we have to think in the place of everybody else. And this, as she puts it via Kant, requires an "enlarged mentality." As she argues:

> Political thought is representative. I form an opinion by considering a given issue from different viewpoints, by making present to my mind, the standpoints of those who are absent; … this is a question neither of empathy, as though I tried to be or to feel like somebody else … The more people's standpoints I have present in my mind while I am pondering a given issue, and the better I can imagine how I would feel and think if I were *in* their place, the stronger will be my capacity for representative thinking and the more valid my final conclusions, my opinion. (1977, 241)

We may remember Arendt's discussion of the public realm evoking the image of the table: people sit around the same table but view it from different perspectives. When she speaks about enlarged mentality and representative thinking, she posits the kind of person as a model who has in his or her mind the standpoints of all those who sit around the table. That is, even though for our common world no common measurement or denominator can ever be devised, we

---

6 On the way in which Kant himself establishes an analogy between aesthetic judgment and moral judgment via his famous claim that "beauty is the symbol of morality," see Timár (2020).

have to imagine how we would feel and think in the place of all those who are present. Meanwhile, quite controversially, when we make a judgment, based on representative thinking, we do not exercise compassion. As Arendt famously puts it, as "a rule, it is not compassion which sets out to change worldly conditions in order to ease human suffering, but if it does, it will shun the drawn-out wearisome processes of persuasion, negotiation, and compromise, which are the processes of law and politics" (1963, 86–87). In fact, we should not exercise compassion, because compassion eliminates the distance necessary for persuasion, negotiation, and compromise. Nor should we become like Adolf Eichmann, who, on the other hand, had the total inability to "ever to look at anything from the other fellow's point of view" (1963: 47–48). Hence, when we make a political judgment properly modeled on Kant's aesthetic judgment, we imagine the perspective of everyone presently involved in the singularly given situation. This is what Arendt elsewhere calls "solidarity" (1963, 88).

As was mentioned above, when making these kinds of judgments, we form an *opinion* instead of declaring some universal truth, a truth that could not be otherwise. That is, what judgments in matters of both taste and politics lack is, precisely, the coercion proper to truth claims. At the same time, and quite conspicuously, as if in a self-contradictory fashion, Arendt herself clearly derives the objectivity, the disinterestedness proper to the truth claims made by science or history writing, from the disinterestedness of art itself, from the disinterestedness of artistic storytelling:

> *The disinterested pursuit of truth* has a long history; its origin, characteristically, precedes all our theoretical and scientific traditions, including our tradition of philosophical and political thought. I think it *can be traced to the moment when Homer chose to sing the deeds of the Trojans no less than those of the Achaeans, and to praise the glory of Hector, the foe and the defeated man, no less than the glory of Achilles, the hero of his kinfolk.* This had happened nowhere before; no other civilization, however splendid, had been able to look with equal eyes upon friend and foe, upon success and defeat. [–] This is the root of all so-called objectivity – this curious passion … for intellectual integrity at any price. *Without it no science would ever have come into being.* (1977: 312–313, emphasis added)

The enlarged mentality of Homer, the storyteller, encompassed the virtues of both the judge of art and the politician: his thinking was representative, his judgment disinterested and impartial. His objectivity could therefore set a model also for those who have been in pursuit of truth itself—as if, without the disinterestedness learned from the reading of literary works, such as the *Iliad*, science could never have come into being. Meanwhile, Homer's words do not correspond exactly to any historical reality; he does not present any propositional truth. Homer's truth is a literary truth, and hence a performative one:

both preserving in his memory and inventing anew what happened, he could both describe and intervene into the world of human affairs.

Taking into account Arendt's discussion of culture, one may conclude that the public character of the literature classroom, which, at the same time, is removed from the everyday world, offers the most exquisite place to enlarge students' mentality. The discussion of literary works helps students engage in representative thinking, as well as practice persuasive and argumentative speech, through an open, agonistic exchange of opinions. Further, at another level, literary works themselves may model enlarged or representative thinking, through the multiplicity of voices and perspectives they present—or, precisely, by staging the absence of certain voices and perspectives.

How Can the Discussion of Literary Works Contribute to the Implementation of Open Society?

In what follows, I will show that an Arendtian approach to the discussion of literature has more potential to pave the way for the implementation of open society than other possible approaches, which place more emphasis on literature's capacity to generate compassion for the marginalized and the dispossessed. In fact, thinkers as different as Lynn Hunt, the historian,[7] or Martha Nussbaum, the moral philosopher,[8] agree that literature can transform us into better citizens precisely by enlarging our sympathetic imagination. In the same vein does Richard Rorty argue that "sad and sentimental stories," alert us to others' suffering, and these "suggestions of sentiment" are much more effective than the commands of reason in building a culture of human rights based on solidarity (quoted in Phillips 2015, 49). As a contrast, as we have seen, Arendt dismisses the politically benevolent effects of empathy and argues *against* the exercise of compassion in the public sphere, while her understanding of "solidarity" as a "dispassionate" and "deliberate" "community of interest" is almost the opposite of Rorty's. To clarify what I mean by an Arendtian approach to the discussion of literature in the literature classroom, let's see an example of the way in which attention to uniqueness, disinterestedness, representative thinking, and open discussion can be taught to students through the teaching of literature.

This demonstrative example will be a familiar one—a short passage from *Robinson Crusoe* by Daniel Defoe. *Robinson Crusoe* was canonized as the first English novel and was published in 1719. It is the fictional autobiography of a sailor, called Robinson Crusoe, who suffers shipwreck and ends up on a desert island, where he grows plants, hunts animals, and survives. The narrator of the story is Robinson himself; we can only hear his voice and can only get to know

---

7 Hunt (2007) claims that it was eighteenth-century sentimental literature that paved the way for the emergence of the idea of universal human rights.
8 Nussbaum (1997) argues that judges should read novels, especially novels by Charles Dickens, to learn how to empathize with people in need.

his perspective, throughout the book. This is one of the many reasons why readers have tended to identify with him all through the centuries. Near the end of the novel, Robinson comes upon footprints in the sand, and it turns out that there is a cannibal feast nearby. He rescues the would-be victim from imminent death. The story, written in first-person singular, reads as follows:

> At last he [the man he saved] lays his Head flat upon the Ground, close to my Foot, and sets my other Foot upon his Head … to let me know, how he would serve me as long as he liv'd; I understood him in many Things, and let him know, I was very well pleas'd with him; in a little Time I began to speak to him, and teach him to speak to me; and first, I made him know his Name should be Friday, which was the Day I sav'd his Life; I call'd him so for the Memory of the Time; I likewise taught him to say Master, and then let him know, that was to be my Name; I was greatly delighted with him, and made it my business to teach him everything that was proper to make him useful, handy, and helpful; but especially to make him speak, and understand me when I spoke; and he was the aptest scholar that ever was; … I [also] began to instruct him in the knowledge of the true God.

Literary works often generate readerly compassion with the main character, especially when the main character is also the narrator. Whenever we read the first-person account of the sufferings and struggles of an individual, we tend to take on his perspective. Readers of Robinson Crusoe's story identified with him and accepted his authority through centuries. This resulted in readings that unwittingly endorsed or became accomplices in perpetuating the colonialist ideology proper to Robinson himself. However, as Arendt warns us, one has to keep a certain distance from both everyday events and works of art. This distance helps us to form judgment and also prevents us from falling into the trap of compassion, which actually eliminates all distance between people. Indeed, an Arendtian reading of *Robinson Crusoe* would suggest that instead of empathizing/identifying with the narrator, as we generally do when we read autobiographies, we should start to engage in "representative thinking." In this case, we may also "present to [our] mind the standpoints of those who are absent" (1977: 241) to realize that both the perspective and the voice of "Friday" are lacking from Crusoe's narrative. This disinterested reading would also make us ask: Why is it absent? Does this absence have a meaning? This 1719 novel was typically written from a colonizer's perspective, and this colonizer, Robinson Crusoe, is presented as the only, and, therefore, authoritative locus of voice, vision, and meaning. Of course, good books are not necessarily like Defoe's *Robinson Crusoe*; ideally, they themselves present a plurality of voices and perspectives, or reflect on their absence, thereby representing what Arendt calls enlarged mentality. For example, *Foe*, the twentieth-century re-writing of *Robinson Crusoe*, by the Nobel Prize–winning J. M. Coetzee is a case in point: Coetzee has a female narrator, and the book presents the absence of Friday's voice and perspective as the unresolved, and perhaps unresolvable, enigma of the story (see also Timár 2021).

At the same time, Arendt would disagree with those who consider literature as a mere tool to advance the cause of "identity politics," that is, with readings that would concentrate solely on the ways in which Defoe erases, while Coetzee wishes to give voice to, the "likes" of Friday. She famously opposes the subsumption of human uniqueness and plurality under the homogenizing rule of the same: her ironic take on the "woman question" and the challenges she poses to the concept of "Jewishness" all indicate that the sacrifice of human uniqueness and plurality is in close kinship with totalitarian thinking. Indeed, storytelling is especially relevant in this context, since it has the potential to resist any ideology based on the rule of the same: as Arendt famously puts it, "storytelling reveals meaning without committing the error of defining it" (Arendt 1968, 109). Storytelling can reveal "who" somebody is (their human uniqueness as disclosed in speech and action) in contradistinction to "what" he is (i.e., "his qualities, gifts, talents, and shortcomings"): as Arendt puts it, "*who* somebody is or was we can know only by knowing the story of which he is himself the hero" (1998, 179, 186; see also Meretoja 2017: 80–81).

Conclusion

Following Arendt, one may conclude that the literature classroom as a space of solidarity allows for the open, plurivocal, and critical discussion of the various perspectives represented or, on the contrary, left unrepresented in the literary work; in other words, it allows for a critical reflection on both monologic and dialogic, both homophonic and polyphonic texts.[9] At the same time, slowing down the reading process, it also permits close attention to the singularity of literary texts, which attention can in itself offer a resistance to totalizing ideologies. For apart from the critical reflection on literary devices (such as the narrative techniques discussed above), the literature classroom can equally disclose and make students reflect upon the workings of language per se, thus fostering the development of a critical awareness of the ways in which language can or cannot be put to ideological use. The free, open discussion of aesthetic *and* political opinions formed about literary works, and the exercise of critical thinking, predicated on both critical distance and imaginative engagement, can thus offer some essential contributions to the implementation of the idea of open

---

9 The twentieth-century literary theorist Mikhail Bakhtin presents something very akin to what Arendt calls "enlarged mentality," when he speaks about the "dialogical," "polyphonic" character of Dostoyevsky's novels. As he puts it, "not a single one of the ideas of the heroes—neither of 'negative' nor 'positive' heroes—becomes a principle of authorial representation, and none constitute the novelistic world in its entirety." For "One should learn not from Raskolnikov or Sonya, not from Ivan Karamazov or Zosima, ripping their voices out of the polyphonic whole of the novels (and by that act alone distorting them)—one should learn from Dostoevsky himself as the creator of the polyphonic novel" (Bakhtin 1984, 25, 36).

society. Differently put, rather than discussing what open society *is*, the literature classroom allows for students to experience the workings of a model of open society. For a variety of reasons, the small community of a classroom cannot stand for, or be representative of, a larger political community, and its practices cannot be unproblematically transferred to and implemented in the practical world. However, the literature classroom can certainly show up the ideal of a space of solidarity in which multiple perspectives can be imagined and in which the plurality of singular voices can yield discussion, argument, agonistic contest as well as, perhaps, compromise. Indeed, it is by showing up a perhaps utopian ideal of solidarity, in the sense understood by Arendt, that it can serve as a place of resistance to authoritarian regimes.

Bibliography

Arendt, Hannah. 1963. *Eichmann in Jerusalem*. New York: Viking Press.
Arendt, Hannah. 1963. *On Revolution*. New York: Viking Press.
Arendt, Hannah. 1968. *Men in Dark Times*. New York: Harcourt, Brace.
Arendt, Hannah. 1977. "'The Crisis in Culture', 'Truth and Politics'. In *Between Past and Future. Eight Exercises in Political Thought*, Edited by. Jerome Kohn, 197–264; 265–82. London and New York: Penguin Books.
Arendt, Hannah. 2018. *The Human Condition*. Chicago: University of Chicago Press.
Bakhtin, Mikhail. 1984. *Problems of Dostoyevsky's Poetics*. Edited and translated by Caryl Emerson, Introduction by Wayne C. Booth. Minneapolis: University of Minnesota Press.
Derrida, Jacques. 1986. "Declarations of Independence." *New Political Science* 7 (1): 7–15.
Honig, Bonnie. 2017. *Public Things: Democracy in Disrepair*. New York: Fordham.
Hunt, Lynn. 2007. *Inventing Human Rights*. New York: Norton & Co.
Ignatieff, Michael. 2018. "Introduction." In *Rethinking Open Society*, edited by Michael Ignatieff and Stefan Roch, 1–16. Budapest and New York: Central European University Press.
Meretoja, Hanna. 2017. "On the Use and Abuse of Narrative for Life." In *Life and Narrative*, edited by Brian Schiff, A. Elizabeth McKim, and Sylvie Patron, 75–98. Oxford: Oxford University Press.
Nancy, Jean-Luc. 1990. *The Inoperative Community*. Edited by Peter Connor, Translated by Peter Connor et al. Minneapolis, MN: University of Minnesota Press.
Nussbaum, Martha. 1997. *Poetic Justice*. New York: Beacon Press.
Phillips, Anne. 2015. *The Politics of the Human*. Cambridge: Cambridge University Press.
Timár, Andrea. 2020. "'The Human Form': Aesthetic/Political Disinterest in Matthew Arnold and Immanuel Kant." In *The Human Form*, edited by Andrea Timár, 69–85. Budapest: Eötvös Kiadó.
Timár, Andrea. 2021. "Dehumanization in Literature and the Figure of the Perpetrator." In *The Routledge Handbook of Dehumanization*, edited by Maria Kronfeldner, 214–29. New York: Routledge.
Timár, Andrea. 2022. "Against Compassion: Post-Traumatic Stories in Arendt, Benjamin, Melville, and Coleridge." *Arendt Studies,* 2022/6 in advance: https://doi.org/10.5840/arendtstudies202211444.
Villa, Dana. 2021. *Arendt*. London: Routledge.

8

CAN BERGSON'S DEFINITION OF OPEN SOCIETY BE USEFUL TODAY?

Jean-Louis Fabiani

Henri Bergson coined the term "open society" in *The Two Sources of Morality and Religion*, his last important book, published in 1932. At that time, he was no longer "the most celebrated philosopher in the world," despite his Nobel Prize, awarded in 1928. Extremely productive during the pre–First World War decade, and very active in diplomacy and politics during the war and its aftermath, Bergson became quite silent after 1923, when he tried to challenge Einstein in *Duration and Simultaneity*: it was a bold but unsuccessful attempt to engage philosophically with a scientific revolution in physics.

As many other European intellectuals, Bergson was deeply stricken by the absurd violence of the war on a continent that esteemed itself as the most civilized in the world. The ghost of the war is everywhere in the *Two Sources*, as an inherent feature of sociality as such: closed societies are based on the identification of the Other as the enemy to get rid of. Especially in France, where academics viewed themselves as republic-builders and as providers of the principles of a society still to be fully constructed, the death of the early promise of a new world, namely implementing the civilizing process (in Norbert Elias's terms) through expansion and education, created an atmosphere of despair. Young generations in the 1930s were mostly angry young men, furious against prewar academics as they seemed to embody the values of a murderous bourgeois world. The Hungarian émigré Georges Politzer targeted Bergson for that reason: his élan vital was nothing but the rallying sign of the dominating class (Politzer 1968). Albeit unfair, the attack was quite successful: Bergson became rather isolated in the intellectual field. He was himself torn between his wish to turn to Christian faith and his preoccupation with the growing anti-Semitism that plagued Europe. He did not convert because he did not want to betray his people. However, the religious preoccupation, as shown in the book, was an attempt to address fundamental questions concerning social organization in the present.

The most French of the French philosophers was in fact from Polish Jew descent. Although he rarely spoke about it, as his fellows secularized Jews in academia, he could see clearly that republican self-proclaimed universalism did not work at all in the country that identified itself to Enlightenment. This kind of silent despair is not particular to France, as Freud's example clearly shows in his anthropological texts: there, the death drive seemed to rule, and civilization was nothing but a fragile varnish. Civilization was no longer what it claimed to be. It seemed impossible to get out of the national box, which is both the condition of a functional society and a huge obstacle to envisage humanity as a unit. As such, the Bergsonian open society is not a kind of a new project of society, as in Popper. It is a way out of society, an a-society, an absence of society, as it is always defined by contrasting us and them, in an operation of closure that is constantly reiterated.

Although Popper made a quite different use of the notion, and seemingly a more practicable one, it is worth coming back with fresh eyes to a text that looks totally out of fashion with its reference to mysticism and its Christian overtones. As Dante Germino writes, "for Bergson, the open society stands forth as a paradigm of development for the community of man" (Germino and von Beyme 1974: 2). Human societies can be said closed since they are based both on inclusion and on exclusion: exclusion is the very condition of inclusion, something that the motto of inclusive society largely misses. Our present is trapped in a double bind: on the one hand, we ask for the inclusion of the social margins; on the other hand, we rely on the tools of identity politics, which are based on the distinction of "us" and "them" and the radical critique of Western universalism. Bergson's two sources of morality and religion allow us to supersede a major contradiction of our times, if our goal is, like his, to prevent the wars to come by understanding how war is inherent to closed societies. However, can the open society become a real society, as in Popper, or is it only a fiction based on the exceptionality of mysticism in society as it is embodied in exceptional individuals regularly qualified as an "elite"?

Understanding the Bankruptcy of Our Values

I want to refresh the analysis of the *Two Sources*, which was considered in the 1930s, mainly by Marxists and the Left, as a conservative attempt to restore an opposition between the masses (as expressed in the notion of closed society) and the elite (the mysticism as a condition of the open society through exceptional personalities). If we leave aside its outdated vocabulary and its anchoring in a peculiar vision of Christianity, we may access a more critical conception of identity politics and restore universalism as a common goal while not being trapped in the expression of Western locality as universal. As Freud, Bergson is obsessed by the discrepancy between the language of values (solidarity, unity of humankind) and the behavior of nations. Bergson's diplomatic action during the war shed light on a huge contradiction: How can we simultaneously consider peace as a universal goal and call for war?

"If you want peace, prepare for war" is a contradiction in terms. Bergson, as all the other prominent French academics of his time, was an ardent prowar militant. Well-versed in German academic culture, very often neo-Kantians (with the striking exception of Bergson who recognized in Kant's work the limitations of rationalist critique), French thinkers wrote extremely violent pamphlets against the "Boches" (Germans) and participated in the war effort. Their war writings were in sharp contrast with what they wrote just before, and they denied the fact that they had borrowed a lot from Germany (in terms of concepts as well as for academic reconstruction after the defeat in Franco-Prussian War). Bergson went a few times to the United States to encourage America to join the conflict on the right side. He withdrew from the frontstage after the war, but he remained interested in political issues. Contrary to Popper, Bergson's open society is never thought in political terms and its conditions of feasibility are never addressed. Politzer would explain this strange withdrawal by the fact that the philosopher systematically refuses to engage into action and therefore into politics. His *élan vital* remains a fully abstract and verbose thing. The notion of "philosophical parade" is used by Politzer to show how Bergson has developed a sort of "mock philosophy" that just pretends to act while it aims to preserve the ideological eminence of the bourgeoisie (Politzer 1968).

Politzer is obviously unfair. His book is not good. However, it is necessary to try to understand why Bergson was so shy in never addressing a political issue (violence in society and its roots in identity) and had to translate it into other terms: morality and religion. Here we can see an escape strategy through mysticism. As the philosopher defines his own argument as only "plausible" (*vraisemblable*) and develops it in the form of a very cautious exploration, he avoids strong political statements. The open society is a way out of society but also out of politics, as if his previous experience led him to withdraw and led him to the isolation of a certain type of mystical experience. Perhaps I am exaggerating at this point, since the last chapter of the book is rich in political remarks, particularly about the Society of Nations or population issues that show a concrete interest in political decision. What is interesting in his attempt is the fact that if one wants to think about politics in nontraditional political terms, it is absolutely necessary to make a detour through morality and religion. The notion of detour might not be the best one here since the new path is also a way out of ordinary politics. Here we can find the right ground for further action, but it seems not to be the task of the philosopher. As Bruno Karsenti rightly says it in his recent and excellent French republication of the book, the central question is: How to act right now? (Bergson 2012). I would add how to act after what happened and that was unthinkable before it happened. At this point, post–First World War is not so far from post–Second World War: it made the thinkers mute; old answers were void.

However, it remains difficult to see to what extent the book is a call for political "*ressaisissement*" (both reclaim and recovery). The message is simply too vague to be identified. What is interesting is that it is never a prophecy (as in Marxism) or a political program (like the open society in Popper's terms). Large societies, characterized by a complex division of labor, are not fundamentally different from simpler groupings: they exist insofar as they are framed by a closure. Any form of social organization requires it as it stems from a social instinct that gives strength to a closed form of morality. In many ways, the modern nation-state is an elaborated form of the closure. One can say that it has triggered unprecedented levels of hatred leading to extermination, exacerbating the contradiction between the discourse of civilization and the actual functioning of modern societies. Right after the end of the First World War, Paul Valéry said that now we knew that civilizations were mortal. Bergson and Freud added something to the statement: civilizations might be not civilized at all. Contrary to Freud's bleak pessimism, Bergson opened a window that was obviously not realistic, as great mystics are always in short supply in society, particularly in those based on rationality and contract. In this respect, *The Two Sources* takes us back to a form of utopia: there is no *topos* for an open society, since place making is always the expression of a closure, spatial as well as mental.

A Paradoxical Quest

Looking for the sources might be close to John Dewey's concept of inquiry. *The Two Sources* is the account of a quest to get back to the origins of social life, through two contradictory elements: a subjective search that goes back to the sources; an objective gathering of anthropological facts. The first (and the most important) is introspection, an inward search that is necessarily solitary and close to French "spiritualist" subjectivism as initiated by Maine de Biran in the first part of the nineteenth century. One knows that Michel Foucault (Foucault 1985) opposed two major trends of philosophy in France, the first being the philosophy of the subject (from Maine de Biran to Bergson) and the second being the philosophy of the concept (from Auguste Comte to Bachelard, Cavaillès, Canguilhem, and Bourdieu).

Here, Bergson inscribes himself in the first, as he claims to derive the two sources from mere introspection. We are far from Dewey's inquiry, as looking into oneself is by definition an experience that cannot be communicated as such. More surprisingly, he draws on anthropology and sociology, particularly when it comes to the functioning of a closed society. A source is both an origin and a force of irrigation (remaining active through quite different times). It is always reachable through a "vigorous effort of introspection," but it makes sense only if it is related to an anthropological gaze. The link is not clearly established by Bergson. *The Two Sources* is undoubtedly the author's most anthropological book, drawing critically on the Durkheimian school. There is a risk inherent to the method: the sources may be the expression of an individual subjectivity, located in history and in ideology. Contrary to Durkheim, Bergson considers that in morality, consent matters much more than constraint. The constraint is on the side of the closed: envisaging society as a system of constraints, even if they remain infra-conscious and are not felt as oppressive, amounts to denying morality as such. On the contrary, there is a sort of spontaneous commitment to moral action, which cannot simply be derived from social obligation. This view is quite Bergsonian, but it is also a very peculiar conception of morality if one considers the empirical observation of its mundane manifestations. The concept of source requires that we can link all forms of social behavior to their origins: according to the philosopher, there is no such thing as the "heredity of acquired features." The human mind remains the same throughout history and always starts from the same point in all individuals at all times. Bergson strived to get this idea recognized as it seems so counter-intuitive. We ordinarily prefer to think that we acquire new traits as our cognitive experience gets more developed. This is a claim against the idea of "primitive mentality" that was very strong in French anthropology in the interwar period (Lucien Lévy-Bruhl wrote six books on the topic). Consequently, the notion of progress is not a universal category. Bergson is clearly anti-evolutionist in this respect and considers that the usual anthropological vectorization of human history is inaccurate. Undoubtedly, the book is the most sociological of Bergson's works. He pays a lot of attention to anthropological concepts, although he envisages religion in a very different way: for Durkheim, religion can be defined as society worshipping itself and reinforcing its bonds (and in some way its closure, if we translate Durkheim's vision in Bergsonian terms) through rituals; for Bergson, religion is never reducible to the symbolic forms through which it represents or asserts the collective. On the contrary, it is more of an instinctual disposition linked to biological forces. The use of instinct may be misleading as human life is characterized by a degree of indetermination. Compared to animal life, it is based on the existence of intelligence and of sociability. It opens a space for contingency, but also for tension and for destruction. We can speak of the ambivalent dimension of human life: relative freedom has very contrasted results and opens a new space where we constantly oscillate between smartness and dumbness. Irrationality is no longer reserved to the so-called primitive people; intelligence may turn against itself and produce negative effects. Here, Bergson situates himself against the grain of Enlightenment that pervades all the French republican ideology through a common reference to Kant. This is the reason why he can be reconfigured as the first thinker in the twentieth century who contested all the great concepts of the social sciences (modernization, rationalization, civilizing process), all oriented by a vector that moves societies from the simple to the complex and from nature to culture. The antihistoricist stance is central: a peaceful and open society would never be the outcome of a modernizing trajectory since there is nothing of this type in history. In this respect, Bergson stands in sharp contrast to the mainstream thought of his time: accounting for the war necessitates a withdrawal from the idea of progress as well as the idea of modernity. The re-enchantment of the world implies a way out of the world as it can be described in terms of ordinary morality and obligation, subsumed under the matrix of social contract. The society based on the concept of humanity is not to be found in any historical process. It presupposes a form of moral conversion based on the belief in the eternal dimension of religion, a clear antisecularist point of view. For Bergson, the idea of a way out of religion, shared by many republican thinkers of his time, including through a transfer of sacrality in Durkheim's conception, is a nonsense.

Two Societies

Sourcing morality and religion reveals two streams. The first appears in the features of closed society and static religion, which is, to put it simply, society as we know it. Here, Bergson takes a clear anti-Durkheimian stance. Morality does not appear as an explicit pressure of society over individuals: it may be an exceptional case, but, generally speaking, human beings do not feel the weight of obligation as coming from above. Society is never envisaged by Bergson as a totality or an objective reality. The adjustment to norms is rather spontaneous and almost "automated." Bergson writes: "The members of a society hold together like the cells of an organism. Habit, served by intelligence and imagination, introduces among them a discipline resembling, in the interdependence it establishes between separate individuals, the unity of an organism of anastomotic cells" (Bergson 1977: 13–14). However, consciousness brings in the idea of an individual personality incommensurable to the others. Man is both intelligent and social. Intelligence develops unexpectedly and challenges the limitations of nature.

The first morality is supposed to be immutable ("If it changes, it immediately forgets that it has changed, or it acknowledges no change") (Bergson 1977: 58). The second morality is totally different: it is a "forward thrust; it is the very essence of mobility" (ibid.). Unfortunately, it is less easy to define than the first, and this will apply to the two sources of religion too. Dynamic "reabsorbs the static, the latter then becoming a mere particular instance of the former" (:59). Between the closed and the open, there is a "transition stage" (:63) that shows the sign of an insufficient impetus. It is very important to note that the closed morality is defined as infra-intellectual and the open as supra-intellectual. Here we can touch Bergson's anti-intellectualist orientation. Closed morality is almost "automated." It is clearly prereflexive and the outcome of natural interaction. Human intelligence is not needed. This is not far from the Bourdieuan habitus—a form of bodily adjustment to the flux of interactions (Bourdieu 1990). Closed morality is on the side of nature, since it is "the counterpart of certain instincts in animals" (Bergson 1977: 64). Thus, it is inferior to intelligence. The open morality is "inspiration, intuition, emotion, susceptible of analysis into ideas which furnish intellectual notations of it and branch out into infinite detail" (ibid.). Thus, it is more than intelligence. Only the first morality can be defined as "purely social," as it is based on impulsion (instinctual in character); the second is "supra-social" as it transcends the social organization. Again, there is an anti-Durkheimian tone. An open morality cannot be defined in terms of mere social function. Movement implies the "fluidification" of ordinary social arrangements. There is always something beyond the social in an open society.

This excess, if one may say, has always something to do with the emergence of strong personalities. Bergson never uses the word, but there is some possible connection with the concept of charisma that Weber derives from theology to apply it to secular situations (Weber 2019), even when a rational-legal logic dominates, as in modern societies. Charismatic domination, wrote Franz Neumann, "is a phenomenon as old as politics itself." In his book on national socialism, he considered the Nazi phenomenon as its extreme form (Neumann 1983). Since Max Weber made charisma a sociological concept, the word has been in regular use in history and the social sciences. Gradually, the term has been appropriated by common language, to the point that its analytical power may have been lost sight of. The popular uses of the term make it an extraordinary property of the individual who holds it, which allows him to stand out from the mass and to exercise his power over it. However, there are specific historical conditions that allow individual characteristics to be apprehended as extraordinary: charisma is therefore always relational, because it presupposes collectives ready to receive the messages that are expressed and to recognize them, most often in an emotional register.

In secularizing the notion of charisma from his reading of the work of the theologian Rudolf Sohm, Weber retained the extraordinary and emotional dimension that characterized the early Christian Church, but he included it in a notional network that reconfigured its meaning: it is obviously from the tripartition between three main forms of domination that the political and sociological definition of this exceptional disposition is articulated in a typology whose purity is always theoretical, inasmuch as impure forms can always be observed in history. Charismatic domination is thus opposed both to the "eternal yesterday" on which traditional domination is based and to the "belief in the legality of rules that makes the strength of rational-legal domination," characteristic of political modernity. The two forms opposed to charisma are thus characterized by a particular form of belief, either in tradition or in reason. The charismatic form also supposes that one believes in its effectiveness. In a world characterized by the existence of a purely rational-legal set of rules and beliefs, charismatic power would be meaningless: there is no room, at least in theory, for the emergence of an emotionally based relationship, which would inevitably destabilize the regular functioning of bodies based on rational principles. However, this is not the case since Weber leaves room for charismatic domination within democratic systems, thus opening up a whole range of questions about the nature of power within them. Indeed, Weber's definition of charisma remains very close to his theological definition, insofar as it continues to include, beyond exceptional properties, a relationship to the divine.

Going back to Bergson, we can say that static religion is first defined through the lens of superstition and irrationality. Contrary to Durkheim, this type of religion cannot be the first matrix for science, as in Durkheim for whom it is the primary source of any type of scientific thinking. We must admit that *Homo sapiens* is the only animal species that can be called unreasonable. Here we find again the structuring dis-adjustment between mere instinctual properties and the space for uncertainty and contingency that society opens. "There has never been a society without religion" (Bergson 1977 112): the statement implies that there will never be a society without religion; I don't speak here of any form of civil religion that would supersede "religious religions." Bergson does not envisage the end of religion. On the contrary, an open society is grounded on a religious move out of closed morality and religion.

Static religion is opposed to dynamic religion. The first is basically defined by its functionality. It concerns the preservation of society. The first is designed to "ward off the dangers to which intelligence might expose man; it was infra-intellectual" (Bergson 1977: 186). Dynamic religion is "coupled doubtless with higher intellectuality, but distinct from it" (ibid.). It is, as in the case of morality, supra-intellectual. The first maintains social life; the second expands humanity through mysticism.

Here, two things must be noted: (1) mysticism is defined by its relation to a "vital impetus" (Bergson 1977:213); (2) true mysticism is rare, which renders open society exceptional. Hence, even if we include in mysticism the attraction exerted by great personalities on disciples, dynamic religion has a minority status, often defined as restricted to elites. I certainly don't want to propose a "sociological" reading that would restrict open society and dynamic religion to a social group, but the repetition of the word "elite" must be noted. It has often been used against Bergson to show his class bias, but I am not sure that it is the main point, which is the short supply of mysticism. This scarcity is solved by the fact that "whose who have, from afar off, bowed their heads to the mystic word, because they heard a faint echo of it within themselves, will not remain indifferent to its message" (Bergson 1977: 215).

At this point, you might think that religion is the solution to social problems. Bergson takes pains to show that the great mystics are not fools and that they are "generally endowed with superior common sense" (Bergson 1977: 245). You may tell me that the "sharp distinction" between the closed and the open is very unlikely to solve many of the problems that plague late modernity. Very few of you will be denigrating Greta Thunberg's action for climate, although she could be included in the category of great mystics. This is often used as an argument against her activism. However, for young people, she embodies quite naturally a form of mysticism based on knowledge, a very original form of sanctity.

Despite this example, you may remain convinced that Bergson is dead wood. I am very skeptical about the efficacy of Bergson's distinction and will never deny its socially outdated vision of social relationships. We live in a time of horizontality, and we fear asymmetrical relations, with few exceptions. It seems impossible to get back to a closed society, which would solve many problems by linking the individual together through symbolic bounds that would remain unnoticed or, at least, preconscious. This option has little chance to fly, as we live in what Ulrich Beck and others have defined as "reflexive modernity," which is not far, if you look at it closely, from Bergson's supra-intellectuality. Besides, mysticism is the other name of the love of humanity, thought as an open unit, which is unthinkable as long as collective entities are defined by the closure of religious denominations and national obligations. The mystic is the one who may show to the world that identities are murderous and are most of the time the main cause of war.

Is Bergson antimodern and committed to put an end to the mechanization of the world? Frédéric Worms, one of the best among Bergson scholars, does not think so: "Bergson in no way condemns us to a terrible choice between purely warlike 'mechanization' and an ecstatic 'mysticism' without any technical support! We can leave that to others. The freedom of humanity, 'now', requires this new alliance between mechanism and mysticism, one beyond the dark, doubly closed one by the war, where technological power serves not mysticism but myth, mythology, ideology and fabulation" (Lefebvre and White 2012: 30). The Bergsonian mystic is able to show the closed dimension of identity politics and say "One World" without being laughed at. If we look at our present condition, we must acknowledge that neoliberalism has increased inequalities in the world and that decolonization has not reduced the weight of racism. Should we resign ourselves to the claim of asymmetry by returning to a premodern vision of social organization where the group takes precedence over the individual? Or should we, on the contrary, criticize the presuppositions of political liberalism and propose an alternative that would put solidarity at the center of action as well as the implementation of systems to control the effectiveness of the application of rights?

Beyond the current ideological disputes, which often mark struggles for power in the world of intellectuals, there is no salvation in a "differentialism" in which the dominated sanctify their domination in the name of the identity that the master has lent them and which, contrary to what they think, will not turn out like a glove. The challenge of the climate emergency today cannot be satisfied with an identity-based response. It is time for political imagination: this cannot be reduced to the replication of old models, in particular the nationalist model, which, in its supposedly renewed form, goes very well with illiberalism, as Viktor Orbán shows with inventiveness, nor with the regression that constitutes the confusing world of multiculturalism. Realizing myself may mean tearing myself away from my native soil and my foster mother, even if I choose to return from time to time. Although Albert Camus preferred his mother to justice, it is doubtful that justice gains by being tied to the game of identities. Universalism is the enemy—it has been said a lot during the last forty years. Undoubtedly, there is a false universalism, which is the screen of the Western domination. It is used by conservatives who ignore the fact that it has long been a disguised localism, and that it was one of the modes of justification among others of the colonial enterprise. There is another, to be constructed, which involves a radical questioning of the logic of identity.

As Bruno Karsenti aptly writes, the love of humanity, the only true love, involving neither possession nor jealousy, develops at its best beyond the social, as it is both supra-intellectual and supra-social (Bergson 2012: 59). Human beings must withdraw from de facto solidarity and from institutionalized religion to enter a new world, not precisely defined, where a new entity can at last be born: the universal, cosmopolitan, and unbounded community.

Bibliography

Beck, U., A. Giddens, and S. Lash. 1994. *Reflexive Modernization*. Stanford, CA: Stanford University Press.
Bergson, H. 1977. *The Two Sources of Morality and Religion*. Translated by R. Ashley Audra and Cloudesley Brereton, with the assistance of W. Horsfall Carter. Notre Dame: University of Notre Dame Press (first English translation 1935).
Bergson, H. 2012. *Les deux sources de la morale et de la religion*. Introduction, notes, chronologie et bibliographie par Bruno Karsenti, édition établie sous la direction de Paul-Antoine Miquel. Paris: Garnier-Flammarion (first edition 1932).
Bourdieu, P. 1990. *The Logic of Practice*. London: Polity Press.
Foucault M. 1985. "La vie, l'expérience et la science." *Revue de métaphysique et de morale* 1: 3–20.
Germino, D. and K. von Beyme. 1974. *The Open Society in Theory and Practice*. The Hague: Martinus Nijhoff.
Lefevbre, A. and M. White. 2012. *Bergson, Politics and Religion*. Durham, NC: Duke University Press.
Neumann, F. 1983. *Behemoth. The Structure and Practice of National-Socialism (1933–1944)*. London: Buccaneer Books.
Politzer, G. 1968. *Le Bergsonisme. La fin d'une parade philosophique*. Paris: Pauvert (1932).
Weber, M. [1920] 2019. *Economy and Society*. Cambridge, MA: Harvard University Press.

PART II
National and Regional Perspectives on Open Society

9

THE GENDER OF ILLIBERALISM: NEW TRANSNATIONAL ALLIANCES AGAINST OPEN SOCIETIES IN CENTRAL AND EASTERN EUROPE

Katalin Fábián

Anti-gender movements—which blame feminism for a "global sexual revolution" that threatens freedom, the family, and the survival of humankind—pose serious challenges to the idea of open society. While the original architects of the concept of open society (such as Henri Bergson or Karl Popper) lamentably did not engage with the notions of feminism or the more recent idea of gender, it is nonetheless easy to perceive that a clear commitment to plurality and diversity drives their conceptions (Bergson 1935; Popper 2020). Open society stands as a powerful idea against xenophobia, misogyny, and homophobia—that have all repeatedly served as catalysts for ushering in exclusion, oppression, and genocide. The recent rise of state-sponsored anti-gender movements in post-communist countries is, thus, an important and deeply concerning phenomenon that flies in the face of the very spirit of an open society.

While the anti-gender movements began in the West, they have thus far been more influential and governmentally supported in Hungary, Poland, and Russia. To be sure, the electoral victories of nationalist-conservative parties and populist politicians since 2010 in these countries have attracted considerable attention in both the media and scholarly literature.[1] However, few observers have noted how transnational anti-gender movements played a role in this important transformation. In fact, conservative-nationalist political parties, especially those in governing positions—such as the Law and Justice Party (*Prawo i Sprawiedliwość*, PiS) in Poland, Fidesz and the Christian Democratic People's Party (*Kereszténydemokrata Néppárt*, KDNP) in Hungary, and the United Russia Party (*Yedinaya Rossiya*) in Russia—have made optimum use of local equivalents of the transnational anti-gender crusade to retain and broaden their support.

These anti-gender movements are part of a more comprehensive, flexible, and adaptable ideological construct usurping ordinary anti-feminism,

---

1 Numerous notable scholarly journals have recently dedicated sections or special issues to the analysis of variants of populism in world politics (e.g., *Foreign Affairs* [October 2016]; *International Political Science Review* 38, No. 4 [2017]; *Slavic Review* 76, No. 1 [2017]). Populism has adopted a right-wing, conservative-nationalist form in most Central and Eastern European countries, but there are left-leaning variations. See, for instance, Ganev (2017).

anti-liberalism, and selective anti-globalization by replacing individual (human) rights with the "rights of the family" and linking procreation with demographic nationalism. Local anti-gender movements have supported and contributed to restrictions on reproductive rights and to increased anti-abortion campaigns; resistance to lesbian, gay, transgender, trans, and queer (LGBTQ+) rights; opposition to laws against domestic violence; the introduction of anti-immigrant policies; and a misogynist turn in the representational politics of gender roles.[2]

In this chapter, I aim to contribute to the literature on open society by addressing two specific questions about anti-gender movements. First, why did anti-genderism as a specific authoritarian trend develop and become pronounced in these otherwise very different post-communist countries? Second, why do the anti-gender movements matter for democracies and open societies? I argue that a marked reappearance of conservative, expressively masculine, and populist forces in post-communist politics has led to the embracing of anti-genderism in different national contexts, with the Hungarian, Polish, and Russian cases offering three similar but distinct variations in the political trajectory of their respective movements. Over the last decade, anti-genderism has served multiple functions to entrench what proponents label as traditional values, while promoting specific class and racialized interests in the cloak of rejecting both the communist past and Western European political and social expectations. This matters for democracies and open societies as these movements resemble the proverbial canary in the coal mine: with the insistence on their monopoly to define sexual roles, these developments signal the instability of democracy and how much exclusionary nationalism has strengthened, along with the normalization of anti-European Union and anti-immigration sentiments and Islamophobia.

In what follows, I will describe and analyze three main triggers, both ideational and institutional, of the Central and Eastern European anti-gender movements. Subsequently, I will bring to the fore the significance of the anti-gender movements for democratic politics. I conclude with an overview of the continuing debates around defining the anti-gender movements both globally and regionally, revealing the significance of this countermovement in the most recent post-communist era.

1. Why There? Why Then? Three Main Triggers

Why was (and is) the Central and Eastern European post-communist region so receptive to the arguments of anti-gender movements? Although most sources

---

[2] While both sexism and misogyny maintain the patriarchal order, Manne (2017, 78) distinguishes misogyny as establishing a barrier and functioning to police and enforce (not just threaten and demarcate, as per sexism) the powers of prevailing gender norms and expectations. Misogyny includes a whole range of actions (e.g., hostility, shaming, shunning, and exclusion) and also inaction (e.g., lack of cooperation).

locate the origin of the European anti-gender movements to Croatia in 2007, Slovenia in 2009, and Spain in 2012, Poland and Russia have been at the forefront of these matters at least as long, with Hungary joining by 2010 (Graff and Korolczuk 2021; Zacharenko 2016). It appears that the confluence of economic crisis and inward-turning, nationalist social changes produced a significant transition: in many countries, particularly Poland, Russia, and Hungary, the relatively stable international human rights consensus has fractured and produced problematic domestic and foreign policy consequences beginning in 2012. This fracture spawned the emergence of a counter-movement challenging gender equality, sex education, and the rights of sexual minorities. Church officials, right-wing party functionaries, and faith-based organizations began conducting similar and sometimes coordinated rhetorical attacks often followed by policy changes against gender equality measures.

The combined effect of three main triggers appears to be at the root of the Central and East European anti-gender movements: (1) an ambiguous relationship to globalization, (2) the European Union (EU) as a stand-in for feminism and liberalism, and (3) a transnational conservative people-to-people diplomacy.

An Ambiguous Relationship to Globalization

Like many other transnational social networks, the anti-gender movements have a complex relationship to globalization. They are the product of increasing political, economic, and cultural connectivity, yet their proponents argue that they aim to curtail what they consider harmful international influences. The many schools that analyze globalization as long-standing phenomena of increased interconnectedness recognize that the exchanges are fundamentally unequal in their effects both within and across states. Anti-genderism can use globalization as a scapegoat to critique and undermine accompanying change, including the emergence of liberalism, feminism, and the rights of sexual minorities. On the one hand, the anti-gender movements are products of globalization, relying on transnational ideational exchanges and importing ideas and techniques. These movements' physical and economic hardware (e.g., international mail, personal travel, and online social networks) as well as software (ideas) come from many parts of the world. Central and Eastern European churches, nationalist parties, and their sympathizers connect to each other both regionally and globally. For example, the Hungarian Catholic Church translated and promoted a letter from the Conference of Bishops of Slovakia in December 2013 on the dangers of "gender ideology" and how standing "against God's order is the promotion of the culture of death," giving it an audience in not one but two countries (Terenzani 2013). In the same year, in Hungary, female members of the youth division of Jobbik, a right-wing nationalist party established connections with the anti-feminist Polish women's movement Women for the Nation (*Kobiety dia Narody*). They created a shared Facebook page called "Christian women against Femen" (https://www.facebook.com/ChristianWomenAgainstFemen?fref=ts), referring to the Ukrainian-French feminist group internationally known for organizing topless protests in defense of women's rights (Ackermann 2014). This page attracted support from, among others, Australia, Brazil, Croatia, France, Italy, Lebanon, Mexico, and the United States (Piasecka-Łopuszańska 2013). The anti-genderists appear oblivious to the irony of relying on extensive transnational networking while branding other forms of globalization (e.g., the United Nations, EU, and World Health Organization) as oppressive and undemocratic.

When critiquing globalization, anti-genderism plays the nationalism card. By reclaiming unfettered state sovereignty and creating a false or exaggerated ideal about the past greatness of the nation, anti-genderism further enhances demographic nationalism. With an increased focus on what they see as a demographic decline, demographic nationalism represents a dominant response to the challenges of globalization in post-communist European countries. First, the reassertion of religion in the form of the churches' increased political influence works in tandem with a political effort to recreate a sense of exclusivist national identity. This appeals to conservatives because religion can provide a feeling of stability in contemporary post-communist contexts. Second, Central and Eastern European churches gained renewed political opportunity and social strength after the fall of the Iron Curtain in 1989, but had to devise ways to deal with pluralism in politics and culture while often facing new religious influences and institutions as well as the residual effects of decades-long secularism. The local anti-gender movements provided an opportunity for the churches to mobilize a significant portion of the population.

The earliest initiator of the anti-gender movement appears to be the Vatican. The Roman Catholic critique of gender began under more obviously conservative Papal leadership (John Paul II and Benedict XVI) but has continued under the leadership of the more liberal-leaning Pope Francis. In Tbilisi, Georgia, Pope Francis argued: "A great enemy of marriage today is the theory of gender" (San Martín 2016). The Vatican has been a leading opponent of women's reproductive freedom, but related rhetorical debates on reproductive rights have moved far beyond Catholic circles. With debates about gender now in mainstream political and public discourse, broader moral and political values beyond theological doctrine are often brought in.

In addition to the churches (themselves transnational in both ideology and structure), new international nongovernmental organizations (INGOs) (e.g., the World Congress of Families [WCF]) have provided extensive ideological and institutional support for anti-gender activists to organize (Human Rights Campaign 2014). Russian conservatives played a central role in the founding of WCF in 1995. Alexey Komov, WCF's regional representative, touted Russia's leading role in the global "pro-family movement," arguing that "Eastern Europe can really help our brothers in the West" to resist the "new totalitarianism" associated with "political correctness and the sexual revolution" (Stroop 2016). WCF held three of its recent global events in post-communist Central and Eastern Europe: in Prague, Czech Republic in 1997, in Tbilisi, Georgia in 2016, and in

Budapest, Hungary in 2017. It would have held a fourth in the region, but the US-based organizers had to relocate the 2014 gathering from Moscow in the wake of Russia's occupation of Crimea and the Western sanctions (Belz 2017). WCF is one of the largest US-based organizations offering ideological content and traveling speakers, connecting the anti-gender movement abroad with the religious right in the United States. While WCF is US-based, its close relationship with Russia is based on synergy and common interests, not a simple transfer of ideas. Their common vision of the impending death of humanity and civilization is fueled by demographic panic over the diminishing white Christian flock.

The EU as a Stand-In for Feminism and Liberalism

The foremost transnational institutional target of the Central and Eastern European anti-gender movements is the EU. Anti-gender movements often blame EU integration and its associated challenges for moral, family, and societal declines due to more progressive gender policies and prohibitions against gender discrimination. With EU member states obliged to adopt the *acquis communautaire* (the accumulated body of EU law and obligations since 1958), legislators and judges in post-communist countries have repeatedly expressed hostility toward gender-progressive regulations, arguing that laws need to be objective and neutral. They describe anti-discrimination law and mandated pay equity as incompatible with freedom. The essentialist understanding of the sexes in the post-communist region has resulted in resistance to EU-endorsed gender-progressive regulations of social relations on the basis that they are an unacceptable interference with the "natural social order" (Havelkova 2017).

Anti-gender activists have systematically portrayed the EU's gender mainstreaming principle as ideologically driven and anti-men. Churches and conservative politicians, therefore, began calling for "family mainstreaming" (vs the EU's "gender mainstreaming") to address what they see as a serious European demographic values-based cultural crisis. In addition to serving as a rhetorical adversary, the EU plays a central role as a pragmatic policy target. The first internationally coordinated campaign concerning "gender ideology" took place at the European Parliament (EP) during the 2013 drafting of and debate on the *Estrela Report*, named after MEP Edite Estrela, coordinator of the *Report on Sexual and Reproductive Health and Rights*. The report recommended that "high-quality abortion services should be made legal, safe, and accessible to all within the public health systems of the Member States" and that "sex education classes [be] compulsory for all primary and secondary school children" (Estrela 2013). The counter-mobilization movement based primarily online argued that the EU has no business talking about these issues. The anti-gender movements' interactive CitizenGO website (https://www.citizengo.org/) coordinated many activities aimed at promoting Christian values and agitating against abortion and same-sex marriage (Whyte 2017). Gabriele Kuby, a notable anti-gender ideologue, and her institute, the European Dignity Watch, coordinated the activities of the transnational World Youth Alliance-Europe, with the Federation of Catholic Family Associations in Europe (FAFCE). Kuby said that "what it [the Estrela Report] offered was free and safe access to abortion on demand. This is neither health care, not support for women, but it profoundly disrespects women, their dignity as well as the dignity of children yet to be born" (Pialoux 2013). The continent-wide mobilization included sending tens of thousands of critical and sometimes threatening messages to each MEP involved in the report. Stunning liberals on International Human Rights Day (December 10), the Estrela report's proposed non-binding resolution on women's health and reproductive rights failed by seven votes. Despite irregularities in counting the votes, the alternative resolution of the right-wing European Conservatives and Reformists (backed by the European People's Party) was adopted instead (Humanist Federation 2013). The alternative resolution rejected what conservatives perceived as the EU Commission's aiming to define sexual and reproductive health as rights and stated that "no human right to abortion exists." It pushed discussions of reproductive rights and sexual education to the member states rather than permitting further discussions at the EP and specifically held that medical personnel have the right to conscientiously object to abortion (Belder et al. 2013).

Further challenges to gender equality policies and LGBTQ rights also came from within the EU. A conservative and Eurosceptic group of MEPs raised numerous legal concerns and argued that the concept of gender was not in the Treaty on the Functioning of the EU, and therefore could not be introduced and applied in human rights conventions and as a basis of conducting EU foreign policy. Three MEPs in particular—Anna Záborská, Ryszard Legutko, and Zbigniew Ziobro, from Slovak and Polish conservative-nationalist parties—regularly raised critical objections to contemporary liberal democracy, as they claimed it allowed "no serious conservative opposition within this system, because the respectable opposition on the Right feels driven to argue that they too are open, pluralistic, tolerant and inclusive, dedicated to the entitlement of individuals and groups, non-discriminatory and even supportive of the claims of feminists and homosexual activists" (Gottfried 2017).

Anti-gender activists and politicians argue that they act in the name of an oppressed and silent majority while they effectively represent a well-organized Christian fundamentalist minority. They have combined grassroots and institutional forces, efficiently using tools to their benefit that were intended to address the democratic deficiencies of the EU. The subsidiarity principle and European citizens' initiative (ECI) procedures, for example, were designed to promote and strengthen democracy but have been used for anti-gender purposes. Conservatives have used ECI procedures repeatedly and effectively to oppose gender-equality-related developments being considered by the EP. An ECI has to be backed by at least one million EU citizens, coming from at least seven out of the twenty-seven member states, thereby forcing the European Commission to commence a debate on the issue. EP votes in 2014 on the *Lunacek Report* on homophobia, for example, have become more contentious because of the coordinated interventions of conservative-nationalist MEPs challenging the concept of gender and other ECIs on the EP reports (Tarabella 2015). The first ECI was the "One of Us" campaign in Poland in 2013 which aimed to prevent the financing of abortions via EU funds and gathered over two million signatures (European Federation for Life and Human Dignity). In December 2015, the "Mum, Dad & Kids: European Citizens' Initiative to Protect Marriage and Family" (http://www.mumdadandkids.eu/ [last accessed August 2017; now offline]) called for EU regulation that would define "marriage" as "a union between a man and a woman" and "the family" as "based on marriage and/or descent." With excellent transnational organizing, this ECI reached one million confirmed signatories. The Mum, Dad & Kids ECI emerged from one of the largest conservative Christian legal advocacy organizations in the world, ADF International, a branch of the US-based Alliance Defending Freedom, which uses litigation to "defend religious freedom, the sanctity of life, and marriage and family."[3] Parallel to attempts to defund Planned Parenthood in the United States, ADF International cooperated with numerous MEPs (notably Miroslav Mikolášik from Slovakia and Michaela Šojdrová from the Czech Republic) and the anti-reproductive choice European People's Party (EPP) Working Group on Bioethics and Human Dignity. During the #DefundIPPF campaign, they argued, incorrectly, at meetings and symposia in the EP in October 2015 and in April 2016 that the International Planned Parenthood Federation (IPPF) profited from abortion by trading baby organs (Truth about IPPF 2016).

The 2011 Istanbul Convention further illustrates the power of the idea of the traditional family in political debates and the role of churches in debates about gender. Polish and Slovak bishops issued a declaration arguing that the Convention relies unduly on the concept of gender and thus "contradicts human experience and common sense," violating religious freedom and parents' right to the education of children (Zvolensky 2016). Relying on their strong relationships with governments, church leaders demanded that their respective governments resist international pressure and not ratify the Convention. Indeed, while most Central and Eastern European delegates signed the Istanbul Convention, thus far Bosnia-Herzegovina, Croatia, Estonia, Georgia, Moldova, Montenegro, North Macedonia, Romania, Poland, Serbia, Slovenia, and Ukraine had ratified it as of November 2022. Uproars followed the Polish center-left government's ratification of the Convention in 2015 and the European Commission recommendation that the EU ratifies and thus makes it part of EU law (European Commission 2016).

Some of these value and policy conflicts pit national governments and sizable segments of local populations against EU norms, laws, and institutions, as the

---

3 The Alliance Defending Freedom (ADF), founded in 1994, works with more than 3,000 lawyers to advance its causes around the world. It is one of the largest legal advocacy groups in the United States, holding US$65.1 million in revenue for the 2019–20 tax year. It acts globally, supporting cases in Belize, India, and Russia, describing "the alliance's involvement in both countries [India and Russia] as 'a small group of attorneys' who wanted 'to resist the foreign activists that were trying to challenge their public health law.'" See Peters (2017).

recent case of Adrian Coman, a Romanian national who was under review in the European Court of Justice (ECJ), shows. The case revolved around whether the term "spouse" includes a same-sex married partner. Romania is one of six EU member states with no legal recognition for same-sex relationships, thus Coman's American husband, whom he married in 2010 in Belgium, could not obtain a residency permit there (Court of Justice of the European Union 2018a). The case and the corresponding debates extended far beyond legal ramifications. For instance, in early 2016, three million Romanians signed a petition calling for the constitutional definition of marriage to be altered from a union between two spouses to one specifically between a man and a woman. Yet, the Romanian Constitutional Court accepted the validity of Coman's case in July 2016, and a hearing was held by the ECJ in November 2017. The ECJ ruled that "although the Member States have the freedom whether or not to authorise marriage between persons of the same sex, they may not obstruct the freedom of residence of an EU citizen by refusing to grant his same-sex spouse, a national of a country that is not an EU Member State, a derived right of residence in their territory" (Court of Justice of the European Union 2018b). Despite this ruling, as of September 2021, Coman's spouse has still not been issued a residency permit from the Romanian authorities (Boffey 2021). How the rights of sexual minorities have become one of the most substantial wedge issues in post-communist Central and Eastern European countries is closely entwined with the emergence of local equivalents of the transnational anti-gender movement.

Foreign Policy by Other Means

A convergence of domestic and international factors produced potent Central and Eastern European anti-gender movements, but much of the movements' success in the region originates from elsewhere. Applying lessons learned in the United States and some African countries, the Vatican successfully used the concepts of rights and freedom to weigh in on the conceptualizations, media debates, and policies in Central and Eastern Europe, where religion is enjoying renewed appeal. In the post-Cold War geopolitical environment, the post-communist region and the Global South are now courted as new "virgin" lands for Catholic influence because they were (supposedly) untouched by the sexual revolution of the 1970s.

In the context of a growing international appeal of rights, the Catholic Church began a counter-offensive in the 1990s to argue for a core of differently conceptualized rights, centered on the right to freedom of religion and the rights of the family (Tomasi 2017, 12–26, 95–97). The Roman Catholic Church has encouraged its followers to fight for the public role of religion, asking parishioners to defend and promote their ideas publicly, to mobilize politically both on the streets and online. Moving dramatically away from a self-perception of marginalization in the international human rights discourse, the Vatican boldly challenged the views of feminists and Western governments at the 1994 Cairo and 1995 Beijing UN conferences on women, critiquing "'gender' feminism" as representing a "culture of death," allegedly exemplified by the acceptance of abortion, euthanasia, and gay marriage (Pope John Paul II 1995). The perceived threat of gender as a common conceptual framework enticed many of its various opponents to a multidenominational "Baptist-burqa" network that includes Evangelical Christians and orthodox adherents of Islam who aim to preserve the previous patriarchal and hierarchal order (Clifford 2010). Global right-wing activism overlaps with this rhetorical and strategic framework, adding the language of defending democracy and protecting the child and the family and critiquing liberal elites.

The US example of linking the "old Right" (also labeled "informal conservatism," especially between 1910 and 1940) with the "new Right" (institutionalized and often evangelical conservative ascendency in the late twentieth century) has also been applied in Central and Eastern Europe. The Vatican and the US Christian Right shared some common ground in making legislation concerning gender, and especially sexual matters, highly controversial and prompted these issues to dominate public discourse. In the 1990s, the emerging Christian Right in the United States selected sex education as one of its first political battlegrounds. Debate about sex education has long occupied a strategic place in the history of efforts to regulate sexual morality, transforming US politics both domestically and in its foreign relations (Irvine 2002).

By the late 1990s, the anti-gender movements had become a global conveyor of the so-called "culture wars" that began in the United States in the 1970s (Webb 2006). US-based religious conservatives found partners abroad after seeming to lose ground at home, especially on the issues of reproductive and gay rights. The anti-gay message resonated in many African countries (Williams 2013) and conservative US activists also found an unexpectedly strong and willing partner in Putin's Russia. The legacy of the Cold War makes it difficult for many observers to recognize contemporary Russia as a conservative state aiming for leadership in global right-wing politics. However, Russia has financially supported numerous right-wing parties in Europe in part to counter EU influence (Datta 2021). The contemporary right-wing iteration of Russian moral exceptionalism entirely overlaps with US conservatives' desire to revive what they see as the Christian roots of European and even, more broadly, Western civilization.

Progressives had successfully employed online organizational models (e.g., MoveOn.org) in the United States and successfully operated feminist and human rights NGOs in Central and Eastern Europe—so-called "NGOization" (Jacobsson 2016). European conservatives followed suit with similar NGOs and websites for transnational mobilization for their own causes. The conservative CitizenGo.org website appears in twelve languages (not including numerous English, Spanish, and Portuguese regional variations, with plans to add Arabic and Chinese), informing and connecting activists. The internet-based networks both connect and support the financing of conservative Christian networks in various countries to further specific policy aims in various large umbrella organizations, such as the WCF (Feder 2014).

Conservative-nationalist politicians in Central and Eastern Europe, especially in Poland, Hungary, and Russia, have successfully built on ideas of national exceptionalism and defending their country, to claim that they protect the nation against ill-intentioned foreign influences. Arguing that they fight for "Europe" and "Christian Europe," the contemporary Polish, Hungarian, and Russian governments are pushing back against the EU and other international agencies. This can be seen in the Hungarian and Polish rhetoric and policy choices opposing the United Nations High Commission for Refugees concerning the migration crisis in 2015 and EU positions to maintain the independence of the judiciary (Euronews 2017). In these contexts, the Polish and Hungarian governments relied on anticolonial arguments as a counterargument for deflecting international organizations' concerns about these countries' democratic backsliding signified by the loss of oversight on part of an independent judiciary, the media, civil society, alongside the degradation of ethnic and sexual minorities' human rights.

Immediately after the regime changes in Central and Eastern Europe, celebrations to assert newly gained or regained state independence were joined by movements against reproductive rights in nearly every country of the region. Poland became, and has remained, a major site of conflict in values and policy in this regard (Davies 2016; Mishtal 2015). After the regime change, the new political elites promoted "neo-traditional," hierarchical gender roles as ideal and healthy, arguing that their communist predecessors had forced equality by requiring that women enter paid labor and politics, traditionally seen as men's purview. The "traditional values" that the anti-gender movements and conservative-nationalist politicians frequently reference are a superficially constructed category ascribing highly positive values based on a simplified, apparently timeless projection of gender relations. They ignore historical change, regional variety, ethnic and religious diversity, sexual and class oppression, and violence. The main elements of ideal gender and family relations are, according to the traditional national ideal, heterosexuality, marriage, robust patriarchy, extremely restricted grounds for divorce, respect for elders, and at least three children per family to revitalize the population of the nation. As more progressive gender ideals challenge the simplistic nature, normativity, and value of these perceived traditional principles, the concept of gender becomes a wholesale threat.

Layers of Significance in the Anti-gender Movement

Why are the Central and Eastern European anti-gender movements important? Among the many mobilizations in Central and Eastern Europe in the last decade, the anti-gender movements became important markers of the vitality of democratic politics. The rise of anti-gender sentiments reveals the instability of democracies, with increasingly blurred boundaries between church and state and the strengthening of exclusive nationalism. The anti-gender movements offer two pragmatic benefits to buttress and legitimatize a conservative political turn: (1) the issues related to gender equality and sexual minorities provide a broadly accessible theme that serves as a political wedge to divide and antagonize already polarized populations, and (2) they provide a façade of democracy in the form of social movement support to otherwise authoritarian tendencies.

Gender is an effective wedge issue to divide populations. As human societies develop any regulation of sexual behavior, the emerging division of norms and tasks often becomes central to the functioning of those societies. Arguing that foundational societal norms and rules are in danger can successfully engage people who are already in precarious (social and economic) positions and may perceive a loss of privileges. In this regard, these issues resonate especially well in Central and Eastern Europe because "a significant segment of the population in each of these countries feels that they have been robbed of something, been misled and cheated" (Erlanger 2017). The contemporary relevance of such a generated sense of crisis is that it can attract the attention of enough voters to sway national elections in a democracy. The adaptation of the language of freedom, anti-colonialism, and at least rhetorical rejection of neoliberalism greatly expanded the appeal of the anti-gender movement, and with it the global political Right, while dramatically reducing the discursive space and policy options of the political Left.

Cultural elements that debate the meanings of rights associated with gender and minorities, especially sexual minority rights, have become increasingly acrimonious even in long-established democracies. Contentious "identity politics" divide groups more willing to embrace diversity from those who see such differences as threats, undermining achievements associated with nation, state, or other entities, such as "Europe." The lack of accessible, affordable childcare, for example, leads many Central and Eastern Europeans to migrate to capitals and Western Europe to be able to support their families. Instead of addressing relevant economic issues that affect families and women, politicians and religious authorities attack feminist and progressive gender ideas, policies, and institutions.

Conclusion

This chapter set out to explore the characteristics and significance to open societies of the Central and Eastern European anti-gender movements by locating their triggers and applications. A review of the evolving definitions of the anti-gender movements reveals the development of an intensifying conflict over interpretations of globalization, human rights, and individual vs. group rights. Gender has become one of the most politically expedient themes of contemporary times to raise attention and rally citizens.

Conservative activists have learned to organize globally by adapting the organizational techniques of their opponents—the international women's and LGBTQ movements. They co-opted and further developed earlier progressive (left-wing) framing, tactics, and strategies to express their fundamental disapproval of what they claim as the unrelenting march of expanding women's rights and reproductive options and legal as well as cultural acceptance of LGBTQ people. Combining political, economic, cultural, and especially religious forces and arguments, the post-communist Central and Eastern European region has become a fertile ground to further the transnational anti-gender movements. Using gender to delineate "us" vs. "them" in Central and Eastern Europe, the anti-gender movements have propelled the new culture wars over identity to become increasingly international, even as these groups claim to fight globalization in their attempts to reclaim a fictive and romanticized past.

The conservative turn in the region is not conservative in a classic sense but rejectionist and reductionist in understandings of concepts like order, norms, appropriateness, and other concepts related to interpersonal behavior and state relations. The ruling conservative actors in Central and Eastern Europe rhetorically reject both the Soviet past and the contemporary global order and are searching for a substitute ideology that would mark them as undeniably "sovereign," "independent," and proudly "traditional." In conservative-nationalist actors' minds, the greatest threat to the state and nation is globalization, which surreptitiously chips away at their alleged unique and superior national identity. The increased nationalist fervor generates frequent perceived crises about demographic decline, the disappearance of the nation, and international conflicts that both individually and especially in combination with one another further legitimate internal (national or regional) siege-mentality that tolerates no challenge, nuance, or alternative viewpoint. Such a generation of crises produces long-term consequences that maintain only a façade of democracy and replace tolerance with violence under the cover of state-approved misogyny, homophobia, and xenophobia.

Bibliography

Ackerman, Galia. 2014. *FEMEN*. Malden, MA: Polity Press.
Belder, Bastiaan, Rolandas Paksas, Tadeusz Cymański, and Philippe de Villiers. 2013. *Motion for a Resolution (Rule 157(4) of the Rules of Procedure) Replacing Non-Legislative Motion for A Resolution*. A7-0306/2013. Brussels: European Parliament. https://www.europarl.europa.eu/doceo/document/A-7-2013-0306-AM-001-001_EN.pdf.
Belz, Emily. 2017. "An Ally at Arm's Length?" *World Magazine*, March 15. https://wng.org/articles/an-ally-at-arms-length-1617305830.
Bergson, Henri. 1935. *The Two Sources of Morality and Religion*. London, United Kingdom: Macmillan.
Bob, Clifford. 2010. *Globalizing the Culture Wars: The United Nations Battle Over Sexual Rights*. SSRN Scholarly Paper ID 1642070. Rochester, NY: American Political Science Association 2010 Annual Meeting. https://papers.ssrn.com/abstract=1642070.
Boffey, Daniel. 2021. "MEPs Condemn Failure to Respect Rights of Same-Sex Partners in EU." *The Guardian*, September 14. https://www.theguardian.com/world/2021/sep/14/meps-condemn-failure-respect-rights-same-sex-partners-eu.
Court of Justice of the European Union. 2018a. "C-673/16 - Coman and Others." Case C-673/16. Luxembourg: European Union. https://curia.europa.eu/juris/document/

document_print.jsf?docid=202542&text=&dir=&doclang=EN&part=1&occ=first&mode=lst&pageIndex=0&cid=467914.
Court of Justice of the European Union. 2018b. "The Term 'Spouse' within the Meaning of the Provisions of EU Law on Freedom of Residence for EU Citizens and Their Family Members Includes Spouses of the Same Sex (Judgment in Case C-673/16)," June 5, 2018, sec. Press and Information.
Davies, Christian. 2016. "Polish Women Vow to Step Up Pressure over Abortion Restrictions." *The Guardian*, October 25. https://www.theguardian.com/world/2016/oct/25/polish-women-step-up-pressure-abortion-restrictions.
Datta, Neil. 2021. *Tip of the Iceberg: Religious Extremist Funders against Human Rights for Sexuality and Reproductive Health in Europe, 2009–2018*. Brussels: European Parliamentary Forum.
Erlanger, Steven. 2017. "In Eastern Europe, Populism Lives, Widening a Split in the E.U." *The New York Times*, November 28. https://www.nytimes.com/2017/11/28/world/europe/populism-eastern-europe.html.
Estrela, Edite. 2013. *Report on Sexual and Reproductive Health and Rights*. A7-0306/2013. Brussels: European Parliament, Committee on Women's Rights and Gender Equality. https://www.europarl.europa.eu/doceo/document/A-7-2013-0306_EN.html.
Euronews. 2017. "EU-Poland Row Gets Personal as War of Words Heats Up." July 27. https://www.euronews.com/2017/07/27/eu-poland-row-gets-personal-as-war-of-words-heats-up.
European Commission. 2016. "Commission Proposes EU Accession to International Convention to Fight Violence against Women." *European Commission – Press Corner*, March 4. https://ec.europa.eu/commission/presscorner/detail/en/IP_16_549.
European Federation for Life and Human Dignity. 2016."History." *One of Us*. https://oneofus.eu/about-us/history/.
Feder, Lester. 2014. "The Rise of Europe's Religious Right." *BuzzFeed News*, July 28. https://www.buzzfeednews.com/article/lesterfeder/the-rise-of-europes-religious-right.
Ganev, Venelin I. 2017. "'Neoliberalism Is Fascism and Should Be Criminalized': Bulgarian Populism as Left-Wing Radicalism." *Slavic Review* 76 (S1): S9–18.
Gottfried, Paul. 2017. "Ryszard Legutko and the Failings of Democracy." *American Thinker* (blog), September 3. https://www.americanthinker.com/articles/2017/09/ryszard_legutko_and_the_failings_of_democracy.html.
Graff, Agnieszka, and Elżbieta Korolczuk. 2021. *Anti-Gender Politics in the Populist Moment*. London: Routledge.
Havelková, Barbara. 2017. *Gender Equality in Law: Uncovering the Legacies of Czech State Socialism*. Portland, Oregon: Bloomsbury Academic.
Human Rights Campaign. 2014. "The World Congress of Families (WCF)." August. Accessed August 9, 2017. http://www.hrc.org/campaigns/exporters-of-hate.
Humanist Federation. 2013. "Distorted Vote on the Estrela Report." *Humanist Federation*, December 19. http://humanistfederation.eu/news-fhe.php?pages=distorted-vote-on-the-estrela-report-the-european-parliament-shows-continuous-support-for-srhr.
Irvine, Janice M. 2002. *Talk about Sex: The Battles Over Sex Education in the United States*. Berkeley and Los Angeles: University of California Press.
Jacobsson, Kerstin, and Steven Saxonberg, eds. 2016. *Beyond NGO-Ization: The Development of Social Movements in Central and Eastern Europe*. 1st ed. New York: Taylor & Francis Group. https://www.routledge.com/Beyond-NGO-ization-The

-Development-of-Social-Movements-in-Central-and-Eastern/Jacobsson-Saxonberg/p/book/9781138279650.
Manne, Kate. 2017. *Down Girl: The Logic of Misogyny.* New York: Oxford University Press. https://doi.org/10.1093/oso/9780190604981.001.0001.
Mishtal, Joanna. 2015. *The Politics of Morality: The Church, the State, and Reproductive Rights in Postsocialist Poland.* Athens, Ohio: Ohio University Press.
Peters, Jeremy W. 2017. "Fighting Gay Rights and Abortion with the First Amendment." *The New York Times*, November 22. https://www.nytimes.com/2017/11/22/us/politics/alliance-defending-freedom-gay-rights.html.
Pialoux, Priscille. 2013. "The Estrela Report: Battle at the European Parliament." *World Youth Alliance.* https://www.wya.net/op-ed/the-estrela-report-battle-at-the-european-parliament/.
Piasecka-Łopuszańska, Maria. 2013. "Keresztény nők a FEMEN ellen." *NOVOpress*, May 6. https://fr.novopress.info/136981/rencontre-avec-la-responsable-des-christian-women-against-femen/.
Pope Paul, John II 1995. "Gospel of Life [Evangelium Vitae]." *The Holy See*, March 25. https://www.vatican.va/content/john-paul-ii/en/encyclicals/documents/hf_jp-ii_enc_25031995_evangelium-vitae.html.
Popper, Karl. 2020. *Open Society and Its Enemies.* Princeton, NJ: Princeton University Press.
San Martín, Inés. 2016. "Pope Calls Gender Theory a "Global War" Against the Family." *Crux*, October 1. https://cruxnow.com/global-church/2016/10/01/pope-calls-gender-theory-global-war-family.
Stroop, Chrissy. 2016. "A Right-Wing International? Russian Social Conservatism, the U.S.-Based WCF, & the Global Culture Wars in Historical Context." *The Public Eye* 85: 4–22.
Tarabella, Marc. 2015. *Report on Progress on Equality between Women and Men in the European Union in 2013.* A8-0015/2015. Brussels: European Parliament, Committee on Women's Rights and Gender Equality. https://www.europarl.europa.eu/doceo/document/A-8-2015-0015_EN.html.
Terenzani, Michaela. 2013. "Criminal Complaint Over Pastoral Letter Filed." *The Slovak Spectator*, December 30. https://spectator.sme.sk/c/20049343/criminal-complaint-over-pastoral-letter-filed.html.
Tomasi, Silvano M. 2017. "'I.1: Right to Life' and 'I.6: Rights of the Family'." In *The Vatican in the Family of Nations: Diplomatic Actions of the Holy See at the UN and Other International Organizations in Geneva*, 12–26 and 95–97. New York: Cambridge University Press.
"Truth about IPPF (#TruthAboutIPPF)." 2016. *Facebook.Com.* https://www.facebook.com/hashtag/truthaboutippf/.
Webb, Adam K. 2006. *Beyond the Global Culture War.* New York: Taylor & Francis Group.
Whyte, Lara. 2017. "They Are Coming for Your Children": The Rise of CitizenGo." *OpenDemocracy*, August 9. https://www.opendemocracy.net/en/5050/the-rise-of-citizengo/.
Williams, Roger Ross. 2013. "God Loves Uganda." Accessed August 9, 2017. http://www.godlovesuganda.com.

Zacharenko, Elena. 2016. "Study for Policy Makers on Opposition to Sexual and Reproductive Health and Rights in Europe." *European Parliamentary Forum on Population and Development.* Accessed August 9, 2017. https://heidihautala.fi/wp-content/uploads/2020/01/SRHR-Europe-Study-_-Elena-Zacharenco.pdf.

Zvolenský, Stanislav. 2016. "Statement by the President of the Slovak Bishops' Conference on the Istanbul Convention." November 25. Accessed August 9, 2017. https://www.eurocathinfo.eu/index.php/en/news-bc-slovakia/94-25-11-2016-bc-slovakia-statement-by-the-president-on-the-istanbul-convention.

10

OPEN SOCIETY CONTESTED: LIBERAL UNIVERSALISM VERSUS AUTOCRATIC FUNCTIONALISM IN HONG KONG

Kenneth Ka-Lok Chan

Post-1997 Hong Kong has been dubbed "a city of protest," but the city was literally "on fire" during the 2019 unrest (BBC 2019; Dapiran 2017; Dapiran 2020). Under the "One Country, Two Systems" policy, the Hong Kong Special Administrative Region (HKSAR) has long suffered from chronic antagonisms between the pro-Beijing "patriots" who are in power by default and the predominantly prodemocracy population. In 2019, what was described as "the largest and perhaps the most relentless protest movement" during that year was triggered by a government proposal to allow extradition of suspects from Hong Kong to Mainland China for trial (Lührmann et al. 2020, 22). Although the government was eventually forced to abandon the controversial bill after millions of citizens took part in sustained demonstrations across the territory, the clashes between the police and a "leaderless struggle for democracy" turned increasingly violent (Freedom House 2020; Lai and Sing 2020). Between June 2019 and May 2020, police fired 16,223 rounds of tear gas, 10,108 rubber bullets, 1,885 sponge grenades, 2,033 beanbag rounds, and 19 live rounds of ammunition (Leung and Cheung 2020). As of January 2022, at least 10,496 protesters have been arrested and 2,909 prosecuted (Kang 2022).

In the aftermath of the political crisis, Beijing imposed its version of National Security Law (NSL) on Hong Kong, bypassing the city's usual legislative processes and derogating from its own Basic Law, according to which it is for the HKSAR to enact such legislation on its own (HKSAR Government 2020). The law is intended to make criminal any act of secession, subversion, terrorism, and collusion with foreign forces that interfere in Hong Kong. According to the law, jury trail can be denied, and complicated cases can be transferred to courts in Mainland China (Davis 2020). Moreover, the national security apparatus has resorted to a colonial-era sedition law, despite not being deployed for decades, to persecute dissidents (Lau 2020). From July 2020 to March 2022, 183 individuals were arrested for alleged national security crimes, and the authorities targeted five companies and seized HKD 1.1 billion worth of cash and assets in a series of operations against "local terrorists" (Lai and Kellogg 2022).

The NSL also paved the way for Beijing to overhaul Hong Kong's electoral systems at all levels which have never been free nor fair in any case: the new rules now install the so-called "patriots only" selections whereby the authorities can vet candidates' eligibility and gain near-total control over the process as much as the outcomes of the selection (Wang 2021). The 2020 Legislative Council (LegCo) election was postponed by Beijing for at least one year (citing Covid as a reason), and it was no coincidence that democrats who participated in the primary election in July 2020 as a part of their joint campaign to win more than half of contestable seats were arrested on national security grounds later that year. The landslide victory for the democratic movement in the 2019 District Council election, taking 392 out of 452 seats, was reversed as most democrats resigned or were subsequently disqualified. New oath-taking requirements and compliance tests to ensure the "loyalty" of elected officials and civil servants may result in arbitrary dismissals or disqualifications in order to suppress the anti-mainland, anti-China sentiments ensuing from the long-drawn-out discords over the pace of democratic reform and how to hold the unrepresentative government to account (Chan 2004; Fong 2017; Fung and Chan 2017; Jang 2016; Yew and Kwong 2014; Yuen 2015).

With the leading figures either in prison or in exile, no less than 60 local and international civil society organizations, local political parties, student organizations, and independent media outlets have resolved to disband themselves; human rights advocates and defenders simply become dormant to avoid further persecutions (Kang 2021; Walker 2021; Wong and Kellogg 2021). The few remaining critics of the authorities and independent commentators have become targets of seemingly endless smear campaigns by progovernment figures and mouthpieces.

This chapter seeks to make an original contribution to the inquiry into the prospects of the open society against the backdrop of Hong Kong's autocratization. Our inquiry will encompass (1) an overview of the origins of the contestation between Autocratic Functionalism and Liberal Universalism in Hong Kong; (2) the perils of Autocratic Functionalism which led to the city's integration and convergence with China in line with Beijing's ideological predilection and the elites' interest, and the growing determination to struggle for the city's liberal way of living under the auspices of Liberal Universalism; and (3) why and how the pursuit of the open society is akin to a Sisyphean task in the face of Hong Kong's dysfunctional polity and the deterioration of its autonomy at the wake of the NSL. With the closing of civic spaces in the domestic political and policy domains, we submit that norm entrepreneurship and contestations along the global-local nexus will provide valuable insights about the opposing expectations stemming from China's long-standing hostility toward the open society. Our study concludes that in Hong Kong's case, the pursuit of the open society is increasingly dependent on the development of a generic identity that is both global and local, post-sovereign and post-national—or else it will fail to resist the increasingly oppressive environment.

Bringing the Global-Local Nexus Back In

Hong Kong's distinctiveness is first and foremost a Cold War legacy when, as a British outpost in the Far East, it served as a conduit between the world and Communist China (Roberts and Carroll 2016). For much of its colonial period, the emergence of the city's international profile was generic and unplanned. Its rise to global prominence as an economic miracle was largely attributable to its strategic location in the Asia Pacific region, the facility and attraction of a free port, an extensive transportation and communication network, the enterprising spirit and managerial professionalism of its business elites, its renowned competitiveness, and the supportive role of Chinese and overseas investments (Hsiung 1998, 242). Despite its lack of sovereignty, Hong Kong's presence on the international stage was unquestionable. Ever since its admission to the Asian Development Bank in 1969, Hong Kong had enjoyed considerable autonomy from London to participate in a wide range of international treaties and organizations, including fifty-six international bodies, twenty-nine of which were limited to states when the city was reverted to China (Chan 2019, 165).

Sassen (2001, 174) has noted that as a global city, Hong Kong has been known as "a key intersection of different worlds," a unique quality which has boosted the city's self-esteem and constituted its distinct identity apart from China's. In a similar vein, Beck (2012, ix–x) has coined the notion of "Global Domestic Politics" (*Weltinnenpolitik*) in an attempt to delineate what politics is like for cities like Hong Kong. In his words:

> Especially world cities are example of this reality: they are part of the world … but are still part of their nations. They exemplify the logic of "both/and"—of both globalism and localism, of the transnational that cohabits with the national—which is in fact the logic of global domestic politics (rather than "either/or").

Importantly, during the Sino-British negotiations in the early 1980s, both sides agreed that in order for Hong Kong to continue to operate as an international financial and trade hub, international backing was imperative. According to the Joint Declaration of 1984, the HKSAR would be vested with specific powers to develop external relations with states, regions, and international organizations after the handover. The Basic Law, which is HKSAR's mini-constitution, delineates Hong Kong's autonomous status in wide-ranging "external affairs" (Basic Law 1990). What is important is the continuous application of international treaties, including those concerning human rights, in Hong Kong after 1997. Article 39 of the Basic Law expressly states that "the provisions of the International Covenant on Civil and Political Rights (ICCPR), the International Covenant on Economic, Social and Cultural Rights (ICESCR), and international labor conventions as applied to Hong Kong before 1997 shall remain in force."

In the aftermath of the June 4th Tiananmen Square crackdown in 1989, stronger international ties were developed in order to maintain local and international confidence in Hong Kong, as instanced in the adoption of the 1992 United States-Hong Kong Policy Act.[1] Against this background, Hong Kong has been afforded different treatment from China by the international community as a recognition of the city's autonomous status which includes not only trade and financial services but also the commitment to human rights and democratic developments. The multilateral ties have not only helped state and nongovernmental actors to nurture international solidarity but have also enabled the international community to champion for the city's autonomy and distinct global identity (Chan and Chong 2019; Ting 2004).

Given the strong and long-standing aversion of the population toward the Communist one-party regime in China, one salient characteristic of the politics of Hong Kong has been its liberal leanings—a strong commitment among citizens to democratic and liberal values as universal values which has brought about a resilient prodemocracy movement vis-à-vis the Chinese Communist regime since the 1980s. The autonomous status of the city has rendered it possible for the city's inhabitants and its civil society to engage in open deliberations and debates over such "core values" as civil liberties, democracy, the rule of law, clean government, and human rights, as well as the standards and procedural requirements that are seen as appropriate and meeting the needs of Hong Kong (Hong Kong Institute of Asia-Pacific Studies 2014). Not surprisingly, the Hong Kong identity has never been successfully assimilated into the political identity in the manner that Beijing has wanted (Fung 2010).

In line with Liberal Universalism, Hong Kong has been described in a majority of scholarly work as a quasi-state with an international personality and de facto sovereign powers over a wide range of international activities (Mushkat 1992; Mushkat 1997a, 1997b; Tang 1993; Gordon 2018). Yahuda (1996, 131–4) was among the astute observers to suggest that Hong Kong's "international profile" may be used to measure "the degree of autonomy that the Hong Kong Special Administrative Region will be allowed to exercise in practice." Hong Kong has developed traits of paradiplomacy of a nonsovereign political entity with growing capacity to conduct external affairs in the international community (Tavares 2016; Duchacek et al. 1988; Keating 1999; Kuznetsov 2015; Aldecoa and Keating 1999). To the extent that its inhabitants are free to take advantage of the intersecting political space it has occupied, Hong Kong should be able to extend its remit beyond the conventional domains of trade and finance into norm entrepreneurship on the legal, political, and social fronts for post-1997 Hong Kong to articulate its identity (Chan 2017; Hsiung 1998; Mushkat 2006).

In contrast, to those who are mindful of the nature of the Chinese Communist regime, there are reasonable doubts that Beijing would allow the city to explore and develop itself into a nonsovereign international actor. Hence, Nossal (1997,

---

1 Accessed June 6, 2020. https://www.govtrack.us/congress/bills/102/s1731.

88) has maintained that "the way to ensure that Hong Kong continues to be enmeshed in the international system is to maintain a high degree of ambiguity about the political components of the HKSAR's international relations." In practice, that means Hong Kong's engagement with the international community must remain essentially unpolitical because Beijing is known to be easily discomfited by any attempt to internationalize the internal affairs of Hong Kong. As China has become more vocal and powerful in geopolitical rivalries with the "western, hostile forces," the aversion toward Liberal Universalism has morphed into Autocratic Functionalism—an overarching banner under which strange bedfellows including the communists, the capitalists, sympathizers of "enlightened autocracy," and others echo the view that the interest of China's one-party regime must always prevail (Buckley 2013; Gan and Lau 2015; Gang 2021; Lippert and Perthes 2020; Xie 2020).

It is not hard to see where Liberal Universalism and Autocratic Functionalism have fundamental disagreements over the prospects of the open society as far as Hong Kong is concerned. To the former, the interpenetration of the global and the local arenas can bolster domestic and international checks and balances which not only safeguard the city's long-standing liberal foundations vis-à-vis the Chinese regime but also develop the open society as a result. Moreover, the city's dependency on China, if unchecked by institutional, political, and other means, could bring about the decay and decline of the autonomous status through integration-cum-convergence in economics, politics, and an expanding range of policy domains.

Norm entrepreneurship reckons that the inclusivity and mutuality of the open society is critical in upholding the city's autonomy and enables activists to engage the global community in a meaningful fashion. That is how Hong Kong is of especial interest to the intellectual inquiry about the contours of contestation along the oft-neglected global-local nexus over the open society. Popper (2013, 92) seemed confident that we shall prefer freedom to slavery. In his words:

> We do not choose political freedom because it promises us this or that. We choose it because it makes possible the only dignified form of human coexistence, the only form in which we can be fully responsible for ourselves.

Popper (1997, 43 and 81) submitted that one's "activism to resist tyranny is a moral duty, to do nothing is inhuman and morally wrong." From time to time, the lure of the tyrant's grandiose visions of the stronger, greater, mightier future may be hard to resist. He pithily argued that any claim to base a political project or utopian social engineering on knowledge of the future must be rigorously rejected. For one thing, one's claim to have anticipated events and gained control over the unknown is questionable because "the future is very open and it depends on what you and I and many other people do, today, tomorrow, and the day after tomorrow." For another thing, there is always a dangerous tendency to deny the people their inalienable freedom and rights in the face of a destiny that is said to be inevitable or insurmountable.

The Perils of Autocratic Functionalism

"Leveraging Hong Kong's Advantages, Meeting the Country's Needs" has become one of the most used slogans among the business and political elites in Hong Kong and China in recent years (HKSAR Government 2018). During his term as the Chief Executive of the HKSAR, Leung Chun-ying (2017) positioned Hong Kong instrumentally as a "super-connector" for China and the world, while his successor Carrie Lam (2018b) has pledged to take full advantage of what the government thought to be the significant opportunities under the Belt and Road Initiative (BRI) and the Guangdong-Hong Kong-Macau Greater Bay Area (GBA) Development by enhancing the city's own competitiveness and explore new areas of economic growth.

It is impossible to lose sight of the economic significance of Hong Kong to China (Ting 2004, 2007; Yue 2007; Béja 2008; Ting and Lai 2012; Shen 2016; Herrero and Ng 2020). The city has long served the Chinese enterprises as a springboard to enter the global economy and simultaneously a conduit for international traders and investors to enter the Chinese market. The financial environment has provided an important strategic platform for internationalizing the Renminbi (RMB). Hong Kong plays a key role as a private wealth management center for high-net worth individuals from Mainland China, including many members of the political and economic elites.

How has Hong Kong's contribution to China's growth with respect to global trade and finance been translated into favorable conditions for its pursuit of the open society? Rezvani (2012) has submitted that "(Hong Kong) is a partially independent political entity which exercises constitutional powers that are robustly defended by the political-economic influence (rather than constitutional influence) which it exerts upon China's central government … prevents maximalist interference from Beijing." What this line of analysis refers to as "maximalist interference" is not clear, but more importantly, the assumption about the political-economic influence that Hong Kong musters on Beijing and its actions toward the city is clearly misplaced.

Concerns about threats to Hong Kong's autonomy have largely intensified since Beijing published on June 10, 2014, a White Paper entitled *The Practice of the "One Country, Two Systems" Policy in the Hong Kong Special Administrative Region* (State Council 2014), according to which the so-called Central Leadership now "directly exercises jurisdiction over the HKSAR" through the National People's Congress and its Standing Committee, the President of the State, the Central People's Government, and the Central Military Commission. The former LegCo President Jasper Tsang has described the White Paper as a "turning point" in China's policy toward the city because such notions as "comprehensive jurisdiction" and "supervisory power" did not appear in the Basic

Law and—prior to the White Paper—they were not mentioned by Chinese officials. It goes without saying that veteran politicians and business elites from the pro-Beijing camp like Tsang were quick to adapt to a new stage of Autocratic Functionalism (Cheung 2017).

The crux of the matter is that the elites have to display their loyalty toward Beijing to remain in the game. When the crunch comes, these elites find themselves immediately deprived of the very thing that they have claimed to have, namely the political-economic influence over China. That economic integration with China has weakened, not strengthened, the city's autonomy became obvious during the heats of the 2019 protests in Hong Kong as Beijing made several bizarre moves against the city's business sector. For example, China threatened to block Cathay Pacific flights from using the air space if the company failed to make sure its pilots and crew members were not supportive of the protests. As a result, dozens of employees were either sacked or advised to resign voluntarily, some merely for displaying their sympathies toward the protesters on social media (Branigan and Hale 2019). Even more perplexing was the story that the American Chamber of Commerce Hong Kong President, Tara Joseph, and Chair, Robert Grieves, were refused entry to Macau to attend an AmCham event. No reason was given (AFP 2019). In the past few years, Hong Kong has witnessed the expulsion of foreign correspondents and barring of international observers, parliamentarians, and researchers from entering the city (Zhou 2020).

Actions like this would only undermine international confidence in Hong Kong's autonomy and signal the beginning of the end of the "One Country, Two Systems" policy as we know it. Can Hong Kong's political entity be aptly described as "partially independent" when Carrie Lam (2018a) advised the people of Hong Kong "to fully or better integrate with national development as laid down by President Xi Jinping in his report to the 19th National Congress of the Communist Party of China"? The answer can only be in the negative. Speaking at a briefing with foreign journalists in Hong Kong in October 2017, Song Ruan, Deputy Commissioner at the Chinese Foreign Ministry's Office in Hong Kong, reportedly declared that, under President Xi Jinping's leadership, the "One Country, Two Systems" policy now "has a new political position in the overall work of the party and the state since Hong Kong was reincorporated into the national governance system" (Cheung 2017).

The Resilience of Liberal Universalism

In *The Open Society and Its Enemies*, Popper (1945) empathically observed that "one hears too often the suggestion that some form or other of totalitarianism is inevitable … [But] the future depends on ourselves, and we do not depend on any historical necessity." Hence, he defined the open society as one in which individuals are confronted with personal decisions, stressing that "if we wish to remain human, then there is only one way, the way into the open society …

into the unknown, the uncertain and insecure." According to Popper, participation in public life is not only desirable but also necessary, a moral obligation which one's preference for political freedom entails. In pursuit of a dignified form of human coexistence, people who have chosen freedom have to learn to take responsibility for the choices they make, including all the entailing consequences, intended as well as unintended.

Over the past twenty-five years, the mainstay of the Hong Kong society has long displayed an unequivocal commitment to the moral, institutional, and policy values of the open society. There have been copious endeavors by nonstate actors and the citizenry at large to take advantage of the opportunities available along the global-local nexus to safeguard the city's norms and values. Liberal Universalism has informed many concerted campaigns in both local and international arenas to stand up for the open society and to hold the ruling elites to account. The formation of two human rights coalitions to engage the United Nations Human Rights Council's 2018 Universal Periodic Review on Hong Kong's human rights condition brought together ninety-one civil society organizations and political groupings from Hong Kong, whose testimonies embodied a free, open, and democratic vision of Hong Kong (Hong Kong Human Rights Monitor 2018; HKUPRC 2018; United Nations Human Rights Council 2018). Cycles of mass protests and ad hoc mobilization broke out from time to time in response to perceived threats to freedom and the city's unique identity, while the democratic opposition squeezed its way into the restrictive electoral arena to articulate and channel people's dissent and aspirations for change. Before the 2019 protests against the extradition law, the world witnessed some determined pushbacks against authoritarianism such as the anti-national security law movement in 2003 (Fu et al. 2005) and during the 2014 Umbrella Movement, when tens of thousands of citizens occupied the main streets in three districts for no less than seventy-nine days to demand full universal suffrage (Cheng 2016; Veg 2017; Wong and Chu 2017).

But it was the 2019 anti-government movement which reached out to the international community and cities around the world on an unprecedented scale. For example, "Stand with Hong Kong. Fight for Freedom" surged within a short period of time to become a global movement, accounting for fifty-eight events in 2019 that took place at either national or regional levels across Australia, Germany, the United Kingdom, the United States, and Canada (Stand With Hong Kong 2019). Importantly, a number of large-scale, sustainable, and multilingual campaigns were initiated by netizens to rally international support for Hong Kong, including a crowdfunding action which raised HK$5 million (US$643,000) within just a few hours for an international advertisement campaign to urge leaders attending the G20 Summit in Osaka in June 2019 to speak out on Hong Kong (Cheng 2019). On September 29, Hong Kong was the focus of a worldwide anti-authoritarian rally involving twenty-four countries and sixty-five cities.

According to *Anti-Extradition Bill Movement: People's Public Sentiment Report*, which has been jointly carried out by the Hong Kong Public Opinion Research Institute and Project Citizens Foundation (2020, 57–58),

> The Anti-Extradition Bill Movement in Hong Kong is not simply a movement of Hong Kong people protesting against a specific bill or against a local government, its police force, or even against a regime, it is a clash between liberalism versus paternalism … The Hong Kong experience will provide an important reference on the future development of the world.

Notably, new "citizens diplomacy" platforms gained momentum with the help of activists from Hong Kong, such as Network DIPLO (Wong 2020), as well as the Hong Kong Democratic Alliance of Overseas Postgraduates which was founded by a group of overseas Hong Kong postgraduate students (HKAOPS 2019). For its part, the Hong Kong Higher Institutions International Affairs Delegation (HKHIIAD 2019), whose members appeared in parliamentary hearings to give evidence and meet with officials to lobby for Hong Kong, described its mission as "mobilizing international support for the protection of human rights, autonomy, and democracy in Hong Kong through citizen diplomacy." There were numerous online petitions to foreign governments and parliaments for new legislative and executive measures in response to the deterioration of the situation in Hong Kong, which resulted in the passage of the Hong Kong Democracy and Human Rights Act[2] and another one to prohibit the commercial export of covered munition items to the Hong Kong Police Force[3] in the United States toward the end of the year (Hung 2018).

The Open Society: Down, but Not Out

Autocratic Functionalism, which is deceptively apolitical, calls for a convergence of local and national interests. In the name of national security, the authorities have proceeded to remold Hong Kong on all fronts. Although the NSL provides that human rights shall be respected and protected, the law requires the government to "take necessary measures to strengthen public communication, guidance, supervision and regulation over matters concerning national security, including those relating to schools and universities, social organizations, the media and the internet." Within months, public libraries removed titles about the June 4th Tiananmen Square crackdown and books authored by the opposition figures from their shelves, new powers are

---

2 Accessed June 11, 2020. https://www.govinfo.gov/content/pkg/PLAW-116publ76/pdf/PLAW-116publ76.pdf.
3 Accessed June 12, 2020. https://www.govinfo.gov/content/pkg/PLAW-116publ77/pdf/PLAW-116publ77.pdf.

given to film censors, schools and universities are required to propagate the NSL and assist in the promotion of national education. Student organizations, exhibitions, media, pollsters, lectures, and seminars are closely monitored and targeted for suspected national security violations (Davis 2021; Hong Kong Journalists Association 2021). To intimidate activists overseas, no less than six warrants are issued for democrats who are called by officials as "criminals" and "fugitives." Moreover, the NSL authorizes extra-territorial operations, for example, London-based Hong Kong Watch is targeted: its website blocked in Hong Kong, its chief spokesman received death threats, and lately warnings from the National Security Department (Hong Kong Watch 2022). International solidarity with Hong Kong's uphill battle against an overpowering one-party regime was dismissed by Beijing and the HKSAR government as a violation of Chinese sovereignty.

Paradoxically, the more China attempts to flex its muscles over Hong Kong, net confidence in the "One Country, Two Systems" policy reached its new low as a result (Hong Kong Public Opinion Research Institute 2022). The normative appeal of the open society as a custodian for the city's distinctive values and identity is expected to grow against the backdrop of the moral and institutional decay of the official, "Orwellian," realm. While organized dissent is enfeebled due to the combined effects of mobilization fatigue, oppression, and intimidation, this must not be mistaken as servility so far as the majority of the people seem prepared to carry on rejecting it, as one of the prodemocracy leaders in exile, Nathan Law (2021, 114), has observed:

> Confronted by the most powerful, controlling and repressive authoritarian power, protesters must be like water. We must be able to flow over any obstacle and take on any form.

To the extent that fear is a powerful ally of the autocratic regimes, the community of the oppressed would have to learn to manage fear and to mitigate the harmful effects and costs inflicted on the people at large. Small acts of resistance and large-scale nonconformity against the moral and institutional decay, albeit assuming unorganized and leaderless forms, were evident during the Legislative Council election on December 19, 2021. To prevent any attempt to turn the fake polls into a de facto referendum, the government has outlawed calls to cast blank ballots, arrested those for publicizing such calls and threatened pollsters asking the public about their voting intentions. In the event, the democratic opposition resolved to ignore the elections altogether. The prodemocracy voters stayed away from the poll in a form of silent protest (Yeung 2021). The turnout was 30.2% by close of polls, the lowest ever since the first few directly elected seats were introduced in the 1990s, far lower than the previous record high of 58% in the last legislative election five years ago, or the 71.2% turnout at the 2019 District Council Election which unequivocally delivered a victory for the democracy movement. The silent protest spoke volumes.

Conclusion

That international factors matter is an observation shared widely in the literature on Hong Kong Studies. It is a geopolitical as well as a geoeconomic reality. The aim of this chapter is to critically reflect on the relevance the open society to the debates about Hong Kong's relations with China and the world from two lenses, namely Liberal Universalism and Autocratic Functionalism. The open society undoubtedly has many fair-weather friends, but it is most relevant to circumstances in which the advocates are found fighting uphill battles such as those in Hong Kong. Twenty-five years after the handover, our analysis has shown that Hong Kong suffers from a series of chronic contradictions which have eventually undermined both internal and external autonomy. The city's civil society and the prodemocracy movement seen to be "endangering national security" have been dealt a fatal blow by the vaguely termed national security crimes. Paradoxically, as Hong Kong is left with a dysfunctional polity buttressed by the omnipresent interventions from Beijing, the norm contestation around the open society has been rendered more, not less, pertinent along the global-local nexus. By way of closing, the defense of Hong Kong as the open society against autocratization has resembled that of a norm entrepreneur focusing on the logic of appropriateness and the development of soft power buttressed by universal norms and local core values.

Bibliography

AFP. 2019. "Hong Kong American Chamber of Commerce Chair and President Denied Entry to Macau." *Hong Kong Free Press*, December 8. Accessed January 15, 2022. https://www.hongkongfp.com/2019/12/08/hong-kong-american-chamber-commerce-chairpresident-denied-entry-macau.

Aldecoa, Francisco and Michael Keating. 1999. *Paradiplomacy in Action: The Foreign Relations of Subnational Governments*. London and Portland, OR: F. Cass.

Basic Law of the Hong Kong Special Administrative Region. 1990. "Chapter 7 External Affairs." Accessed 30 March 2022. https://www.basiclaw.gov.hk/en/basiclaw/chapter7.html.

BBC. 2019. "Hong Kong: Timeline of Extradition Protests." *BBC*, September 4. Accessed January 15, 2022. https://www.bbc.com/news/world-asia-china-49340717.

Beck, Ulrich. 2012. *Twenty Observations on a World in Turmoil*. Cambridge: Polity Press.

Béja, Jean-Philippe. 2008. "An Exception to the Growing Emphasis on Multilateralism: The Case of China's Policy towards Hong Kong." In *China Turns to Multilateralism: Foreign Policy and Regional Security*, edited by Guoguang Wu and Helen Lansdowne, 253–63. New York: Routledge.

Branigan, Tania, and Hale, Erin. 2019. "Cathay Denounced for Firing Hong Kong Staff after Pressure from China." *The Guardian*, August 28. Accessed January 15, 2022. https://www.theguardian.com/world/2019/aug/28/cathay-pacific-denounced-for-firing-hong-kong-staff-on-china-orders.

Buckley, Chris. 2013. "China Warns Officials Against 'dangerous' Western Values." *New York Times*, May 13. Accessed January 15, 2022. http://www.nytimes.com/2013/05/14/world/asia/chinese-leaders-warn-of-dangerous-western-values.html.

Chan, Kenneth Ka-Lok. 2004. "Taking Stock of 'One Country, Two Systems'." In *One Country, Two Systems in Crisis: Hong Kong's Transition since the Handover*, edited by Yiu-chung Wong, 35–60. Lanham: Lexington Press.

Chan, Kenneth Ka-Lok. 2017. "Towards a Partnership for Global Norm Diffusion: The Strategic Importance of Hong Kong in EU-China Relations." *Asia-Pacific Journal of EU Studies* 15: 1–26.

Chan, Kenneth Ka-Lok, and Chong Eric King-man. 2019. "A Critical Appraisal of the International Factors in 'One Country, Two Systems' and Democratization in Hong Kong." *Asian Education and Development Studies* 8: 208–16.

Chan, Wai Yin. 2019. "The Soft Power and Paradiplomacy of Hong Kong." *Asian Education and Development Studies* 8: 161–72.

Cheng, Edmund Wai. 2016. "Street Politics in a Hybrid Regime: The Diffusion of Political Activism in Post-Colonial Hong Kong." *The China Quarterly* 226: 383–406.

Cheng, Kris. 2019. "Hongkongers Raise over HK$5m for Front-page Newspaper Ads Urging G20 Action over Extradition Crisis." *Hong Kong Free Press*, June 25. Accessed January 15, 2022. https://hongkongfp.com/2019/06/25/hongkongers-raise-hk5m-front-page-newspaper-ads-urging-g20-action-extradition-crisis/.

Cheung, Karen. 2017. "Ex-LegCo Head: 2014 White Paper Was Turning Point of Beijing Exercising 'Overall Jurisdiction' in Hong Kong." *Hong Kong Free Press*, November 20. Accessed January 15, 2022. https://www.hongkongfp.com/2017/11/20/ex-legco-head-2014-white-paper-turning-point-beijing-exercising-overall-jurisdiction-hong-kong/.

Cheung, Tony. 2017. "Beijing Official Says Xi Jinping Has Given 'One Country, Two Systems' a Status Boost." *South China Morning Post*, October 31. Accessed January 15, 2022. https://www.scmp.com/print/news/hong-kong/politics/article/2117827/beijing-official-says-xi-jinping-has-given-one-country-two.

Dapiran, Antony. 2017. *City of Protest: A Recent History of Dissent in Hong Kong*. London: Penguin.

Dapiran, Antony. 2020. *City on Fire: The Fight for Hong Kong*. London: Scribe.

Davis, Michael C. 2020. *Making Hong Kong China: The Rollback of Human Rights and the Rule of Law*. Ann Abor, MI: Columbia University Press.

Davis, Michael C. 2021. "Hong Kong: How Beijing Perfected Repression." *Journal of Democracy* 33: 100–15.

Duchacek, Ivo, Daniel Latouche, and Garth Stevenson. 1988. *Perforated Sovereignties and International Relations: Trans-sovereign Contacts of Subnational Governments*. New York: Greenwood Press.

Fong, Brian Chi Hang. 2017. "One Country, Two Nationalisms: Centre-Periphery Relations between Mainland China and Hong Kong, 1997–2016." *Modern China* 43: 523–56.

Freedom House. 2020. *Freedom in the World 2020: A Leaderless Struggle for Democracy*. Accessed January 15, 2022. https://freedomhouse.org/report/freedom-world/2020/leaderless-struggle-democracy.

Fu, Hualing, Carole J. Petersen, and Simon N. M. Young. 2005. *National Security and Fundamental Freedoms*. Hong Kong's Article 23 Under Scrutiny. Hong Kong: Hong Kong University Press.

Fung, Anthony. 2010. "What Makes The Local? A Brief Consideration of the Rejuvenation of Hong Kong Identity." *Cultural Studies* 15: 591–601.

Fung, Anthony, and Chi Kit Chan. 2017. "Hong Kong Youth Identity (2006–2016)." *Journal of Youth Studies* 20: 27–35.

Gan, Nectar, and Lau Stuart. 2015. "Hong Kong's Occupy Protest 'Was an Attempt at Colour Revolution': PLA General." *South China Morning Post*, March 3. Accessed January 15, 2022. https://www.scmp.com/news/hong-kong/article/1728027/hong-kongs-occupy-protest-was-attempt-colour-revolution-pla-general.

Gang, Wen. 2021. "CPC Leadership Highlighted in Advancing 'One Country, Two Systems.'" *China Daily*, June 14. Accessed January 15, 2022. https://www.chinadaily.com.cn/a/202106/14/WS60c6959fa31024ad0bac6903.html.

Gordon, Nicholas. 2018. "One Country, Two Systems: An Example of Divisible Sovereignty?" *Hong Kong Studies* 1: 26–40.

Herrero, Alicia Garcia, and Gary Ng. 2020. "Hong Kong: One Country, Two Systems, Three Challenges." In *Between Politics and Finance: Hong Kong's Infinity War?*, edited by Alessia Amighini, 80–91. Italy: Italian Institute for International Political Studies. Accessed January 15, 2020. https://www.ispionline.it/sites/default/files/pubblicazioni/ispi_report_china_2020_0.pdf.

HKAOPS. 2019. *Hong Kong Democratic Alliance of Overseas Postgraduates*. Accessed March 2, 2022. https://www.facebook.com/hongkongaops/.

HKSAR Government. 2018. *Press Release: Seminar on Strategies and Opportunities under the Belt and Road Initiative—Leveraging Hong Kong's Advantages, Meeting the Country's Needs to be held in Beijing*. January 26. Accessed March 2, 2022. http://www.info.gov.hk/gia/general/201801/26/P2018012600312.htm?fontSize=1.

HKSAR Government. 2020. *The Law of the People's Republic of China on Safeguarding National Security in the Hong Kong Special Administrative Region*. Accessed March 2, 2022. https://www.isd.gov.hk/nationalsecurity/eng/law.html.

HKUPRC. 2018. *Joint Civil Society Submission from the Hong Kong UPR Coalition*. Accessed March 2, 2022. http://www.justicecentre.org.hk/framework/uploads/2018/UPR/HKUPRC_Submission_MARCH2018.pdf.

Hong Kong Human Rights Monitor. 2018. *Joint Submission of NGOs for the Universal Periodic Review. Hong Kong Special Administrative Region (HKSAR) China*. (unpublished).

Hong Kong Institute of Asia-Pacific Studies. 2014. *Hong Kong's Core Values Survey*. Accessed March 2, 2022. http://www.cpr.cuhk.edu.hk/en/press_detail.php?id=1915.

Hong Kong Journalists Association HKJA. 2021. *Freedom in Tatters: 2021 Annual Report*. Accessed April 1, 2022. https://www.hkja.org.hk/wp-content/uploads/2021/07/HKJA_AR2021_eng_outline_single-1.pdf.

Hong Kong Public Opinion Research Institute. 2022. *Net Confidence in 'One Country, Two Systems'*. Accessed March 2, 2022. https://www.hkupop.hku.hk/pori_table_chart/Trust/K006_Conf_OCTS/K006_halfyr_chart.html.

Hong Kong Public Opinion Research Institute & Project Citizens Foundation. 2020. *Anti-Extradition Bill Movement Public Sentiment Report*, Revised ed. Accessed March 31, 2022. https://www.pori.hk/anti-extradition-bill-report-3.

Hong Kong Watch. 2022. *Hong Kong Watch co-founder and CEO Benedict Rogers Threatened under National Security Law*. March 14. Accessed March 30, 2022. https://www.hongkongwatch.org/all-posts/2022/3/14/hong-kong-watch-co-founder-and-ceo-benedict-rogers-threatened-under-national-security-law.

Hsiung, James C. 1998. "Hong Kong as a Nonsovereign International Actor." *Asian Affair* 24: 237–44.

Hung, Ho-fung. 2018. "Sanction Hong Kong, for Its Own Sake." *Journal of Political Risk* 7 (10). Accessed February 14, 2022. http://www.jpolrisk.com/sanction-hong-kong-for-its-own-sake/.

Jang, Jinhyeok. 2016. "Competing Political Visions in the Legislative Council of Hong Kong." *Journal of Chinese Political Science* 21: 89–102.
Kang, Tsung-Gan. 2021. "The Chinese Communist Party is Decimating Hong Kong Civil Society." Accessed March 2, 2022. https://kongtsunggan.medium.com/the-chinese-communist-partys-decimation-of-hong-kong-civil-society-679c914f9fe9.
Kang, Tsung-Gan. 2022. "Arrests and Trials of Hong Kong Protesters and Opposition Leaders." Accessed March 2, 2022. https://kongtsunggan.medium.com/arrests-and-trials-of-hong-kong-protesters-and-opposition-leaders-2144f5d6895b.
Keating, Michael. 1999. "Region and International Affairs: Motives, Opportunities and Strategies." In *Paradiplomacy in Action: The Foreign Relations of Subnational Governments*, edited by Francisco Aldecoa and Michael Keating, 1–16. London and Portland, OR: F. Cass.
Kuznetsov, Alexander. 2015. *Theory and Practice of Paradiplomacy: Subnational Governments in International Affairs*. London: Routledge.
Lai, Eric Yan Ho, and Ming Sing. 2020. "Solidarity and Implications of a Leaderless Movement in Hong Kong: Its Strengths and Limitations." *Communist and Post-Communist Studies* 53: 41–67.
Lai, Eric Yan Ho, and Tomas Kellogg. 2022. "Arrest Data Show National Security Law Has Dealt a Hard Blow to Free Expression in Hong Kong." April 5. Accessed April 8, 2022. https://www.chinafile.com/reporting-opinion/features/arrest-data-show-national-security-law-has-dealt-hard-blow-free.
Lam, Carrie. 2018a. "Transcript of Remarks by CE at Media Session before ExCo Meeting." Accessed March 2, 2022. http://www.info.gov.hk/gia/general/201801/16/P2018011600427.htm.
Lam, Carrie. 2018b. *The Chief Executive's 2018 Policy Address*. Accessed March 2, 2022. https://www.policyaddress.gov.hk/2018/eng/speech.html.
Lau, Chris. 2020. "Explainer: What is Hong Kong's Colonial-Era Sedition Law, and How Does it fit into Landscape of National Security Legislation?" *South China Morning Post*, September 9. Accessed January 15, 2022. https://www.scmp.com/news/hong-kong/politics/article/3100740/what-hong-kongs-colonial-era-sedition-law-and-how-does-it.
Law, Nathan with Evan Fowler. 2021. *Freedom: How We Lost It and How We Fight Back*. London: Bantam Press.
Leung, Christy, and Gary Cheung. 2020. "Hong Kong Protests: United States, Taiwan Interference Played Role in Anti-government Movement, City's Security Chief Says." *South China Morning Post*, June 9. Accessed January 15, 2022. https://www.scmp.com/news/hong-kong/law-and-crime/article/3088271/hong-kong-protests-united-states-taiwan-interference.
Leung, Chun Ying. 2017. "Speech by the Chief Executive at Thematic Session on Financial Connectivity of Belt and Road Forum for International Cooperation." Accessed March 2, 2022. http://www.info.gov.hk/gia/general/201705/14/P2017051400571.htm.
Lippert, Barbara, and Volker Perthes. 2020. "Strategic Rivalry between United States and China Causes, Trajectories, and Implications for Europe." German Institute for International and Security Affairs SWP Research Paper 4. Accessed March 2, 2022. https://www.swp-berlin.org/fileadmin/contents/products/research_papers/2020RP04_China_USA.pdf.
Lührmann, Anna Maerz, Seraphine F. Maerz, Sandra Grahn, Nazifa Alizada, Lisa Gastaldi, Sebastian Hellmeier, Garry Hindle, and Staffan I. Lindberg. 2020. *Autocratization Surges – Resistance Grows. Democracy Report 2020.*" Varieties of

Democracy Institute (V-Dem). Sweden: Department of Political Science, University of Gothenburg. Accessed April 2, 2022. https://www.v-dem.net/media/filer_public/f0/5d/f05d46d8-626f-4b20-8e4e-53d4b134bfcb/democracy_report_2020_low.pdf.

Mushkat, Roda. 1992. "Hong Kong as an International Legal Person." *Emory International Law Review* 6: 105–70.

Mushkat, Roda. 1997a. "Hong Kong's Status in International Law." In *One Country, Two International Legal Personalities*, edited by Roda Mushkat, 1–41. Hong Kong: Hong Kong University Press.

Mushkat, Roda. 1997b. "Managing the Transfer of Sovereignty over Hong Kong: The Case for Continuity of Treaties." In *Hong Kong SAR: In Pursuit of Domestic and International Order*, edited by Beatrice Leung and Joseph Cheng, 161–76. Hong Kong: Chinese University Press.

Mushkat, Roda. 2006. "Hong Kong's Exercise of External Autonomy: A Multi-Faceted Appraisal." *The International and Comparative Law Quarterly* 55: 945–61.

Nossal, Kim Richard. 1997. "A High Degree of Ambiguity: Hong Kong as an International Actor after 1997." *The Pacific Review* 10: 84–103.

Popper, Karl R. 1945. *The Open Society and Its Enemies*, 2 Vols. London: Routledge.

Popper, Karl R. 1997. *The Lesson of This Century with Two Talks on Freedom and the Democratic State. Karl Popper interviewed by Giancarlo Bosetti*. London: Routledge.

Popper, Karl R. 2013. *All Life is Problem Solving*. London: Routledge.

Rezvani, David A. 2012. "Dead Autonomy, A Thousand Cuts or Partial Independence? The Autonomous Status of Hong Kong." *Journal of Contemporary Asia* 42: 93–122.

Roberts, Priscilla, and John M. Carroll. 2016. *Hong Kong in the Cold War*. Hong Kong: Hong Kong University Press.

Sassen, Saskia. 2001. *The Global City*. Princeton, NJ: Princeton University Press.

Shen, Simon. 2016. *Hong Kong in the World: Implications to Geopolitics and Competitiveness*. London: Imperial College Press.

Stand with Hong Kong. 2019. *Stand with Hong Kong. Fight for Freedom*. Accessed March 31, 2022. https://www.facebook.com/standwithhk/.

State Council, The People's Republic of China. 2014. *The Practice of the 'One Country, Two Systems' Policy in the Hong Kong Special Administrative Region*. Accessed March 6, 2022. http://www.fmcoprc.gov.hk/eng/xwdt/gsxw/t1164057.htm.

Tang, James Tuck Hong. 1993. "Hong Kong's International Status." *Pacific Review* 6: 205–15.

Tavares, Rodrigo. 2016. *Paradiplomacy: Cities and States as Global Players*. New York: Oxford University Press.

The Hong Kong Higher Institutions International Affairs Delegation (HKHIAD). 2019. Accessed March 18, 2022. https://www.facebook.com/HKHIIAD/.

Ting, Wai. 2004. "An East-West Conundrum: Hong Kong in between China and the United States after the Chinese Resumption of Sovereignty." In *One Country, Two Systems in Crisis: Hong Kong's Transition since the Handover*, edited by Yiu-chung Wong, 187–208. Lanham: Lexington Press.

Ting, Wai. 2007. "Hong Kong in between China and the Great Powers: The External Relations and International Status of Hong Kong after the Chinese Resumption of Sovereignty." In *The Hong Kong Special Administrative Region in Its First Decade*, edited by Joseph Cheng Y-S, 261–304. Hong Kong: City University of Hong Kong Press.

Ting, Wai, and Ellen Lai. 2012. "Hong Kong and the World." In *Contemporary Hong Kong Government and Politics*, edited by Wai-man Lam, Percy Luen-tim Lui, Wilson Wong, and Ian Holliday, 349–70. Hong Kong: Hong Kong University Press.

United Nations Human Rights Council (UNHRC). 2018. *Universal Periodic Review: China. Third Cycle.* Accessed March 2, 2022. https://www.ohchr.org/EN/HRBodies/UPR/Pages/CNIndex.aspx.

Veg, Sebastian. 2017. "The Rise of "Localism" and Civic Identity in Post-handover Hong Kong: Questioning the Chinese Nation-State." *The China Quarterly* 230: 323–47.

Walker, Tommy. 2021. "Hong Kong Civil Society Keeps Shrinking." *Voice of America*, October 7. Accessed January 15, 2022. https://www.voanews.com/a/hong-kong-civil-society-keeps-shrinking/6260793.html.

Wang, Maya (2021) Hong Kong Imposes Sham Election Beijing Ensures No Opposition in Vote for Legislature. Human Rights Watch. Available at: https://www.hrw.org/news/2021/12/17/hong-kong-imposes-sham-election (accessed 15 February 2022).

Wong, Lydia, and Thomas Kellogg. 2021. "Individuals Arrested under the Hong Kong National Security Law or by the National Security Department." *China File.* Accessed February 1, 2022. https://www.chinafile.com/individuals-arrested-under-hong-kong-national-security-law-or-national-security-department.

Wong, Rachael. 2020. "Network DIPLO." *Hong Kong Free Press.* Accessed March 2, 2022. https://hongkongfp.com/tag/network-diplo/.

Wong, Wilson, and May Chu. 2017. "Rebel with a Cause: Structural Problems Underlying the Umbrella Movement of Hong Kong and the Role of Youth." *Asian Education and Development Studies* 6: 343–53.

Xie, Feng. 2020. "The International Community Needs a Full and Accurate Understanding of the Basic Law." *South China Morning Post*, April 21. Accessed January 15, 2022. http://www.fmcoprc.gov.hk/eng/zydt/t1772337.htm.

Yahuda, Michael B. 1996. *Hong Kong: China's Challenge.* London: Routledge.

Yeung, Jessie. 2021. "Hong Kong Sees Record Low Voter Turnout in First "China Patriots Only" Election." *CNN*, December 20. Accessed January 15, 2022. https://edition.cnn.com/2021/12/19/asia/hong-kong-election-turnout-intl-hnk/index.html.

Yew, Chiew Ping, and Kin-ming Kwong. 2014. "Hong Kong Identity on the Rise." *Asian Survey* 54: 1088–112.

Yue, Ren. 2007. "Hong Kong in the Eyes of the International Community." In *The Hong Kong Special Administrative Region in Its First Decade*, edited by Y.-S. Joseph Cheng, 305–32. Hong Kong: City University of Hong Kong Press.

Yuen, Samson. 2015. "Hong Kong after the Umbrella Movement: An Uncertain Future for 'One Country, Two Systems'." *China Perspectives* 2015 (1):49–53.

Zhou, Cissy. 2020. "China Expels American Journalists from 3 US Newspapers: The New York Times, Wall Street Journal and Washington Post." *South China Morning Post*, March 18. Accessed January 15, 2022. https://www.scmp.com/news/china/diplomacy/article/3075647/china-revokes-press-credentials-american-journalists-3-us.

11

"SOROSOIDS": USES OF LABELING IN BULGARIA

Lubomir Terziev

Over the last two decades, the media-fueled neologism "sorosoid" (*соросоид*) has established itself as a buzzword with a strongly pejorative connotation in the lingo of Bulgarian gurus of neoconservatism of all hues. It refers to an individual or an organization allegedly relying on Soros's funding to promote ideas and values which, according to these ideologues, undermine inherently national cultural traditions. From this tribalistic perspective, which is gaining ground in Bulgarian society, the two most obvious culprits for the supposed disintegration of national identity are liberal attitudes to gender and immigration. In what follows I will trace the peculiar uses of the word "sorosoid" in Bulgarian public discourse, and I will also focus on some of its dehumanizing connotations. The chapter will be divided into seven sections. The first one will focus on what I consider the two fundamental targets of neoconservative ideology in Bulgaria and on the reason why they are incompatible with the idea of open society. In the second section, I will give a brief overview, based on relevant quotations from Bulgarian media, of some current uses of the word "sorosoid." The third section will provide a semantic analysis of the dehumanizing potential of the inflection "-oid." Following on that, I will elaborate on three figures of the "non-human" that the inflection invokes: the animal, the machine, and the figure of divinity. In the seventh section, I will suggest two strategies of assertion of the values of open society in Bulgaria. The conclusion will briefly elaborate on the role of the supporters of open society in Bulgaria in the current political situation.

The Two Pillars of Neoconservatism and Open Society

There are a number of predicates that inform the anti-sorosoid rhetoric: sorosoids are West-backed brokers of the Green Deal; sorosoids are atheists; sorosoids want to separate children from their (violent) parents; sorosoids want to grant equal rights to the lazy and good-for-nothing Roma minority. In this section, I will draw attention to the two most prominent anti-sorosoid mantras: sorosoids want to tamper with our (children's) biological sexes and sorosoids want to let in millions of alien immigrants who will assimilate our nation.

Importantly, the neoconservative ideological stance cuts across the left wing vs. right wing divide. Thus, for instance, the leadership of the Bulgarian

Socialist Party (successor of "real socialism's" Bulgarian Communist Party) have declared their categorical opposition to the ratification of the Council of Europe's Istanbul Convention on Violence against Women because, according to Kornelia Ninova, the party's leader, "[the party] had to choose between the country's constitution and laws, the opinion of the Orthodox Church, the values of the Christian family on the one hand, and this resolution on the other" (Ninova 2018).¹ The contentious term that allegedly undermines "the values of the Christian family" is, of course, "gender," which the Convention defines as "the socially constructed roles, behaviours, activities and attributes that a given society considers appropriate for women and men" (2011). In a classic example of the straw man fallacy, the opponents of the Convention have interpreted "gender" as superseding and negating the "normal/natural" distinction between biologically determined sexes. They have envisaged a terminological slippage from the God-sanctioned male vs. female dichotomy to a social construct which challenges the sacred binary opposition by validating the existence of subversive options between or beyond the poles. The socialists' support for this interpretation has co-opted them into the camp of right-wing nationalists and conservatives. In their declaration, Bulgaria's Conservative Youth Club, for instance, dismiss the Convention on identical grounds: "we cannot help but voice our misgivings about some particular content in the Convention. One example is the attempt to replace the biological term for sex with a political equivalent" (Position 2018).

As I have pointed out already, the other key pillar of neoconservative ideology targets Bulgarian liberals' support for immigrants regardless of their race or religion. These attacks gained momentum during the influx of refugees from predominantly Muslim countries like Syria and Afghanistan a few years ago. Sorosoids were represented as the "fifth column" of these threateningly numerous outsiders who, because of their peculiar manners and mores, would never be able to graft themselves onto the organic fabric of the Bulgarian nation and would linger like a canker on this nation's body. Predictably, in these neoconservative quarters, the election of President Trump was seen as an event redeeming the West and Bulgaria (sic!) from the menace of a Muslim takeover. Thus, for instance, writer and publisher Ivan Granitski acknowledges Trump's contribution to "annihilating Islamic State and blocking those hordes of invaders from Africa and the Middle East who pass for immigrants."² Quite logically, Granitski believes that "sorosoids are worried because the cutting off of their food source is nigh" (2016). In what sense are these attitudes inimical to the concept of open society? Their irrationality and their inveteracy aside, the anti-gender and the anti-immigrant responses to the realities of the globalized world envision a utopian combination between what Ferdinand Tönnies dubbed, back

---

1 All translations from Bulgarian are mine.
2 The portrayal of immigrants as pretenders implicitly contrasts with the genuineness of national belonging.

in the nineteenth century, *Gemeinschaft* (community) and *Gesellschaft* (society). For Tönnies, *Gemeinschaft* is a tradition-oriented, collectivist social formation premised on organic, tight-knit bonds among its members. There are some specific characteristics of this closed structure. First of all, it revolves around the economy of "mutual possession and enjoyment and also possession of and enjoyment of common goods" (Tönnies, 1957, 50). The apposite symbolic center of this physical togetherness is the home with "[its] hearth fire and [its] table" (Tönnies 1957, 54). In a post-Romantic vein, Tönnies associates the transition to *Gesellschaft*, that is, the social order based on commerce beyond the confines of the local community, with the loss of organicism: "In the conception of Gesellschaft, the original or natural relations of human beings to each other must be excluded" (1957, 77). The community of the "hearth fire and the table" is replaced by an atomized society in which "every person strives for that which is to his own advantage" (1957, 77). At the same time, however, Tönnies highlights the merchant's cosmopolitan cultural openness: "He is without home, a traveler, a connoisseur of foreign customs and arts without love or piety for those of any one country" (1957, 168). The merchant, then, may epitomize, *mutatis mutandis*, what Karl Popper refers to as "the spirit of the search for truth, as opposed to the belief in its possession" (1966, 136). For Popper, Socrates, as opposed to Plato, epitomizes this preference for search rather than possession: "Socrates had stressed that he was not wise; that he was not in the possession of truth, but that he was a searcher, an inquirer, a lover of truth" (1966, 137).

Where do (Bulgarian) neoconservatives fit in this picture? As I have suggested, they seem to be pursuing the utopian agenda of getting the best of both worlds by returning to the organic values of *Gemeinschaft* without sacrificing the material benefits associated with *Gesellschaft*. On the one hand, they lay claim to the right to "common possession and common enjoyment of *their* land" as well as to privileged possession of the truth about the values of the home. At the same time, they would rather live in a world where they have Facebook installed on their Apple smartphones. Ironically, on Facebook, they contend that the narrow and perfectly transparent interests of the Bulgarian nation come first for them. Of course, as Tönnies knew, "common possession and common enjoyment" entail protection of the closed community, and hence, the construct of the "common enemies." The "genders" (*джендъри*)[3] are a threat to the natural enjoyment of living in one's own land "comparable to the inhalation of atmospheric air." The immigrant "hordes" are a threat to the Bulgarian people's physical possession of the land and their symbolic possession of the truth of the land.

What about "sorosoids"? Why are they such an eyesore to the neoconservative gaze? An analogy with an eighteenth-century conservative literary text comes to mind. In Book IV of Jonathan Swift's *Gulliver's Travels*, the Houyhnhnms, a rational race of horses (the sole possessors of truth), have built their world order around an indefeasible binary opposition: they represent perfect reason whereas

---

3 A pejorative label for the supporters of LGBTQ rights.

the Yahoos (a subhuman race supposedly devoid of reason) represent absolute instinct. Gulliver, a human being who looks like a Yahoo, quickly learns the Houyhnhnms' language, which brings into play a new category: the teachable Yahoo. This puts at risk the immutability of the binary opposition—Gulliver stands for the supplementary middle ground that defies the logic of polarity. Logically, the Houyhnhnms relegate him to the status of a Yahoo, and at the end of the book, they expel him from their homeland because they cannot accommodate him in it. By way of analogy, we could say that the Bulgarian sorosoid is Gulliver in Houyhnhnmland.

What Is a Sorosoid?

The multifarious neoconservative voices, united around the quasi-nationalist, anti-minority-rights agenda, perceive sorosoids as their ideological Other. The semantic content of the term "sorosoid" consists of two discrete components which form a holistic *Gestalt*. Obviously, the stem of the word alludes to the influence of the Hungarian-American businessman-cum-philanthropist and all the individuals affiliated with the Open Society Foundation in Bulgaria. According to Georgi Lozanov, media expert and professor of journalism at Sofia University, "the use of Soros' name as a pejorative appellation" has served as a pillar in the reductive rhetoric adopted by the advocates of Christian and national values:

> What could be a more effective way of overcoming the universal fear and consternation [due to the financial crisis and the refugee wave] than finding a culprit for all social ills and point a finger at him. (2019)[4]

Lozanov's explanation draws upon an ironic invocation of the aggressive rhetorical labeling that anti-sorosoids employ. Here is an example of this aggressive rhetoric. In a recent article published in the *Trud* newspaper, columnist Kristiyan Shkvarek comes up with four defining characteristics of the sorosoid creed:
The sorosoid always believes in the following:

1. The West, the EU, and NATO are sacred cows … The sorosoid is a supporter of the West so strongly indoctrinated that one could hardly find an equivalent in the Central Committee of the Bulgarian Communist Party.
2. For the sorosoid, religion is an obsolete notion at best or a sinister system of control over the population at worst …

---

[4] Lozanov suggests that the word "sorosoid" was first used "around 2007 by Valentin Fartunov, author and host of a SKAT TV show" (2019). SKAT TV is a channel sponsored by one of Bulgaria's "patriotic" parties. Interestingly, 2007 is the year when Bulgaria acceded to the EU.

3. For the sorosoid, globalism (not to be mistaken for globalization) is the only meaningful identity. To him, notions like tribe, nation, ethnos, people, let alone race, are harmful or stupid.
4. The sorosoid is a functionary of a particular political system, just like the communist before him, and there is no more important goal for him than the construction of Liberal Democracy with all its hollow mantras: "division of powers," "independent media," "the NGO sector and civil society," "equality and the rule of law" … (2021)

The rhetorical and conceptual imperfections of this anti-sorosoid manifesto aside, three significant points deserve attention. First of all, in this symbolic geography, the West is perceived as a homogeneous space which accommodates, without any residue, "Liberal Democracy" and its "hollow mantras." The concoction of diachronically exclusive terms like "tribe" and "nation" in the third point suggests that the anti-sorosoid constructs her meaning around ahistorical, yet supposedly concrete, graspable concepts. The fact that the word "tribe" opens the sequence suggests a deliberate focus on the finiteness of the appeal. From this perspective, the principles of liberal democracy are "hollow mantras" because their content is abstract and volatile. The values and the identity of the tribe never change as they apply to a soundly rooted finite community, whereas the rule of law, for instance, is constantly re-negotiated as it applies to an amorphous mass of unrooted individuals. The local and the global (or the globalistic in this writer's parlance) are irreconcilable, since one is firmly grounded and the other one is dangling in the air of speculation. There is a second motif here that brings the two planes together. The sorosoid's jettisoning of local identity is bound up with her atheistic orientation. In other words, by sleight of hand, the local and the global are conflated: it turns out that the one and only universally valid religion—Christianity—provides the foundation for the locally determined tribe.

In the third significant, albeit oxymoronic nexus, liberal democracy's forever changing dogmas (sic!) are represented as a form of totalitarianism. The allusion to the sorosoid as an "indoctrinated functionary" and the reference to the "Central Committee of the Bulgarian Communist Party" resonates with many in a post-communist country like Bulgaria, where anti-communism/socialism is the dominant attitude toward the recent past. Thus, liberal democracy comes across as just another variant of the communist virus, and the neoconservative doctrine promises an effective vaccine against this disease.

Dehumanization through an Inflection

The image of the disease as a deviation from the norm is discernible in the second semantic component of the term "sorosoid": the inflection. Despite the nebulous mechanisms of this word's incorporation in post-communist Bulgaria's public discourse,⁵ one could assume that "sorosoid" is meant to echo "humanoid." There is both textual evidence (references in media articles) and paratextual evidence (references in readers' comments) that this is the association that resonates with the Bulgarian public. For instance, in Bulgaria's equivalent of *Charlie Hebdo*—*Starshel*—Mihail Mishkoved published a commentary on an interview with Vezhdi Rashidov (the then minister of culture), who referred to Ivo Prokopiev (owner of two influential "sorosoid" newspapers) and Ivan Krastev (an internationally renowned political scientist) as "sorosoids." Mishkoved (the author's nom de plume) writes: "He called them 'sorosoids' – what's that supposed to mean? Maybe it means something like 'humans,' but not exactly …" (Mishkoved 2018). At the paratextual end, here is a comment in response to an article defending the *Charlie Hebdo* journalists published in *Dnevnik* (one of the papers associated with Soros in the public consciousness): "How absurd and hypocritical are today's sorosoid laments! Why were the very same humanoids silent when people were burnt alive in Odessa? Or when the West-backed government in Kiyv killed women and children in Donbas?" (Laments 2018).⁶

It is interesting to note that Bulgarian seems to be practically the only language that features this word form. A Google search for "sorosoid" typed in the Latin alphabet yields predominantly Bulgarian sources in the Cyrillic. For one reason or another, in other languages of the same family, a different suffix has been attached to the same word. Tomasz Kamusella has come up with a fairly comprehensive overview of the word forms in some Slavic languages:

> The neologism соросовец *sorosovets* in Russian (Rozenbergs 2007), соросоид *sorosoid* in Bulgarian (Vodenicharov 2007), *sorosowiec* in Polish (Pająk 2016), or *sorosovec* in Slovak (Havran 2012) was coined in the early twenty-first century from the name of George Soros, and recently—quite ominously—appeared in Russia's English language news outlets, spelled as "sorosite" (rmstock 2016). It is a novel and increasingly accepted term of abuse for the staff of the organizations supported by George Soros as well as for graduates of these organizations' educational branches. (2017, XV)

The suffix "-ets" is not alien to Bulgarian; it is quite productive, its connotation is usually neutral, and it often denotes belonging to a certain nationality (cf. *румънец*/rumanets/Romanian; *германец*/germanets/German). I will leave

---

5 Interestingly, in one of the earliest appearances of the word, a different association comes to the fore: "They are a weird species of humans. Unlike asteroids, they have not fallen from the sky. Like the communists, they have taken shape under the influence of ideas launched by great philosophers. If Marx is the shaping influence for the former, for sorosoids the ideologue is the British, Austria-born philosopher Karl Popper" (Vodenicharov 2007).
6 The pro-Putin–anti-Soros nexus in Bulgaria's public discourse deserves special attention in a separate study, especially in today's political conjuncture.

to Bulgarian linguists, sociologists, and anthropologists the task to investigate the reasons why the semantically charged "-oid" inflection has been added to the "soros" stem in my mother tongue. In this chapter, I will confine myself to exploring the dehumanizing connotations of this neologism.

Let me first provide an authoritative definition of the word "humanoid." According to the *Merriam Webster* dictionary, "a humanoid being [is] a nonhuman creature or being with characteristics (such as the ability to walk upright) resembling those of a human" (www.merriam-webster.com). A glance at the etymology of the suffix yields another significant insight: word-forming element meaning "like, like that of, thing like a _____," from Latinized form of Greek *-oeidēs* (three syllables), from *eidos* "form," related to *idein* "to see," *eidenai* "to know"; literally "to see" (from PIE **weid-es-*, from root **weid-* "to see") (https://www.etymonline.com/word/humanoid). The etymological connection with the Greek *eidos* and its derivatives, albeit imperceptible to contemporary language users, suggests that "-oid" does not simply evoke likeness. There is a supplementary semantic component here: one may assume that referring to a being as a "humanoid" involves a "true" human being's *seeing/knowing* the difference between an essential form and its imitation. The similarity between a human being and a humanoid/sorosoid cannot delude the bearer of this knowledge/insight into believing that *those* creatures, brainwashed by neoliberal propaganda, deserve a higher status than that of the imperfect copy. They are not exactly human; they are, at best, *like* "us," and we are the epitome of essence. It is this self-perception of the neoconservative community in Bulgaria that unleashes the rhetorical potential of belittlement and self-aggrandizement hidden in the peculiarly inflected word "sorosoid."

Let me now elaborate on some of the associative mechanisms that I believe the inflection conjures up. These mechanisms are premised on a definition of the "non-human." In this chapter, I will use, somewhat reductively perhaps, a neat classification provided by Alan Bourassa. Bourassa has argued persuasively that if we approach the definition of the "non-human" as a concern "invoked by the question of language," three "figures of the non-human" can be conceived: "the non-human: the animal, the machine and the divinity." Bourassa goes on to map the manifestations of the "non-human" onto three linguistic modes:

> And these three figures of the non-human are paralleled by three kinds of language, three powers that can be assigned to language and between which our own thinking about language negotiates its uneasy path: semiotics, information and revelation. (2002, 61)

Bourassa's focus on "three powers that can be assigned to language" and on "the three great figures of the non-human: the animal, the machine, and the divinity" tallies with my classification of dehumanizing strategies.

The Figure of the Animal: Semiotics

Here is Bourassa's brief account of the distinction between animalistic semiotics and human semantics:

> Semiotics is grounded in recognition rather than understanding. The animal recognizes a certain sign – the beaver's tail-slap on the water, the honeybee's signal indicating the presence of pollen – because the sign is repeated, either genetically in the animal's innate responses or experientially in its ability to learn. (2002, 61)

The rhetoric of Bulgarian conservatives often reduces the behavior of sorosoids to "recognition rather than understanding." The motives of these quasi-individuals are relegated to the space of behavioristic responses to external, albeit linguistic, stimuli. On this view, there is a finite set of specific words that trigger a sorosoid's actions and reactions. This species of animalized humans never makes it to the Lacanian symbolic order, and hence they never become Lacanian subjects as their language simply mirrors their ego's identifications.[7] The "daily schedule of the sorosoid," published in an anonymous article in one of Bulgaria's news sites, is an example that illustrates the denial of full linguistic subjectivity to sorosoids:

> 10:00 I took part in a conference dedicated to the violation of the rights of the Roma community. I presented my argument that Bulgarians are extremely intolerant of the underprivileged Roma community
>
> 12:00 I appropriated some funding from the Open Society Foundation on a project that involves the re-affirmation of Euro Atlantic values
>
> 14:00 Together with other democratically minded citizens, I waved the rainbow flag in front of the Russian embassy as a sign of protest against the law adopted by the Russian *Duma* incriminating homosexual propaganda
>
> 20:00 Together with other democrats, I protested against the rising wave of xenophobia (2017)

According to this representation, the democrat's day revolves around actions motivated by a few keywords—rainbow flag, Roma, Euro-Atlantic values, xenophobia—which function as stimuli and play the role of Pavlovian signals for an animal. If the sorosoid does not follow the behavioral patterns that ensure

---

7 In the lingo of French poststructuralist thinker Jacques Lacan, "the symbolic order" is the space in which the human subject constructs her communication with others through the medium of language. In the presubjective "imaginary order," the ego, as opposed to the subject, seeks identification with its counterpart in the mirror.

her survival, she would "cease to exist." The simple linearity of the cause-and-effect relationship precludes the possibility of rational inquiry or creative deviation. Sorosoids respond to the rainbow flag and the Roma minority signal just as animals rush toward food. If they were, for some reason, repelled by these stimuli, or if they chose to reason about them, they would strip themselves of the alimentary canal which feeds life into their social body. Any attempt to add complexity to the argument that "Bulgarians are extremely intolerant of the underprivileged Roma minority" would endanger the survival of sorosoids as an animal species.

The Figure of the Machine: Information

In Bourassa's language-centered classification, "the machine is language as information. Information differs from simple signification in that it can rely on a type of coding that can intensify the signifying function of language" (2002, 61). In other words, the machine is effective when it comes to indicating or translating accurately in its functionally limited referential language particular scenarios and states of affairs. Very often, it is the poetic function that is weakened. Pure referentiality is a straitjacket for language and its potential to reach toward creatively conceived truths beyond fact. In Bourassa's words:

> There is … something brutal about this kind of language, its atheistic immediacy, its relentless attachment to the actual. Information is a step up from the pure sign, calling on higher levels of organization and memory, but neither form of language can justify a claim to truth. (2002, 62)

My contention is that the opponents of open society in Bulgaria represent sorosoids as mere mechanical transmitters of versions of "the actual" conceived in a space beyond the Bulgarian *Gemeinschaft*. In other words, sorosoids are machine-like entities that are totally, and without any residue, dependent on external geopolitical sources beyond their ken and control. Sorosoids are stripped of autonomous agency and are only capable of translating "verbatim" the scenario of neoliberal democracy without any awareness of its inapplicability to the local environment. The Bulgarian internet space abounds in examples of this form of dehumanization. In an interview for a Bulgarian news site, for instance, Vassil Prodanov, PhD, introduced as a professor of national and world Economy at Sofia University, responds to the question whether he expects a "color revolution in Bulgaria if a left-wing party wins the election":

> It is difficult to say at this stage. If by "color revolution" we mean protests whose core consists of individuals connected with the so called "sorosoids," *paid and supported by external powers* [my emphasis], then the prime time of "color revolutions" was four or five years ago. Their

last success was in Ukraine in 2013 … At present, the public image of "sorosoids" is more negative than that of "communists." (2017)

The poorly grounded parallel between liberals and communists is, predictably, drawn again. What concerns me in this quote, however, is the emphasis on change in post-communist societies as possible only if there is intervention that comes from a locus beyond the confines of the nation. Apart from alienating sorosoids geographically from their own motherland, this rhetorical focus reduces them and those affiliated with them to the status of automatons. Sorosoids are denied the privilege of acting on their volition, since the precepts of the West incapacitate each sorosoid's personal judgment. Not only are sorosoids mentally incapacitated, they are paid to perform their automated actions. This reduces them to the absurdly humiliating status of money-driven machines. On this view, there is no hierarchy that sets apart one source of funding from another. Vested interest and a possibly philanthropist agenda are pigeonholed into the category of less-than-idealistic motivation. Sorosoids will transform any funding into ideology. To put it aphoristically, sorosoids are vending machines: they deliver what the coin in the slot tells them to deliver.

Divinity: Dehumanization through Self-Aggrandizement

I want to suggest, finally, that Bulgarian neoconservatives indirectly dehumanize sorosoids by denying them access to the immutable truths that express the very essence of nationhood. If we revisit our language-based classification, this "third language … is the language of revelation" (Bourassa 2002, 62). This language works in mysterious ways indeed. It is both rooted in history and it transcends it. My claim is that, in the Bulgarian case, and beyond, I suppose, the language of neoconservatives seeks to conflate the mythical with the historical. A peculiar literal imagination informs the prophet's rhetoric. Prophetic discourse blithely bridges the gap between the literal space and the imaginary universally symbolic space. The following example from a recent article on the *Консерваторъ* website shows that this universalization of the local applies to time as well. The text is so rich in allusions that it deserves a longer quotation:

> Over the last few days[8], the liberal community, well known for its left-wing and progressive messages against concepts like borders and sovereignty, which are retrograde for postmodern man, has embraced nationalism …
>
> Western liberals are famous for their aversion to national flags, and yet a war is raging, and Ukraine has been invaded … These people used to refute the concept of the nation state. They had dedicated their entire

8 The text was published on March 7, 2022.

identities as journalists, activists, professors, political influencers, and TV spokespersons to transforming words like "nation" into hate speech. Especially in Europe.

Most of them are dreaming of and working towards melting all European nations into one multicultural federation without internal and external borders. It is all open to anyone. Two minutes on Stockholm's turf make me a Swede. You pass through Paris – you're French. You've worked in Hamburg for three months – no one is more German than you. You put on a festival costume in Bansko,[9] and you can talk about your proto-Bulgarian roots. (Apostolov 2022)

This text is definitely written from a quasi-divine, privileged perspective. For this writer, the tragic historical events in Ukraine are no cause for empathy; instead, the war serves to vindicate the undebatable accuracy of the conservatives' mythical fore-knowledge. Apostolov always already knew that the multicultural project will come to naught because immersing oneself in the local culture takes … time. The banal dimension of this observation aside, it does give us some food for thought. According to this "I-told-you-so" interpretation of today's historical conjuncture, the war in Ukraine reaffirms the significance of the inalienable identity of the nation. Importantly, "post-modern man" has subverted a sacred state of affairs; in a peculiar mixture of myth and history, the nation—a historical phenomenon that we associate with modernity in Europe—is promoted to the space of the immutable. A temporally localizable phenomenon is universalized. In this light, the liberals are perceived as dreamers who have constructed vacuous utopian scenarios, and now they must bear the burden of disgrace and convert to the religion of nationalism. This quasi-prophetic language belittles liberals/sorosoids by representing them as flawed reasoners who were blind to the one and only valid revealed truth. What is more, they come across as flawed believers whose fickle faith changes under the pressure of concrete historical circumstances. It is worth paying attention to how this writer's nationalist rhetoric progresses from the more abstract references to the localities of Stockholm, Paris, and Hamburg (all of these are, obviously, well put on the map), to the bodily experience of wearing a Bansko (a town of about 20,000 residents) festival costume. The writer's mythopoeic pathos goes toward *showing* that the costume's fabric must rub against your skin for eons before the truth of Bulgarian-ness becomes a tactile sensation. It is this organic voice which speaks, as it were, from the inner recesses of genuine sensuous experience that validates the nationalist perspective.

---

9 A Bulgarian winter resort known for preserving its local culture.

Modes of Resistance

What are the workable modes of resistance to this neoconservative paradigm which seeks to subvert the values of Bulgaria's open society? Let me consider two possible strategies, which I will tentatively dub the rationalist and the affective response.

The rationalist approach will involve revealing the inconsistencies of anti-sorosoids' arguments by focusing on the stem of the sorosoid *Gestalt*. By highlighting the complex philosophical legacy behind Soros's philanthropy, one could hope to counter the reductive, frequently *ad hominem*, claims of open society's opponents. The deconstruction of the nexuses I discussed above will also be part of this response, and it could be combined with historical references to the corrupt genealogy of the term "sorosoid." Fake constructs will be countered with logical argumentation. This strategy of resistance is premised on the Kantian assumption that an enlightened society consists of individuals who "[have left] man's self-caused immaturity" and can communicate freely on the basis of reason:

> All that is required for this enlightenment is freedom; and particularly the least harmful of all that may be called freedom, namely, the freedom for man to make public use of his reason in all matters. (Kant 1995, 56)

The only problem with the enlightened/enlightening approach is that the wall of irrational reasoning may turn out impossible to break. I insist on the phrase "irrational reasoning" because what makes "the public use of ... reason in all matters" difficult is that the opponents of Enlightenment values have their own indefeasible logic. Faced with the wall of irrational reasoning, the level-headed rationalist may turn to the stance of what Sara Ahmed has dubbed the "affect alien," that is, someone who opposes illiberal attitudes on the battleground of affects/emotions. Here is how Ahmed describes the rhetorical/political dilemmas of the "affect alien":

> Let us take seriously the figure of the feminist kill-joy. Does the feminist kill other people's joy by pointing out moments of sexism? Or does she expose the bad feelings that get hidden, displaced, or negated under public signs of joy? The feminist is an affect alien: she might even kill joy because she refuses to share an orientation toward certain things as being good because she does not find the objects that promise happiness to be quite so promising. (2010, 38–39)

Like the "feminist kill-joy," sorosoids should not feel responsible for spoiling the affective atmosphere of nationalist joy or elation shared by many Bulgarians. The "affect aliens" cannot but voice their disagreement with "objects" that bring illusory happiness. Importantly, I want to suggest, they should be ready to accept, despite their belief in the significance of critical thinking, that there are tautological spaces which preclude debate and argumentation.

Let me give a current example. With the wave of Ukrainian refugees in Bulgaria, a peculiar racist rhetoric has made its way into the public discourse. Various public figures, including our otherwise liberal prime minister, have referred to Bulgarians' willingness to accept these refugees because they are Christian and well-educated. It seems to me that one cannot argue with this implicitly discriminatory position which is deeply ingrained in the collective unconscious. One way to oppose it is to repeat tautologically: a refugee is a refugee is a refugee ... *ad infinitum*. *Un point c'est tout*. One of the significant risks associated with this strategy is that the supporters of open society may end up forming a closed ecstatic community with its own well-established affective atmosphere, modeled on that of their opponents. In an attempt to replace anti-sorosoids' arguments with their own, they may well displace themselves from the plane of rational openness to the plane of immanent affectivity. In other words, the tautological defiance of reasoning undermines one of the foundations of open society—rationalism—which Popper describes as "an attitude of readiness to listen to critical arguments and to learn from experience" (1966, 420).

Conclusion

I started writing this chapter three months before Russia's invasion of Ukraine. We are now one month into a war that challenges the Socratic/Popperian quest for truth and the Kantian Enlightenment ideal. How could one keep "the spirit of search for truth" alive if the truth seems so obvious and yet so mind-boggling? How could one "make use of reason ... in all public matters" if the very concept of reason is put to the test? In these new circumstances, the role of the supporters of open society becomes even more crucial, especially in a country like Bulgaria, which has a long-standing and still prominent subculture of Russophilia. As I have suggested, the pro-Putin–anti-Soros nexus often emerges in the rhetoric of Bulgarian anti-sorosoids, and the motif has gained new currency after February 24. The argument appears in many guises, but in its most common, mitigated manifestation, it invokes the benefits of a safely closed society in today's precarious situation: "We had better not do anything that could irritate the 'Russian bear' because the missiles can be targeted at our own Black Sea ports. Keeping a low profile is the best course of action for the time being. From an economic perspective, we should keep the Russian gas and petrol flowing because otherwise the Bulgarian economy will collapse. It's time for us to be Bulgarophiles rather than Russophiles or Americanophiles." In other words, our possession and enjoyment of the "hearth fire and the table" should be a priority.

Against this background, the only stance available to the dehumanized sorosoid seems to be that of the humanist. I want to suggest that it could be conceived as a composite attitude that merges the two strategies I discussed above. The rationalist approach could break through the wall of irrational reasoning because the reality of meaningless death, the ultimate absurdity, is now much more compelling than it was during the Covid-19 pandemic. The affective response could challenge mythopoeic and historicizing interpretations of Putin's decision by pressing one simple point home: an aggressor is an aggressor is an aggressor ….

Bibliography

"Absurd Sorosoid Laments." 2015. https://www.dnevnik.bg/bulgaria/2015/01/08/2450092_predozirane_smeshen_sorosoiden_plach/comments.

Ahmed, Sara. 2010. "Happy Objects." In *The Affect Theory Reader*, edited by Melissa Greg and Gregory J. Seigworth, 29–51. Durham, NC: Duke University Press.

Apostolov, Vassil. 2022. "How Progressivists Embraced Nationalism." https://conservative.bg/kak- progresivistite-pregarnaha-natsionalizma/.

Bourassa, Alan. 2002. "Literature, Language, and the Non-Human" In *A Shock to Thought: Expression after Deleuze and Guattari*, edited by Brian Massumi, 60–76. Routledge.

Flagman. 2017. "What Is a Sorosoid? Can They Thrive in This Country?" https://www.flagman.bg/article/139551.

Granitski, Ivan. 2016. "Sorosoids Are Stressed Because their Food Source Will Be Cut Off." https://www.standartnews.com/.

Istanbul Convention. 2011. https://www.coe.int/en/web/istanbul-convention/.

Kamusella, Tomasz. 2017. *The Un-Polish Poland, 1989 and the Illusion of Regained Historical Continuity*. Palgrave Macmillan.

Kant, Immanuel. 1995. "What is Enlightenment?" In *Sources of the Western Tradition*, Vol. 2, edited by Marvin Perry et al. Houhgton Mifflin Company.

Lozanov, G. What is a 'Sorosoid'? Accessed March 17, 2022. https://www.dw.com/bg.

Mishkoved, Mihail (n.d.) "A Hunt for Sorosoids." https://starshel.bg/2001/lov-na-sorosoidi/.

Ninova, Kornelia. 2018. "Between Bulgaria's Constitution and the Istanbul Convention, I Choose Bulgaria." https://bsp.bg/news/view/15349korneliya_ninova__mejdu_konstitutsiyata_na_bylgariya_i_rezolyutsiyata_za_istanbulska_konventsiya_izbiram_bylgariya_____.html.

Popper, Karl. 1966. *The Open Society and Its Enemies*. Princeton, NJ: Princeton University Press.

Prodanov, Vassil. 2017. "In Public Consciousness 'Sorosoid' Now Sounds Worse Than 'Communist'." https://pogled.info/avtorski/Vasil-Prodanov/v-masovoto-saznanie-sorosoid-veche-e-po-losho-ot-komunist.83105.

Shkvarek, Kritsiyan. 2021. "What Is a Sorosoid in Bulgaria." https://trud.bg.

Swift, Jonatahan. 2003. *Gulliver's Travels*. Barnes & Noble Books.

Tönnies, Ferdinand. 1957. *Community & Society*. Edited and translated by Charles P. Loomis. Harper & Row.

Vodenicharov, Rumen. 2007. "Sorosoids." http://www.novazora.net/2007/issue31/story_07.html.

12

AN AFRICAN BACKGROUND TO THE CONCEPT OF OPEN SOCIETY: *IKENGA* AND *OFO* CULTIC FIGURES AS STRUCTURAL REPRESENTATIONS OF THE ENTERPRISING SPIRIT OF THE IGBO OF NIGERIA

Nwankwo T. Nwaezeigwe

Introduction

The concept of open society in its characteristic form as a society founded on "a flexible structure, freedom of belief, and wide dissemination of information" (Oxford Lexico) and a high degree of social mobility (Popper 2020) is not alien to most traditional African societies, especially the non-centralized polities where the traditional political authority is not autocratic but dispersed among the people. Although the holistic nature of these societies in which political authority is often blended with religious sanctions and socio-economic obligations, might appear contradictory to contemporary notions of open society, but a detailed analysis of the dynamic nature of the society reveals their complementary rather than conflicting roles in the making of the open society character of the polity.

The Igbo of Nigeria represent this category of holistic traditional polity where authority is not only dispersed but where there is no barrier to freedom or opportunities for mobility at different levels of the society both vertical and horizontal sub-structures. Indeed among the Igbo, what acts as the guardian of their open society phenomenon is their social control mechanism which is anchored on their characteristic traditional belief system expressed through tangible and intangible spiritual mediums. This belief system is anchored in a generative life force which recognizes that every individual is born with a distinct destiny made manifest through his associated talent, with talent in turn leading to enterprise and enterprise to advancement and advancement to privilege. This could explain why the Igbo are one of the most distinctly enterprising groups of African extraction with conspicuous presence in all the continents.

The Igbo of Nigeria are one of the most dispersed and highly enterprising ethnic nations in Africa. They are located in the south-eastern part of Nigeria; and form one of the three largest ethnic groups in the country; the other two being the Hausa-Fulani and Yoruba. Mainly located in the present five south-eastern states of Abia, Anambra, Ebonyi, Enugu, and Imo, they are dominantly found in the two Niger-Delta states of Delta and Rivers, with considerable numbers found in the present Edo and Benue states.

The Igbo propensity to always migrate from their homeland to other places in search of greener pastures, their associated enterprising spirit, and the resulting successes, have often led to envy from their host communities; leading to hostilities and in some extreme cases, to outright anti-Igbo riots, particularly in the Muslim-dominated northern states of Nigeria. This characteristic enterprising spirit coupled with bitter experiences in the hands of their host communities has led some people to describe them in different characteristic terms, of which the most popular is their description as the Jews of Africa.

They are markedly the dominant entrepreneurs in small- and medium-scale industrial and commercial activities in the Nigerian nation today. In fact over 70 percent of Nigeria's commercial activities are carried out by people of Igbo ethnic extraction. In other words every major market in every major Nigerian city is under the economic grip of the members of the Igbo ethnic group. Associated with Igbo commercial enterprise is their propensity to travel far beyond the confines of their ethnic boundaries. Hence it is not mistaken evidence that even beyond the confines of the Nigerian nation, prominent Igbo communities have become common features in most African countries, including the Americas, Asia, and Europe, where they represent the conspicuous African population.

Demographic Questions on Igbo Migration

The Igbo have characteristically been compared to the Jews and Irish, as well as such people as the Kikuyu of Kenya, the Chagga of Tanzania, the Ewe of Ghana and Togo, and the Bamileke of Cameroon. LeVine (1966, 7) described these groups as the "examples of groups noted for their opportunism and industry in response to the new situation created by Western institutions in this century." In comparing the Igbo with the Irish, Niven (1970, 18) wrote:

> The Ibo have the same courage and intelligence as the Irish and they had not come under any greater authority than the village nor had they encountered an outsider in the war-path. Every man has always been for himself and has usually done well himself.

The general trend however was for some scholars to associate the Igbo economic adventurism with ecological disadvantages. Coleman (1958, 69) one of the major apologists of this hypothesis writes:

> Ibo land is one of the most densely populated rural areas in the world. In some places the density is more than 1000 persons to the square mile. Moreover, the soil is comparatively poor. As a result, in the past

the Ibo expanded territorially and exported to other areas large numbers of seasonal laborers and even semi-permanent residents. In fact, the Ibo were expanding territorially in many directions at the time of the British intrusion. Since then this outward thrust has continued and has been the source of anti-Igbo feeling among the tribes bordering Iboland.

However, while migration arising from expansion could readily be linked with pressure of the population on the available resources, it is unlikely that such could bring about the culture of high enterprising spirit. To say the least, scarcity of land is not a uniform feature in Igbo land. Most peripheral Igbo sub-groups have relative expansive portions of arable land enough to sustain viable agricultural communities. Linking migration with scarcity of farming lands seems therefore ridiculous in the case of these Igbo sub-groups.

This is evident in the cases of the north-east or *Ogu-ukwu* Igbo sub-group, and communities within the Niger and Anambra River Basins. Apart from possessing enough farmlands relative to their population, and producing enough foodstuff particularly rice and yams in commercial quantities, they paradoxically constitute the bulk of seasonal migrant farm laborers in Igbo land. How then can this be explained in terms of scarcity of land arising from population pressure?

Lee (1966, 48) working in concert with Ravenstein's theory of migration lists factors which account for economic-related migrations, the introduction of bad or oppressive laws, heavy taxations, an unattractive climate, uncongenial social surroundings, as well as compulsion which may arise from either slave trade or transportation. He however went further to opine that none of the above-mentioned factors "can compare in volume with that which arises from the desire inherent in most men to 'better' themselves in material respects."

There is no doubt, as Lee rightly puts it, that it is the desire for better economic attainments more than other motives that pushes the Igbo out of their traditional home base. Yet, it has to be made known that neither the desire for better economic needs nor the propensity to migrate from one's home base is exclusive to the Igbo. Every group of people is imbued naturally with such desires. What then is the uniqueness of the Igbo experience which made them the most shrewd and remarkable in these matters of economic quest and expansion among their neighbors? In their study of Venezuela, Brown and Goetz (1987, 49) stated: "Migration in third world settings as elsewhere, results when opportunities provided by geographic places are not commensurate with the personal need(s) or capabilities of their resident." In the same vein, they attribute outward migration "as a function of both personal attributes and places of contextual characteristics related to development."

Relating the Igbo circumstance to the position of Brown and Goezt, Ottenberg (1959, 130) links the force behind the Igbo tendency to expand beyond their traditional borders to their receptivity to culture change. He goes further to associate this attribute to four major factors. These include: the influence of the European slave trade on them; the nature of direct European contact following the slave trade; the nature and organization of Igbo society and; the Igbo population density. While the first and second factors cannot be exclusive to the Igbo, and the fourth factor—"population density," having been resolved, the third—"the nature and organization of Igbo cultures," appears to particularly agree with the dynamic character of Igbo open society and its inherent enterprising spirit.

Socio-political Structure of Igbo Open Society as the Catalyst to Adventurism

Igboland in its most unadulterated indigenous form shows a markedly high level of political democratization. There is a marked lack of strong centralization of authority on any individual or group of individuals. This situation has often led some scholars to describe the Igbo as forming part of the territorial political complex popularly, but in certain circumstances erroneously, known as "stateless societies" (Horton, 1972).

Horton (1972) in defining a stateless society has identified the following grounds as forming the basis of his classification: firstly, that in a stateless society there is little concentration of authority in which case there exists the difficulty of identifying any individual or limited group of men as the rulers of the society. Secondly, that such authority roles as exist affect a rather limited sector of the lives of those subject to them; while thirdly, the wielding of authority as a specialized full-time occupation is virtually unknown, and finally, that the unit within which people feel an obligation to settle their disputes according to agreed rules and without resort to force tends to be relatively small.

Vansina, Mauny, and Thomas (1964, 87), on the other hand, in defining a state system describes a political structure as one with differentiated status between rulers and ruled, which is founded not only on kinship relations, but also on a territorial basis, with the presence of political offices as an important index of classification. The following episode from Achebe's (1969, 105) iconic novel, *Things Fall Apart*, provides a clear picture of the character of political decentralization among the Igbo, which by extension expresses its inclusive character of open society:

> The missionaries spend their first four or five nights in the marketplace, and went into the village in the morning to preach the gospel. They asked who the king of the village was, but the villagers told them that there was no king. 'We have men of high title and the chief priest and the elders', they said.

Be that as it may, there is more to the characteristic enterprising spirit of the Igbo than the mere lack of central political authority. This is because most other ethnic groups with similar political structure do not possess similar or equal enterprising spirit with the Igbo. Thus, one may ask, what are the forces that propel the characteristic enterprising spirit of the Igbo, as well as their expansionist tenacity outside their traditional homeland?

Relating to the nature and organization of Igbo culture as impetus to their achievement-oriented drive, Ottenberg (1959, 130) believed that its strength lies on, firstly, the emphasis on individual achievement and initiative; secondly, alternatives prestige goals and paths of action; thirdly, a tendency toward equalitarian leadership; fourthly, considerable incorporation of other peoples and cultures; fifthly, a great deal of settlement and resettlement of individuals and small groups; and sixthly, considerable cultural variations.

The foregoing factors, although seemingly evident, are not exclusive to the Igbo. Take for instance, the emphasis on individual achievement and initiative. How could it be explained that no other ethnic group except the Igbo has a sense of individual achievement motivation and initiative? Again, looking at the issue of equalitarian leadership and bringing it alongside the Tiv of Benue State, and even the Ekoi groups of Cross River State of Nigeria, it becomes difficult to define it in exclusive terms in the context of the Igbo impetus for achievement. The same goes with the other factors.

However, that is not to say that these factors do not on their own, to varying degrees, play important roles in shaping the Igbo achievement drive. In actual fact, among the Igbo they form the outward indicators of an inner ideological drive which is not shared with the other groups. This inner ideological drive is expressed by one unique characteristic which the Igbo do not share with the other groups except to some extent the Jews and, this is their sentimental attachment to their traditional homeland.

This Igbo sentimental attachment to their ancestral homeland is cosmologically propelled by a momentum spirit which induces a pattern of habitual but regulated outward migration in search of greener pastures and subsequent home-coming during which one is expected to assess his progress in life. What then is this momentum spirit that seems to have defied all external linkages to exclusively impel the Igbo to a habitual enterprising spirit and adventurism?

This momentum spirit is cosmologically anchored on the belief in a generative life force known as *Ikenga* and structurally represented by a cultic artistic symbolism defined by a ram-headed human figure with a cutlass in the right hand and a booty often represented by a human head on the left hand. *Ikenga* otherwise known as the "cult of the right hand" is believed to be the source of Igbo enterprising instinct and migratory propensity. The *Ikenga* thus is the cosmological basis of Igbo belief in open society, which recognizes that talent leads to enterprise and enterprise to achievement, and achievement to customary privileges. Hence, the Igbo society with its characteristic republicanism is engrossed in a highly competitive personal achievement-driven motivation, which is anchored in *Ikenga*. Allied with *Ikenga* and acting as a spiritual counterbalance is the *Ofo*—another cultic objective defined variously as the ancestral staff of office and staff of justice.

Indeed while *Ikenga* is dictated by a go-getter centrifugal force, the Ofo on the other hand is driven by a stock-taking centripetal force with both acting within a complimentary spiritual orbit that defines the essence and character of traditional African open society. It is against the background of the interplay of these two centrifugal and centripetal cosmological forces that the nexus of Igbo enterprising spirit could be well explained in the context of open society. Allied with this interplay is Igbo socio-political structure which is rooted in their pattern of inheritance and by extension succession to and exercise of political power.

Conceptualizing *Ofo* and *Ikenga* as Open Society Phenomena in the Contest for Political and Economic Powers

The *Ofo* and *Ikenga* when viewed in the context of Igbo cosmology embody the ideological fulcrum on which the Igbo society rests. In other words, a better understanding of the basic character of Igbo way of life explained through their pattern of political behavior and economic enterprise can only be properly understood from the position of the two cosmological concepts of *Ofo* and *Ikenga* in the body of Igbo belief system.

The *Ofo* is the staff of customary authority conferred on the political head of a defined patrilineal level of an Igbo society by right ancestral heirloom generally determined through age ascendency. It is symbolized by the twig of a tree known among the Igbo by the name, but botanically known as *Detarium senegalense*. Its branches fall off naturally on drying. It is this branch that symbolizes the authority of its holder. Since the *Ofo* cannot be cut or broken off by the agency of human activities, but falls off by natural means, it is thus believed that its inherent authority cannot be acquired by the act of human ability or effort but by the commission of transcendental forces defined in this context by *Chukwu-Okike* (God the Creator) through the mediation of Deified Ancestors.

The position of the custodian of the *Ofo* which is defined as *Okpala* (*Diokpala*) cannot be contested but emerges by right primogeniture as symbolized by the manner the twigs of the *Ofo* tree fall off the branches at appointed time. As Ilogu (1974, 18) observed:

> The characteristic falling off of the *Ofo* twigs symbolizes the process of establishing new family and lineage branches among the Igbo. In his words: No cutting of the *Ofo* branch is done. It is believed that Chukwu (the Great God) purposely created this tree to be sacred, and by manner its branches fell unbroken, he (*Chukwu*) symbolizes the way families and lineages grow up and established new extended families and lineages. Therefore the *Ofo* made out of these branches is the abode of the spirit of dead ancestors, hence the authority and the sacredness of the

Ofo as well as the special place given to it as the emblem of unity, truth and indestructibility for the individual or group possessing the *Ofo*.

For an *Ofo* to be traditionally functional, it must first be consecrated. This consecration often takes place on the day a man leaves his father's homestead to establish his own branch of the family by taking a wife. Although having become independent of his father's house by establishing his household, he and his other equally independent brothers continue to maintain a collective allegiance to the authority of their father, which is symbolized by their father's *Ofo*.

On the death of their father, the eldest among the male children inherits their fathers homestead and by extension his *Ofo*, which subsequently signifies the transfer of their father's authority to him. By having custody of the *Ofo*, the eldest son holds every aspect of their father's assets principally his living house, and such others as land and economic trees which he holds in trust on behalf of the others or shares with them afterwards as the case may be. Where the situation concerns a father with many wives, he is equally obliged to take over the responsibility of the widows' maintenance and welfare.

In return, the other sons are expected to transfer the allegiance due to their late father to the first son, who then assumes the role of the political, religious, and juridical head of what becomes the minimal lineage or *Umunna* of their late father who automatically transforms into the class of Deified Ancestors. Thus cosmologically, *Ofo* symbolizes both the Igbo belief in continuity of life after death and unbroken chain of interactions between the living and the dead.

The *Ikenga* on the other hand, symbolizes Igbo adventurism and enterprising spirit. It is the go-getter spirit of the Igbo associated with good fortune, personal ability, war, and general success in life. It is ideologically associated with a man's right hand. Since a man's right hand in Igbo cosmology symbolizes positivism, his ability to utilize it most effectively for a considered goal puts him on the saddle of success and recognition. Among the Igbo, a man's basic strength is believed to be found in his right hand; as Afigbo (1986, 2) aptly describes it as the "cult of the right hand with which a man hacks his way through the jungles of sweat and bitter experiences known as life."

Beyond the authority provided by the *Ofo*, which is only restricted to an individual within a selected kindred group, the *Ikenga* provides a level-playing ground for all the male members of the group, based on their individual abilities to achieve the material goals of their lives. *Both* the *Ofo* and *Ikenga* are therefore based on two mutually opposed, yet complementary patterns of acquisition and exercise of socio-political and economic influences. How then dose this situation act as a lever for the extraordinary enterprising spirit of the Igbo? The answer lies, as earlier pointed out, in the pattern of inheritance among the Igbo, which leaves nearly everything at the disposal of the first son, including his father's liabilities.

Often, in a typical Igbo family, the eldest male child inherits, in strict traditional sense, his father's homestead, the *Ofo* and the ancestral shrine which houses the *Ofo*. These three objects of inheritance represent the most potent evidence of a family's unbroken link with the ancestors. By this unquestionable right of inheritance, the other male children become extended branches of the family, seeking alternative locations for their homesteads. When the eldest son dies, while the homestead often remains within the custody of his first son, the *Ofo* and the ancestral shrine however shift to the custody of the next eldest surviving son among as younger brothers, while his son in establishing another lineage branch with his siblings transfers the allegiance due his father to his uncle.

Thus, within each lineage level, the position of the eldest surviving male child, commonly referred to as *Okpala* or *Diokpa*, remains constant over time. However, as one moves up to the maximal stage and eventually to the village-group level, his authority gradually diminishes, although not actually in importance but in effectiveness. At these upper levels, what accounts most is the evidence of one's achievements in life, which in traditional Igbo society was measured not only in material acquisitions, but the number of scalps brought home.

However, it was in the acquisition of social titles that in most instances one's socio-political influence is measured in his community. If a man has all the things that constitute the status of a wealthy man, but fails to acquire the necessary titles which his level of wealth demands, such a person remains an *Ofeke*, a commoner of no social significant worth in the society. As LeVine (1966), 21) puts it, "among the Igbo the social title system is the one potent means by which a man's wealth could be translated into social and political statuses."

Furthermore, since these titles are graduated into levels of importance in ascending order, it means that as one acquires more titles so his influence in both social and political matters increases. This ascending order also means a corresponding high cost of initiation. This further means that for a man to move from one grade to the other, he must work towards accumulating enough money to cover the cost of initiation rites. Most significant is the fact that a man dies with his title, living his sons to work toward getting theirs. One striking thing about this however is the fact that one cannot acquire the upper levels of these titles in his father's life-time. Thus putting limits as to the degree of one's dependence on his father's wealth.

Among the Igbo therefore, while age is highly respected, a man's achievements based on his personal enterprises are revered. To the Igbo therefore, a man's worth is not measured by his inheritance but by his personal enterprising efforts. The Igbo-born literary icon, Achebe (1969, 6) pictures this vividly through the dramatic rise of his main character, Okonkwo from the level of his father's abject poverty to personal stardom:

> When Unoka died he had taken no title at all and he was heavily in debt. Any wonder then his son Okonkwo was ashamed of him? Fortunately, among these people a man was judged according to his worth and not according to the worth of his father. Okonkwo was clearly cut out for

great things. He was still young but he had won fame as the greatest wrestler in the nine villages. He was a wealthy farmer and had two bans full of yams, and had just married his third wife. To crown it all he had taken two titles and had shown incredible prowess in two inter-tribal wars. And so although Okonkwo was still young, he was already one of the greatest men of his time. Age was respected among his people, but achievement was revered. As the elders said, if a child washed his hands he could eat with kings. Okonkwo had clearly washed his hands and so he ate with kings and elder.

It is in this realm of personal achievement that *Ikenga* takes precedence. Thus, for the greater population of those who were not privileged to exercise the authority offered by the possession of the *Ofo* by right age and by extension inherit the bulk of their father's wealth which would enable them to begin a new life with considerable ease, the *Ikenga* becomes the motivating ideological force. As Boston (1977, 14) put it, "*Ikenga* symbolizes the person as a particular individual contrasting his personal achievements with those which can be ascribed to hereditary qualities or to some other external source." Unlike the *Ofo*, the *Ikenga* is not inherited. Each man is expected to have his own *Ikenga* which ceases to exist on his death. The *Ikenga* is expected to direct his life ambitions and adventures. Whenever he meets with success, he is expected to celebrate victory, which he attributes to his *Ikenga*. On the other hand, if a man meets with repeated failures in the quest for his life objectives, he may re-consecrate his *Ikenga* on account of its ineffectiveness, or attribute the situation to his *Chi* (Personal Guardian Spirit). A man's *Chi* is expected to save him from misfortunes. Thus an Igbo who escape dramatically from accident or an enemy attributes such feats to his Chi. Since someone's *Chi* determines his *Akalaka* (Destiny), repeated efforts to make a breakthrough in life without commensurate results could then be attributed to one's *Akalaka*. Among the Igbo therefore, while a man's achievement, based on his personal ability is recognized and accorded the due respect, there is still a strong belief in the unseen hands of the Supreme God (Chukwu) offering every bit of protection through the man's *Chi*.

The Igbo spirit of enterprise is strongly anchored on the premise that man is created by *Chukwu* (Almighty God) who dumps him with hands and feet in a world-like jungle, giving him the option of either conquering his environment to live or be conquered by his environment. The *Ikenga* in this case provides the impetus for a strong bargaining power. Hence, while intelligence and strength are recognized as natural gifts from *Chukwu*, the ability to harness them into tangible substance is attributed to the *Ikenga*.

This is the basis of the symbolism of ram head. In other words, just as the strength of the ram is its head so a man's head should form the basis of his strength. This is conceptualized through the application of his intelligence in his confrontation with a given venture, which is then transferred to his right hand for execution, and then handed to the left hand for custody.

Jeffreys (1954, 34) explains this in these terms:

> Even if a man is naturally strong and vigorous, this virility is attributed to the power of his *Ikenga*; furthermore, if a weak man by accident throws a stronger one or makes money more easily than others, people give the credit to his *Ikenga*.

This prominent role accorded to *Ikenga* in Igbo philosophy of life was clearly manifested by its widespread presence in Igbo households in the early periods before European influence. Commenting on this with respect to the Igbo spirit of enterprise, Basden (1966, 19) observed:

> Each household contains many sacred objects, but they have not all equal significance, for among the 'god' many and lords many there are higher and lower degrees of importance. The most universal of these household gods, and that which is given first rank, is the *Ikenga*, and no house may be without one. It is the first god sought by a young man at the beginning of his career and it is the one to which he looks for good luck in all his enterprises.

Allied to the individual *Ikenga* is the collective *Ikenga* associated with a group, usually a village or village group community. It is usually associated with the collective interest and advancement of the given community. Unlike personal *Ikenga*, which ceases to exist on the owner's death, the group *Ikenga*, which is normally called *Ikenga-Oha* or the associated suffix, as the case may be, exists as long as the community concerned exists.

One inherent character of both the *Ikenga* and *Ofo* is their tendency to always draw the Igbo toward their ancestral homeland. The *Ofo* is fundamentally a centripetal force which quite often draws the individual Igbo closer to his ancestral home. For instance, in most Igbo communities, any man who attains the status of *Okpala* but is sojourning somewhere outside his ancestral territory is traditionally required to return home and assume the headship of his lineage. The reason being that no other person can occupy the position while such a man lives.

In like manner, a man who sets out for a business adventure needs to return home periodically to give account of his successes and failures whichever is applicable, before his people. Thus, for a man who goes out in search of fame and wealth, it is traditionally imperative for him to engage in periodic homecoming, in what appears to be occasional stock-taking vis-à-vis the virility of his *Ikenga*.

For the Igbo man who goes out in search of fortune, therefore, his occasional home-coming is driven by the following reasons: Firstly, to assure his people as well as his *Ikenga* at home, of his survival in the course of his adventure. Secondly, he is expected to reappraise his successes and failures in a ceremony that leads him to occasionally propitiate his *Ikenga*. Thirdly, he is required to pay periodic homage to his *Okpala* (Head of his lineage and custodian of lineage *Ofo*) who acts as both the guardian of the home front and his link with his ancestors. It is therefore this desire to always keep in touch with one's ancestral home that explains why, in spite of their widely traveled character, the Igbo remain the most active yearly home returnees during occasions of either traditional festival or the modern Christian celebrations such as Easter, Christmas, and New Year.

From all indications therefore, while the *Ofo* emphasizes ancestral linkage, the *Ikenga*, although diametrically opposed to it, especially in matters of mode of status acquisition, complements it by creating alternative means of status acquisition, which lays more emphasis on personal ability. This readily accounts for the seemingly habitual Igbo tendency towards individualism, which in effect produces their characteristic culture of competitiveness, industry, and expansionism.

This is aided by the nature of Igbo socio-political organization which does not recognize classes based on right of birth. Rather it maintains that every freeborn has equal opportunities to attain the highest position in the community like any other person. If God grants you the privilege of long life you automatically become the head of your lineage by virtue of age. Similarly, if you work hard you can become a prominent member of the titled political class through the dint of hard work. From the point of adolescence the individual begins to bear his share of the responsibilities concerning the welfare of his community. These responsibilities which are allotted through the medium of age-grade system became de facto platforms for peer-group competitions and subsequent drive for achieved status.

Conclusion

Such has been the ideology which over the centuries molded the Igbo personality; a personality founded on individualism, go-getter spirit, and close kinship that radiate from the orbit of their characteristic open society. It therefore follows that if the Igbo are seen to be distinct in their struggles to achieve status in such areas as education, politics, business and the modern professional fields against the pace of their neighbors, it has little to do with population explosion or dearth of farmlands.

It is equally obvious that even the socio-political framework of the society cannot by itself provide the needed impetus for their inherent habitual enterprising drive. The force of Igbo spirit of enterprise is therefore deep and powerful, operating from within, and not merely the response to external factors.

It further explains the instinctive republican character of the Igbo, their individualistic orientation, and propensity to change and adapt to new situations without changing their basic primordial character.

In general, the traditional Igbo pattern of status acquisition, which invariably provides the impetus to economic adventurism, tends to maintain a balance between the right of primogeniture explained by the possession of the *Ofo* and the drive for achieved status which is guided by *Ikenga*.

Thus, while *Ofo* as a patrimonial instrument of authority represents continuity, the *Ikenga* on the other hand depicts change as a fundamental element of man's process of achieving his destiny on earth, through the dint of his personal efforts. This spiritual force further accounts for the inherent Igbo protestant spirit, their disdain for monarchical and authoritarian institutions, and subsequent tendency towards democratic principles.

From the foregoing, one can agree that open society is not an exclusive Western concept as generally believed. It is a concept primordially rooted in African society with its unique characteristics founded on the holistic foundation of the society, yet operating with a pattern of flexibility that provides ample allowance for change over time. In essence, the African idea of open society should be seen as a model for the reinterpretation of the concept in Western society.

Bibliography

Achebe, Chinua. 1969. *Things Fall Apart*. New York: Anchor Press.
Afigbo, A. E. 1986. *Ikenga: The State of our knowledge*. Owerri: Rada Publishing Company.
Basden, G. T. 1966. *Niger Ibos*. London: Frank Cass.
Boston, J. S. 1977. *Ikenga Figures among the Northwest Igbo and the Igala*. Lagos: Ethnographica.
Brown, Lawrence A., and Andrew R. Goezt. 1987. "Development Related Contextual Effects and Individual Attributes in Third World Migration Process: a Venezuela Example." *Demography* 24, 497–516.
Coleman, James S., 1958. *Nigeria: Background to Nationalism*. Los Angeles: University of California Press.
Horton, Robin. 1972. *Stateless Societies in the History of West Africa*. New York: Columbia University Press.
Ilogu, Edmund. 1974. *Christianity and Igbo Culture*. New York: Nok Publishers.
Jeffreys, M. D. W. 1954. "Ikenga: The Ibo Ram-headed God." *African Studies* 13, 25–40.
Lee, Everett S. 1966. "A Theory of Migration." *Demography* 3 (1), 47–57.
Levine, Robert A. 1966. *Dreams and Deeds Achievement Motivation in Nigeria*. London: The University of Chicago Press.
Niven, Sir Alex 1970. *The War of Nigeria Unity 1967–70*, edited by William Bascom and Melville Herskovits. London: University of London Press.
Ottenberg, Simon. 1959. "Igbo Receptivity to Change." In *Continuity and Change in Africa Culture*, edited by William Bascom and Melville Herskovits, 1. Chicago: The University of Chicago Press.
Popper, Karl. 2020. *The Open Society and Its Enemies*. Princeton, NJ: Princeton University Press.
Vansina, Jan, R. Mauny, and L.V. Thomas. (eds). 1964. *The Historian in Tropical Africa*. London: Oxford University Press.

13

IMAGINING THE FUTURE OF INTELLIGENCE IN OPEN SOCIETIES: VENTURING BEYOND SECRECY AND SCIENTIFIC PROPHECY AS TOTALITARIAN MODES OF MODERNITY

Anna Eva Grutza

"Who are we? Where do we come from? Where are we going? What are we waiting for? What awaits us?"—these are the questions with which Ernst Bloch ([1947] 1986, 3) introduces the reader to *The Principle of Hope*. They could not resonate more with a contemporary profound loss of certainty and security caused by a violent breakup of the current geopolitical world order. For Bloch, the future contains "what is feared and what is hoped for" (4). The human experience constantly oscillates between two poles: past and future, fear and hope. Bloch's answer to this human condition relates objectivity to subjectivity, openness to closeness, uncertainty to expectation, and determinacy to the process of becoming and a *venturing beyond* on the ground of a dialectic tendency inherent in history.

Equally, Karl Popper's critical approach to scientific inquiry encapsulates both, the indeterminacy of the future and the provisional status of all knowledge. Popper ([1945] 2013) was aware of the social aspects of the scientific method and culture, which stood model for his *open society*.[1] An *open society* resembles a scientific community due their common commitment to the search for truth. In Popper's view, the determinism particular for closed systems is destructive to the idea of creativity, the human ability to create something new. At the same time, Popper's ([1957] 1964) criticism of historicism—sweeping historical prophecies, which attempt to render the future world controllable on the ground of past trends—implies a judgment about historicists' poverty of imagination. An *open society* is a rational society when it is able not only to guarantee the plurality of ideas but to cope with this unstable and changing world, to which solutions and scientific theories always remain tentative and never complete.

While this chapter concentrates on the possible role of secrecy and intelligence *within* an open society like the United States, its overarching goal is a bolder one: it aspires to contribute to the research on *open society* in pointing out

---

1 To which extent this model rather refers to a closed system, see Newton-Smith (2000).

that reflecting upon and safeguarding the values of an *open society* requires to guide one's awareness and thinking into matters of futurity. The pivotal attribute of an *open society*—its openness—designates as well, and even constitutes, as its necessary condition an openness toward the future. The *open society* can be regarded as a vibrant, if not daring, idea and political and social project, whose members and decision-makers do not decide about their future solely on the ground of their past but who move and venture beyond both, past and present, toward the unknown and uncertain. In this sense, it requires citizens and scientists who are prepared and even aspire to be contradicted by reality in regard to their expectations, and who remain open toward encountering the *unforeseen, unintended, unpredictable,* and *unimagined* in what the future reveals. Therefore, this chapter revolves around the hypothesis that whether a society will develop toward a *closed* or an *open society* depends equally on how we approach the uncertainty, unpredictability, and openness, which, on a scientific, political, and social level, we face in regard to the future.

Intriguingly, in practice, the task of forecasting the future and the "taming of chance" (Hacking 1990) has been granted to social scientists and intelligence analysts alike. This asymmetrical because top-down sharing of responsibility and authority in the field has introduced one of the major contradictions within an *open society*. The secrecy and power of intelligence agencies has been interpreted as antithetical to the values of an *open society* and has, historically seen, often dramatically infringed the open culture of scientific practice and, in turn, of *open societies*. At the same time, as I would like to stress, intelligence agencies are one of those particular places within *open societies* that can inform us best about the errors and fallacies of scientific attempts to rationalize uncertainty and the future. As the apotheosis of an *empire of chance* (Gigerenzer et al. 1989), they are the institutions to be studied in order to test some of Popper's most important premises of his ideal of an *open society*.

Furthermore, although neither scientific nor social progress can be achieved if the free flow of ideas and information is jeopardized, this does not mean that intelligence analysts would not be part of the scientific community. They, too, assemble and interpret huge amounts of data employing scientific models and theories, but they do so, as this chapter claims, not to integrate uncertainty as a variable into their matrixes nor to use probability theories as a measurement of ignorance but to downplay, and hence to govern both, ignorance and uncertainty. As shall be shown in this chapter, the intelligence officer qua scientist approaches the realm of future uncertainty in ways that are, due to their rigid determinism, similarly at odds with Popper's ideal type of an *open society* and his definition of the responsibilities of the social scientist.

In addition, being the common denominator of both, the *open* as well the *closed society*, the work of secret services appears as particularly problematic for the former, while often constituting one major pillar of the latter. Secret services are situated at the very line between *closed* and *open societies* constantly endangering the latter to transform into the former. The questions to which this chapter tries to provide tentative answers are: What makes intelligence agencies oscillate toward the extreme of a closed and totalitarian model of society? What would allow them to perform an acceptable function in an *open society*? Next to the problems of power and secrecy, this chapter takes in particular a critical look at the collection and interpretation of data, which plays thereby a significant role. Thomas Richards (1993) notes in *The Imperial Archive* that data "has no inherent function and can just easily lend itself to open societies as closed ones" (73). Richards stresses the fragmented character of all information and its impossibility to be totally assembled. In our data sets, there always remains a gap of epistemic uncertainty, an inherent epistemic incompleteness. Trying to deal with this relative absence of data and knowledge, "probabilistic knowledge is loosened to incorporate assumptions about that which is merely possible" (Amoore 2013, 31). This chapter assumes that secret services tend to disguise this interpretative uncertainty, that is, that future actions and events are only "merely possible."

Finally, does this mean that secrecy and intelligence agencies are the clear enemies of an open society? While Popper himself remains remarkably silent in this respect, this chapter takes a more realist stance by treating intelligence—despite all the previous criticism—as a necessary evil of *open societies*. In line with the arguments of Edward Shils ([1956] 1996) that secrecy as part of security system "is an imperative imposed by the need of society to preserve itself and the values which it embodies" (208),[2] this chapter makes use of Popper's criticism of the historicists' striving for historical prophecies and prediction as a cornerstone for imagining the future of intelligence services within *open societies* by limiting their perils and recognizing and integrating their errors.

Information Wars: A Strategic Turn toward Radical Openness

In *Perception and Misperception in International Politics*, Robert Jervis (1976) departed from the criticism that US deterrence policies produced self-fulfilling prophecies. The unintended consequences of the Cold War security dilemma were, according to the critics, dangerous self-perpetuating misperceptions: "The United States misperceived the Soviet Union as aggressive and, by acting on this belief, led the Soviets in turn to view the United States as a grave threat" (xiii). For Jervis (2009), intelligence continues to be influenced by these processes of perception and purposeful deception. This dilemma has equally haunted the critical assessment of Russia's war plans against Ukraine in 2022.

On February 24, 2022, Russia decided to invade Ukraine after a period of indecision and military provocation. However, already on December 3 and 4, 2021, respectively, *The Washington Post* and *The New York Times* made public information that they had obtained by having been granted access to unclassified

---

2 In this respect, Shils's attitude toward secrecy resonates with more contemporary arguments like those of Pfahl-Traughber (2010).

US intelligence documents. Like Michael Crowley (2021), their colleague of *The New York Times*, Shane Harris and Paul Sonne (2021), both experts in US intelligence and national security, revealed in their article in *The Washington Post* that US intelligence had found the Kremlin was planning a "multi-front offensive as soon as early next year involving up to 175,000 troops, according to US officials and an intelligence document." According to US and Ukrainian officials and military analysts, Russia was preparing a large-scale invasion drawing on its strategy of the 2008 invasion of Georgia (Harris and Sonne 2021).

As much as intelligence might have failed in the past, the future proved these analysts and forecasters to be disastrously right this time. However, the Biden administration's tactic to deny the element of surprise to Russia was weakened through the prevailing uncertainty about Putin's real intentions, which resulted in a strategic limbo and divergent interpretations concerning Russia's "hybrid war."[3] Between early December 2021 and Russia's attack on February 24, 2022, the interpretation of Russia's military maneuvers at its border to Ukraine differed strongly among prominent experts and scientists. Burton Gerber, former chief of the CIA's Soviet section, for instance, was skeptical that Putin planned a big war. To Gerber's conviction, he was following an old-school playbook of strategic ambiguity: "A prolonged, slow-boil conflict that never quite boils over but keeps everyone guessing will eventually make them grow tired of doing so" (Weiss 2022).

In particular, Gerber worried that "America has publicized too much of what it knows—or thinks it knows—about Russia's war plans" (Weiss 2022). Under attack was the White House's information strategy to "leak" military plans and intelligence reports to the public (Lillis, Bertrand, and Atwood 2022). Respectively a former CIA officer showed himself concerned about the long-term credibility of US intelligence in regard to the amount of declassifications: "If it turns out to be wrong, or partially wrong, it undermines how much our partners trust the info we give them, or, frankly, how much the public trusts it" (Toosi 2022).

For Julian E. Barnes and Helene Cooper (2022), the White House was playing a highly unusual gambit: "the extraordinary series of disclosure—unfolding almost as quickly as information is collected and assessed—has amounted to one of the most aggressive releases of intelligence by the United States since the Cuban missile crisis." According to the authors, the Biden administration pursued thereby various goals ranging from the attempt to delay an invasion and winning time for diplomacy to disabling Russia to use any of its disinformation for possible justifications of war.

Although these newly adopted strategic revelations should allow the United States and the West to remain a step ahead regarding Moscow's information

---

3 For a definition of the term, see Galeotti (2019). Galeotti still believed that "the real threat to the West is not hybrid but political war . . . : achieve your objectives by aggressive and sometimes violent political operations that still stay below the true threshold of outright military action" (108).

warfare, this preemptive use of intelligence, as stressed by David E. Sanger (2022), a White House and national security correspondent, was certainly not without risk:

> But the disclosures also raised the issue of whether, in trying to disrupt Moscow's actions by revealing them in advance, the administration is deterring Russian action or spurring it on. ... Democracies are usually terrible at information warfare, and American officials insist there is a difference between what they are doing and the dark arts that Mr. Putin made famous.

The tactic of forecasting war could not only trigger unintended consequences like an actual provocation but reveal crucial information about the CIA's sources and, as the Ukrainian president, Volodymyr Zelensky, strongly worried, display and provoke an "unnecessary fear" (Barnes and Cooper 2022).

One might conclude that the problem of intelligence in an *open society* is neither simply a question about right or wrong forecasts nor about disclosing or keeping secret certain information. As shown, diverse actors worried that the disclosure might not only weaken the security services but prematurely provoke fear and uncertainty among the public or lead to a general distrust in regard to the reliability of the information obtained. It hints at what intelligence services rarely openly admit: intelligence data and interpretations thereof are prone to mistakes; sources are only to a certain degree fully reliable and, as it happened in the past, intelligence analysts may err with their forecasts; their results remain provisional. As a consequence, the solution to the problem of intelligence within an *open society* lies not simply in a radical opening and general accessibility of the output of intelligence.

Open Societies at the Crossroads of National and International Security

In general, openness and transparency are endangering the work of intelligence agencies. Their functioning within *open societies* appears to be a contradiction in terms. Democracies proclaiming to be *open societies* can find themselves in a systemic disadvantage when it comes to information warfare. One of the earliest accounts on this matter directly addressing the notion of *open society* is possibly Walter Laqueur's *A World of Secrets: The Uses and Limits of Intelligence*. For Laqueur (1985), the question of how "secret services function in free societies, and how well they *can* function, given the constraints of their own political and social frameworks" (201) remains less clear under conditions of openness.

These disadvantages concern equally inter-systemic ones. Already during the Second World War, the sharing of sensitive intelligence information among the Allies revealed further weaknesses of *open societies* in comparison to a *closed society* like the Soviet Union. For John Lewis Gaddis (1989), the "intelligence revolution" (191) had a decisive impact on the US Second World War strategies. Remarkably, the sharing of secret information among the allied forces—which from June 1941 included the Soviet Union—was unprecedented in scale. Retrospectively, this might come as a surprise, the more, as Moscow was clearly the great profiteer of this unusual exchange receiving a substantial amount of secret information.

This trust toward the Soviet Union remains even more puzzling given the fact that the Russians were grudging partners and displayed little willingness to submit to the rule of reciprocity. The result was that the Soviet Union was able to establish its own equivalents of US intelligence covert operations. After the war, this led to a strong disadvantage on the Anglo-American side to conduct covert operations within the Soviet Union or Eastern Europe. As they had to operate under a "double disability of having to penetrate a closed society at a time when their own internal security had been severely compromised" (199), their work could hardly be successful. As a consequence, during the first half-decade of the Cold War, the Soviet intelligence was superior to its Western counterparts mainly because of the Soviet Union's "'built-in' advantage of having relatively open societies as their target" (200).

Furthermore, as the sociologist and co-founder of the *Bulletin of Atomic Scientists* and *Minerva*,[4] Edward Shils ([1956] 1996), has analyzed in *The Torment of Secrecy*, the right equilibrium in American post-war political culture between privacy, secrecy, and publicity was highly fragile. Being a severe critic of the misuse of publicity by populist radicals of the McCarthy era, Shils warned that this equilibrium was strongly endangered by a new "irrational" dependency on both secrecy and publicity and their simultaneously political exploitation:

> The past decade has been the decade of the secret. Never before has the existence of life-controlling secrets been given so much publicity and never before have such exertions been made for the safeguarding of secrets. ... The United States has been committed to the principle of publicity since its origin. ... American culture has become "wide open" (36ff.)

In this sense, an excess of openness can likewise infringe the well-functioning of an *open society*. As argued by Gregory Kaebnick (2007), simply more openness does not necessarily lead to better results. At times and in certain domains, secrecy can serve an *open society* more than radical disclosure.

The form of openness incorporated in the "transparent man" is a further step toward the closed society. The pressure of "maximum loyalty" (214) through clearance practices for the sake of totally reliable guardians of secrecy weighed heavily on values like freedom and privacy. This delicate balance between

---

4 About Shils's involvement in the atomic scientists' movement and science policy, see Weinberg (1996).

secrecy, disclosure, and security concerns has reached new dimensions since the Second World War and the military-industrial complex surrounding the invention of the atomic bomb. Especially the latter, according to Shils, became a catalyst of a "pseudo-crisis," which was generated by fears of subversion, secretly working forces, and conspiracy theories. This crisis was even further deepened through a radicalized notion of publicity and secrecy deployed by what Shils called "populist radicals" and their "irrational hypersensitivity" (64) toward such possible threats.

However, the main point in getting back to *The Torment* lies especially in Shils's vision of science and society. It echoes Popper's philosophy of science and its relation to *open society*. For Shils, there exists a high affinity between science and the pluralistic society because the scientific method and the ethos of scientific research are based on a particular form of relationships among scientists, "which is the prototype of the free society. In a microcosm, the scientific community mirrors the larger free society. … The community of science is built around the free communication of ideas" (64). Scientists possess the authority of the judgment over falsehood and truthfulness of research results; their culture is guided by "observation and analysis freely made and freely communicated" (180) and is based on "a system of publicity far from the populistic tradition of publicity" (180). Finally, Shils differentiates between two types of secrecy: a symbolic and a functional one. The former he regards as part of populist dangerous war of fantasy fostering a "pseudo-crisis," the latter as an indispensable part for national security. The distinction between these two forms appears as a first necessary, though by far not sufficient, condition for defining a realm in which secrecy within open societies could function.

At the same time, Shils's view of the functioning of the scientific culture resonates strongly with Popper's (1947) severe criticism of the so-called *sociology of knowledge*, which Popper attacks in *The Open Society and Its Enemies* as a wrong doctrine: "Under the name of 'sociology of knowledge' or 'sociologism', this doctrine has been developed recently (especially by M. Scheler and K. Mannheim) as a theory of the social determination of scientific knowledge" (201). Popper rejected the premises of a sociology of knowledge because, in his eyes, it failed to account for the *"social aspects of knowledge"* (205), which Popper saw as being part and parcel of the scientific method. Like for Shils, for Popper the scientific attempt at reaching scientific objectivity could only become relative success not when a single individual tried to be "objective," but when many scientists decided to cooperate, communicate, and exchange their results. Scientific objectivity hence resulted from the "inter-subjectivity of scientific method" (205) and the "publicity of scientific method" (206); this means free public criticism, open expression of opinions in public, and the public character of the testing of observations and experiments.

These similarities between the two scholars are not a coincidence. In the 1940s, when Shils worked in London for the *Office for Strategic Services* (OSS), the precursor of the CIA, he became acquainted with prominent émigré intellectuals and a highly influential group of scholars, to whom belonged not only Michael Oakeshott, Michael Polanyi, or Isaiah Berlin but also Friedrich Hayek and Karl Popper who distanced themselves continuously from Karl Mannheim's arguments (Turner 1999, 131). Shils deepened these contacts with this circle of scholars further after his appointment as a reader in sociology at the London School of Economics (LSE) in 1946. It was precisely at LSE where both, Hayek and Popper, developed their "critique of Mannheimian planning" (Pooley 2007, 366).[5] According to Jefferson Pooley, Hayek, Popper, and Polanyi had a much more significant influence upon Shils's writing than has been ascribed to Oakeshott or Berlin.

Despite these contacts, there is little mention in Popper's work regarding the possibility and function of secrecy within open societies. The rare moments that Popper invokes the secret services like the Secret Police make it, however, clear that he regards them as an enemy of the open society—an enemy that he enumerates, alongside the Inquisition and gangsterism, as belonging to "the heroic age of tribalism" (Popper [1945] 2013, 189). For Popper, it is *tribalism* that enables the closed society to suppress reason and truth, and which Popper opposed to the *open society*. The lack of reference does not mean, however, that a parallel reading of Shils and Popper would not bring us a bit closer to a tentative solution in regard to intelligence agencies' work in the modern world. Their common idea of the social aspects of knowledge suggest that objectivity, whether in science or intelligence, can only be achieved through open communication and critical testing of research results. As shall be shown in the next part, in particular Popper's critic of prophecy and historicism can contribute in this respect, next to Shils's more direct answer, to a more nuanced understanding of the right scope of agency of secret services within *open societies*.

The Threat of Totalitarianism: Intelligence as Scientific Prophecy

The Yale historian Sherman Kent is often referred to as the father of intelligence analysis. Together with the Harvard historian William L. Langer, he founded the CIA's *Office of National Estimates* (ONE), which was designed as the heart of national intelligence operations:

> ONE was tasked with creating National Intelligence Estimates (NIEs) – the wide ranging [sic] strategic intelligence documents produced by the CIA for policymakers. Through his position, Kent established the basic theory of intelligence analysis that served the agency throughout the Cold War. Kent's intelligence theory and methodology revolved around the collection of the "basic-descriptive" facts and current

---

5 For a systematic comparison of Popper's and Hayek's work and mutual influences, see Hayes (2009).

events of a targeted state. From here, ONE would complete the process by producing a "speculative-evaluative" report on the possible actions of the state and deliver it to policymakers who would then act on it. (Bohland 2013, 17)

Despite this direct acknowledgment of the speculative side of this analytical intelligence work, Kent understood intelligence as scientific through and through. For him, intelligence followed a clear and systematic scientific method. It stemmed not only from a positivistic view of history but above all from the social sciences, which Kent situated closely to the method of the physical sciences. He defined intelligence as "high-level foreign positive intelligence" achieved through "unromantic open-and-above-board observation and research" (Kent 1965, 4) being a fruit of careful surveillance and *research operations*. Surveillance for him needed to be "vigorous and aggressive" (154) allowing to expose a maximum number of phenomena.

The research implied also the "finding of new leads—out of all of which emerges a proposition which seems the truest of all possible propositions. ... In wartime it produces the knowledge of the enemy strategic capacities, enemy specific vulnerabilities" (155). Hence, next to a descriptive form of information, the second form of information was concerned with the future, its possibilities and probabilities. The latter defined the very core of the National Intelligence Estimates (NIEs) produced by ONE. As Chester Cooper remarked in 1972, the "estimates are, by their very nature, a projection into the future: 'What will be the effect of …? What are probable developments in …? [...] What emerges reflects a mass of distilled information'" (Cooper 1972, 224).

Positivism remained at the heart of the early Cold War social sciences. Dominating their falsification and verification methods, it did neither stop at the threshold to the intelligence services. Already during the Second World War, social scientists became, like Shils at the OSS, involved in intelligence work (Backhouse and Fontaine 2010, 186). After the war, they aspired to free science from ideology by trying to attain the highest possible degree of objectivity. As a consequence, they increasingly relied upon positivism putting their trust in numbers and algorithms (Porter 1995). This tendency found its echo in the rise of decision and rational choice theory, game theory, and cybernetics, which were an attempt at de-ideologizing politics: "They seemed to offer nonideological languages of sovereign decision that eschewed the need for democratic decision-making" (Bessner and Guilhot 2019, 14). Against these aspirations, however, the numerical models rather reminded of a totalitarian mode of scientific modernity—a supreme "*Matrix* code of the West" (Abella 2008, 13)—that found its way into the realms of science, policy, security, and intelligence.

Trying to identify causal relationships in human behavior, the social sciences turned toward "a harder, analytical style that used quantitative methods to test hypotheses. They began to treat social systems much like physical systems—that is, subject to discoverable natural laws" (Scoblic 2018, 108). This newly emerging

Cold War rationality (Erickson et al. 2013) was based on models that tried to calculate the options available to a certain actor faced with a decision in a situation of high uncertainty. Nothing has become more of a target for Popper than the attempt if not to predict than at least to control change. This control through large-scale planning constitutes for Popper the actual threat to a democratic society; its actual totalitarian moment.

In *The Open Society and Its Enemies*, Popper ([1945] 2013) asks: "Is it within the power of any social science to make such sweeping predictions?" (xlii). His answer seems to be clear: it is not the task of the social sciences to announce long-term historical prophecies through an alleged discovery of historical laws. Still, in *The Poverty of Historicism*, Popper's ([1957] 1964) reflections are more nuanced: a scientific prediction is by far not a historical prophecy of the kind that Popper termed *historicist*. The important point about a scientific prediction is that, in order not to become *historicist in nature*, scientists should proceed deductively. Scientists should start from the problem and not the data before they test their theories against reality and public criticism (Popper [1957] 1964, 124).

Popper's fight against totalitarianism rested upon his rejection of induction as a scientific method and his quest for objective knowledge through deduction, which is based "on the belief that the prior probability of a law must equal zero" (Redman 1994, 68). The relation between scientific prophecy and totalitarianism has equally been raised by Hannah Arendt (1973):

> Totalitarian propaganda raised ideological scientificality and its technique of making statements in the form of predictions to a height of efficiency of method and absurdity of content because, demagogically speaking, there is hardly a better way to avoid discussion than by releasing an argument from the control of the present and by saying that only the future can reveal its merits. (346)

Arendt analyzed the connection between these scientific predictions and the rise of the masses "who hoped for the appearance of 'natural laws of historical development' which would eliminate the unpredictability of the individual's actions and behavior" (346).

At the same time, especially Marxists from the Frankfurt School started to address the "'totalitarian' effects of modernity" (Suny [2006] 2008, 28). The "blind capitulation to the 'facts' was a leitmotif of the Frankfurt School's critique of positivism. ... Positivism was criticized by critical theory both for its 'ahistorical appeal to raw facts' and for its 'construction of alleged laws from such data'" (Stockman 2021, 55). For Horkheimer, for instance, this process reduced "the objective basis of our insight to a chaos of uncoordinated data', culminating in the identification of 'scientific work' with 'the mere organization, classification, or computation of such data'" (54). Adorno and Horkheimer argued in their critique of the concept of Enlightenment that "mathematical procedure became a kind of ritual of thought" (Horkheimer and Adorno 2002, 19). They attacked

Enlightenment's "numerical totalitarianism" warning of the unintended consequences of replacing natural causes by rules and probability.

Leaving the so-called positivism debate here aside,[6] this authoritarian conception of reason, and the objection to the tyranny of reason and its rules, is only to a certain extent shared by Popper. For him, the "rational society" is not at all a totalitarian one but finally the goal to aim for: namely the *open society*—"a society that tolerates doubt, diversity of views and ways of life, and criticism, and sustains individual liberty, reasonableness, humanity, justice and democracy" (Maxwell 2017, 295). As argued by Nicholas Maxwell (2017), Popper's ideas about science and reason are crucial in this regard. Not only is imagination essential for the scientific method but as well reason "is at loss without imagination" (296). More importantly, a rational and open society necessitates plurality of ideas, the freedom to imagine and to criticize authority and dogma, whereby, however, the scientific method does not deliver "certainty, but rather uncertain progress, improvement, development, growth" (296f.), and degrees of increasing verisimilitude.

This does not mean, as already mentioned, that Popper remained uncritical of the methods of the social sciences. For Popper ([1969] 1976), all science or knowledge "does not start from perceptions or observations or the collection of data or facts, but its starts, rather from *problems*. ... This means that knowledge starts from the tension between knowledge and ignorance" (88). Furthermore, this means that, although some tentative solutions may be gained, this tension is never fully overcome; a certain epistemological uncertainty remains and is healthy for "rational societies." All justifications of knowledge can only be provisional, but, at the same time, "our tentative solutions cannot be shown to be probable (in any sense that satisfies the laws of the calculus of probability)" (90). Popper regards this method as the *critical approach*, which, in strict contrast to any estimation of the future, does not "begin by collecting statistical data, to proceed, next, by induction to generalizations and to the formation of theories" (90).

Conclusion

Facing a threat, political decision-makers and leaders need to rely upon intelligence in moments of distinct uncertainty, which, however, can demand from them highly consequential decisions, so that, as Jervis (1976) argues, "getting it right is crucial to them" (xvii). Intelligence, in turn, has been designed to serve exactly that goal.

However, while "uncertainty remains a prominent factor both on the battlefield and in international affairs" (Jackson 2010), the final output of intelligence analysis rarely discloses what cannot be known and what remains uncertain. Following a positivistic, probabilistic, and inductive approach to data,

---

6 See Adorno et al. (1976); Strubenhoff (2018).

intelligence services rather tend to "eliminate the uncertainty of opinion about how to weigh what information one has, and therefore, about what course of action to pursue" (Gigerenzer et al. 1989, 286). In the words of Louise Amoore (2013), while intelligence seeks to govern "possible futures" (5) by incorporating unknowability and profound uncertainty into urgent decision-making, "contemporary security practice works on and through the emptiness and the void of that which is missing: inferring across the elements, embracing uncertain futures … across the gaps of what can be known" (3).

The parallel strong recourse to positivism, inductive forms of inference through probability, and rational choice or game theory appears anachronistic. To a certain extent, it is an unreasonable step backward to a statistical calculus of the "eighteenth-century probabilists [who] took the conduct of prudent men as an index" (Daston 1988, 107) relying upon inductive inference.[7] In particular, as Gigerenzer et al. have shown (1989), the history of mathematical probability and statistics was often guided by an illusive attempt to escape judgment by probability statements, which facilitated a straightforward yes-no decision:

> Whereas probability once aimed to describe judgment, statistical inference now aims to replace it. … These expectations are fed by ignorance of the existence of alternative theories …, and above all by the hope of avoiding the oppressive responsibilities that every exercise of personal judgment entails. (288)

Among the most severe critics of this type of ignorance based on inductive inference was, as has been argued here, Karl Popper.

It must be remembered that Popper ([1935] 2002) did not reject probability statements as such but was highly concerned with them being "in principle *impervious to strict falsification*" (133) and searched for a new probability theory, through which "*a statement of ignorance … can be empirically tested and corroborated*" (138). This entails Popper's (1947) idea of falsification, namely that scientists should not look out for confirmation but for "facts which may refute the theory" (247). Predictions are only valuable and can be regarded as truly scientific if they have been exposed to unsuccessful attempts of falsification. At the same time, Popper repeatedly argued that social scientists need to study the unforeseen, unwanted, and "unintended repercussions" (90) of human actions. Like historians, social scientists need to recognize "the play of the contingent and the unforeseen" (346).

Moreover, at the core of Popper's critical rationalism is an attitude of intellectual openness that "everybody is liable to make mistakes" (224). This kind of rationalism implies tolerance and emerges, according to Katharina Thalmann (2019), as "the only antidote to authoritarianism and forms the basis of democratic societies" (42). Although no ultimate truth can be reached, for Popper,

---

7 See also Amoore (2013, 29–54).

the search for it necessitates the learning from trial and error, and therefore the criticism of others for the identification of mistakes. In regard to the question of governance and secrecy, one might want to follow Steve Fuller's (2018) suggestion that "fundamental to the governance of science as an 'open society' is the *right to be wrong*" (151), and one might want to add, speaking with Popper ([1969] 1976), that "the logic of knowledge has to discuss this tension between knowledge and ignorance" (88).

A truly scientific and acceptable functioning of intelligence services within an *open society* would make a new "intelligence revolution" imperative. Not only a change in method, like from induction to deduction, would be necessary but one concerning scientific ethics and a renewed culture of open communication, responsibility, accountability, and trust. Certainly, Popper's critical method as the method of trial and error poses particular challenges if one attempts to transfer it to the contemporary work of intelligence agencies. At the same time, as has been discussed, a radical openness of intelligence can strongly backfire.

Nevertheless, if the intelligence officer qua scientist is considered as part of the scientific community, which adheres to rules outlined by both, Shils and Popper, then finally nothing prevents those scientists to follow the same path of trial-and-error elimination through open communication and criticism. To avoid the risk of radical openness, a phased openness might be a partial, though still unsatisfactory, way out of the dilemma. The whole scientific community as the prototype of the *open society* could have a gatekeeping function over decision about intelligence disclosures. Members of scientific community might contest intelligence predictions prior to their public or political use. This privileged role of the scientist and expert in an *open society* would remain, of course, an unsolved riddle.

Bibliography

Abella, Alex. 2008. *Soldiers of Reason. The RAND Corporation and the Rise of the American Empire*. Orlando, Austin, New York, San Diego and London: Harcourt.

Adorno, Theodor W., Hans Albert, Ralf Dahrendorf, Jürgen Habermas, Harald Pilot, and Karl R. Popper, eds. [1969] 1976. *The Positivist Dispute in German Sociology*. London: Heinemann.

Amoore, Louise. 2013. *The Politics of Probability. Risk and Security beyond Probability*. Dunham, NC and London: Duke University Press.

Arendt, Hannah. [1951] 1973. *The Origins of Totalitarianism*. San Diego, New York and London: A Harvest Book.

Backhouse, Roger E., and Philippe Fontaine. 2010. *The History of the Social Sciences since 1945*. New York: Cambridge University Press.

Barnes, Julian E., and Helene Cooper. 2022. "U.S. Battles Putin by Disclosing His Next Possible Moves. Declassified Information is Part of a Campaign to Complicate What Officials Say are Russia's Plans to Invade Ukraine." *The New York Times*, February 12. Accessed April 14, 2022. https://www.nytimes.com/2022/02/12/us/politics/russia-information-putin-biden.html.

Bessner, Daniel, and Nicolas Guilhot, eds. 2019. *The Decisionist Imagination. Sovereignty, Social Science, and Democracy in the 20th Century*. New York and Oxford: Berghahn.

Bloch, Ernst. [1947] 1986. *The Principle of Hope*, Vol. 1. Translated by Neville Plaice, Stephen Plaice, and Paul Knight. Reprint ed. Cambridge, MA: The MIT Press.

Bohland, James. 2013. "The CIA's Past and Future." *Ex-Patt Magazine of Foreign Affairs* Fall: 17–18.

Cooper, Chester. 1972. "The CIA and Decision-Making." *Foreign Affairs* 50 (2): 223–36.

Crowley, Michael. 2021. "U.S. Intelligence Sees Russian Plan for Possible Ukraine Invasion." *The New York Times*, December 4. Accessed April 14, 2022. https://www.nytimes.com/2021/12/04/us/politics/russia-ukraine-biden.html.

Daston, Lorraine. 1988. *Classical Probability in the Enlightenment*. Princeton, NJ: Princeton University Press.

Erickson, Paul, Judy L. Klein, Lorraine Daston, Rebecca Lemov, Thomas Sturm, and Michael D. Gordin. 2013. *How Reason Almost Lost Its Mind*. Chicago, IL: The University of Chicago Press.

Fuller, Steve. 2018. *Post-Truth. Knowledge as Power Game*. New York: Anthem Press.

Gaddis, John Lewis. 1989. "Intelligence, Espionage, and Cold War Origins." *Diplomatic History* 13 (2): 191–212.

Galeotti, Mark. 2019. *Russian Political War. Moving Beyond the Hybrid*. London and New York: Routledge.

Gigerenzer, Gerd, Zeno Swijtink, Theodore Porter, Lorraine Daston, John Beatty, and Lorenz Krüger, 1989. *The Empire of Chance. How Probability changed Science and Everyday Life*. New York: Cambridge University Press.

Harris, Shane, and Paul Sonne. 2021. "Russia Planning Massive Military Offensive against Ukraine Involving 175,000 Troops, U.S. Intelligence Warns." *The Washington Post*, December 3. Accessed April 14, 2022. https://www.washingtonpost.com/national-security/russia-ukraine-invasion/2021/12/03/98a3760e-546b-11ec-8769-2f4ecdf7a2ad_story.html.

Hacking, Ian. 1990. *The Taming of Chance*. Cambridge and New York: Cambridge University Press.

Hayes, Calvin. 2009. *Popper, Hayek and the Open Society*. London and New York: Routledge.

Horkheimer, Max, and Theodor W. Adorno. 2002. *Dialectic of Enlightenment. Philosophical Fragments*. Stanford, CA: Stanford University Press.

Jackson, Peter. 2010. "On Uncertainty and the Limits of Intelligence." In *The Oxford Handbook of National Security Intelligence*, edited by Koch K. Johnson. Oxford University Press. https://www.oxfordhandbooks.com/view/10.1093/oxfordhb/9780195375886.001.0001/oxfordhb-9780195375886-e-0028?q=cognitive+constraints.

Jervis, Robert. 1976. *Perception and Misperception in International Politics*. Princeton, NJ and Oxford: Princeton University Press.

Jervis, Robert. 2009. "Intelligence, Counterintelligence, Perception, and Deception." In *Vaults, Mirrors and Masks. Rediscovering U.S. Counterintelligence*, edited by Jennifer E. Sims and Burton Gerber, 69–80. Washington, DC: Georgetown University Press.

Kaebnick, Gregory. 2007. "From the Editor: Secrets and Open Societies." *The Hastings Center Report* 37 (3): 2.

Kent, Sherman. 1965. *Strategic Intelligence for American Word Policy*. Hamden, CT: Archon Books.

Laqueur, Walter. 1985. *A world of Secrets: The Uses and Limits of Intelligence*. New York: Basic Books.
Lillis, Katie Bo, Natasha Bertrand, and Kylie Atwood, 2022. "How the Biden Administration is Aggressively Releasing Intelligence in an Attempt to Deter Russia." *CNN*, February 11. https://edition.cnn.com/2022/02/11/politics/biden-administration-russia-intelligence/index.html.
Maxwell, Nicholas. 2017. *Karl Popper, Science and Enlightenment*. London: UCL Press.
Newton-Smith, William Herbert. 2000. "Science and an Open Society. Is the Scientific Community a Genuinely Open One?" In *The Paradoxes of Unintended Consequences*, edited by Lord Dahrendorf, Yehuda Elkana, Aryeh Neier, William Newton-Smith, and István Rév, 337–50. Budapest: Central European University Press.
Pfahl-Traughber, Armin. 2010. "Analysekompetenz und Öffentlichkeitsarbeit des Verfassungsschutzes." In *Offener Demokratieschutz in einer offenen Gesellschaft*, edited by Thomas Grumke and Armin Pfauhl-Thraughber, 15–32. Leverkusen: Budrich Verlag.
Pooley, Jefferson. 2007. "Edward Shils' Turn against Karl Mannheim: The Central European Connection." *The American Sociologist* 38 (4): 364–82.
Popper, Karl. [1945] 2013. *The Open Society and Its Enemies*. New ed. Princeton, NJ: Princeton University Press.
Popper, Karl. 1947. *The Open Society and its Enemies. The High Tide of Prophecy: Hegel, Marx, and The Aftermath*. Vol II. London: George Routledge & Sons.
Popper, Karl. [1969] 1976. "The Logic of the Social Sciences." In *The Positivist Dispute in German Sociology*, edited by Adorno, Theodor W., Hans Albert, Ralf Dahrendorf, Jürgen Habermas, Harald Pilot, and Karl R. Popper, 87–104. London: Heinemann.
Popper, Karl. [1957] 1964. *The Poverty of Historicism*. New York and Evanston: Harper Torchbooks.
Popper, Karl. [1935] 2002. *The Logic of Scientific Discovery*. London and New York: Routledge.
Porter, Theodore M. 1995. *Trust in Numbers. The Pursuit of Objectivity in Science and Public Life*. Princeton, NJ: Princeton University Press.
Redman, Deborah A. 1994. "Karl Popper's Theory of Science and Econometrics." *Journal of Economic Issues* 28 (1): 67–99.
Richards, Thomas. 1993. *The Imperial Archive. Knowledge and the Fantasy of Empire*. London: Verso.
Sanger, David E. 2022. "Is Biden's Strategy With Putin Working, or Goading Moscow to War?" *The New York Times*, February 2. Accessed April 14, 2022. https://www.nytimes.com/2022/02/02/us/politics/biden-putin-strategy.html.
Scoblic, Peter. 2018. "Beacon and Warning: Sherman Kent, Scientific Hubris, and the CIA's Office of National Estimates." *Texas National Security Review* 1 (4): 98–117.
Shils, Edward. [1956] 1996. *The Torment of Secrecy. The Background and Consequences of American Security Policies*. Chicago: Elephant.
Stockman, James. 2021. "Pathologies of Reason in Computational Capitalism: A Speculative Diagnosis of Our Computational Worldview." In *Pathology Diagnosis and Social Research. New Applications and Explorations*, edited by Neal Harris, 47–72. Oxford: Palgrave Macmillan.
Strubenhoff, Marius. 2018. "The Positivism Dispute in German Sociology, 1954–1970." *History of European Ideas* 44 (2): 260–76.

Suny, Ronald. [2006] 2008. "Reading Russia and the Soviet Union in the Twentieth Century: How the 'West' Wrote its History of the USSR." In *The Cambridge History of Russia, Volume 3: The Twentieth Century*, edited by Ronald Grigor Suny, 5–64. New York: Cambridge University Press. https://doi.org/10.1017/CHOL9780521811446.

Thalmann, Katharina. 2019. *The Stigmatization of Conspiracy Theory Since the 1950s. 'A Plot to Make us Look Foolish'*. London and New York: Routledge.

Toosi, Nahal. 2022. "Spy World Wary as Biden Team Keeps Leaking Russia Intel." *Politico*, February 8. Accessed April 14, 2022. https://www.politico.com/news/2022/02/08/spy-world-biden-leaking-russia-intel-00006956.

Turner, Stephen. 1999. "The Significance of Shils." *Sociological Theory* 12 (2): 125–45.

Weinberg, Alvin M. 1996. "Edward Shils and the 'Governmentalisation' of Science." *Minerva* 34 (1): 39–43.

Weiss, Michael. 2022. "A CIA Cold Warrior on the Intelligence War Over Ukraine. Burton Gerber, former chief of the CIA's Soviet section, worries America has Publicized too Much of What it Knows – Or Thinks it Knows – About Russia's War Plans." *New Lines Magazine*, February 22. Accessed April 14, 2022. https://newlinesmag.com/reportage/a-cia-cold-warrior-on-the-intelligence-war-over-ukraine/.

14

OPEN SOCIETY IN CRISIS: MAKING SENSE OF PUBLIC HEALTH AND EXPERT ADVICE DURING COVID-19

Tarun Weeramanthri

> All people are intellectuals ... but not all people have in society the function of intellectuals.
>
> —*Gramsci (1971, 9)*

The Covid-19 global pandemic, now in its third year, has seen nation-states respond with a series of public health measures that have been based on expert advice, and had wide economic and societal impacts. No country has been spared from the virus and its effects. Borders have been closed, lockdowns instituted, and vaccines mandated. As such, the pandemic has acted as a stress test on the concept of an open society.

Public health is visible like never before, and decisions based on public health advice, or made by public health specialists, have been widely debated and contested in the public space. The strongest criticism has come from libertarian viewpoints, but such arguments are too simplistic, and fail to recognize that a balance is always needed between usual freedoms and necessary interventions in a time of crisis. A proper framework for how an open society should respond to a crisis must include not just the downsides but also the benefits of such public health actions, the place of science, the protection of vulnerable groups, and the full impact of not taking such measures.

A delicate, dynamic balancing act is necessary, and it is argued in this chapter that the principles, protocols, and practices that result need to be grounded in a new mix of public health, political philosophy, crisis management, and sociology of institutions (including scientific and public health institutions).

Knowledge needs to be generated rapidly for public health action in the midst of pandemic uncertainty. Such knowledge generation relies on experts and expert groups providing advice to government. However, over time the line between expert advice and political decision-making can become blurred. The advice is often then contested by other experts or public commentators, and public trust can be eroded. In an open society, there needs to be transparency not just of the final advice itself but of the whole structure and process of expert advice. These points are illustrated through consideration of Australian expert advice on border closures and lockdowns.

Written by a public health professional, this chapter will make a case that public health action should be precautionary but also balanced, proportionate, and transparent, and then highlight ways that it can be conducted that inspire public trust in an open society. It is this middle or meso-level of administrative actions (in either government or civil society) that links the big picture or macro-level societal levers (political and legal decisions) to the micro-level of policy implementation and ultimate outcomes. The design of this middle level, in which much public health practice is carried out, also allows for feedback from people with lived experience of the pandemic (the "public" of "public health"), which in turn can inform changes to big picture policy (a necessary element of flexible pandemic response).

This chapter will take as its starting point the "public health experience" and draw on the work of theorists from different disciplines to highlight what is at stake and how different interests can best be reconciled in a crisis,[1] so that citizens, experts, and institutions can remain true to the ideals of an open society and avoid pitfalls that come with governmental controls.

Considered in this light, the existential crisis that is Covid-19 is both a lens through which public health and philosophy can peer through and see other disciplines, and a mirror for self-reflection and fundamental reform.

Public Health in an Open Society

Karl Popper (1902–1994) is the philosopher most prominently associated with the concept of an open society (see also Soros 2010, 51–55). Ronald Levinson (quoted in Magee 1973, 93) has described an open society as "an association of free individuals respecting each other's rights within the framework of mutual protection supplied by the state, and achieving through the making of responsible rational decisions, a growing measure of humane and enlightened life."

I have written previously (pre-Covid) about the relationship between open society concepts, Popper's political philosophy, and the practice of public health, highlighting the dangers of authoritarianism and populism, the declining support for key institutions even within democracies, and the gathering implications for public health in the recent Trump and Brexit eras (Weeramanthri 2019). In that article, opposition to vaccination against polio and measles was linked to right-wing nationalism in countries as diverse as Indonesia (McKenna 2019) and

---

1 Labeling Covid-19 as a crisis is my starting point for this chapter. Badiou (2020) has labeled the pandemic "not particularly exceptional," and Roitman (2021) has pointed out the implications of a "crisis" framing. I think the widespread impacts of Covid-19 justify its labeling as a crisis and disagree that such a framing forecloses a discussion about the appropriateness of communicative practice.

Italy (Kennedy 2019), demonstrating that a political crisis can quickly become a public health crisis and vice versa.

The following question was also posed: Can public health and prevention only succeed in an open society? For this chapter, I will reframe the question to "How can public health contribute to an Open Society?" Attempting an answer means looking first more closely at what is meant by public health.

The most cited textbook definition of public health, at least among public health professionals, is that adopted by the World Health Organization, namely "the art and science of preventing disease, prolonging life and promoting health through organized efforts of society."[2] In my experience, this somewhat dry statement fails to excite the layperson seeking to understand public health. That such a definition is favored is consistent with the status of public health as a mostly invisible administrative act, that is mostly ignored and underfunded when working well, yet suddenly called upon in times of crisis.

Academic lawyer and ethicist, John Coggon, avoids such definitional issues and the essentialist dead end laid out by Popper.[3] Instead of asking "What is public health?" he asks "What makes health public?" with particular reference to the "scope of governmental public health in a liberal democracy" (Coggon 2012, ix). He argues that the practice of public health amounts to a series of *claims* that can be tested and outlines various faces or aspects of public health that account for its broad scope and complexity.

At its most basic, Coggon states that public health includes an emphasis on the health of the population as opposed to the individual, and is most often conducted and legitimated by government (including through education and legislation) via the actions of various professional groups. He adds that it has important communitarian features (the "public" in public health) meaning that health is shared, not simply a sum of individual benefits. Perhaps most importantly, he argues that public health carries an implicit political and normative claim that "the health of the people is the highest law." This can become problematic in times such as a pandemic when health has to be balanced against other public goods.

In terms of who can speak about public health, an expert can certainly state that she has a certain level of training in a discipline (such as epidemiology) that relates to the question at hand, or that she has been recognized as a public health practitioner by a learned college. However, Coggon argues that no one (not even such an "expert") can claim to "own" public health or speak on behalf of a unitary and untestable public health view. That does not mean that all views are equal, but it does mean that each view should be examinable.

For practical purposes, I favor a functional, short-hand description of public health in six key words, namely that public health aims to "promote health,

---

2 https://www.euro.who.int/en/health-topics/Health-systems/public-health-services
3 Popper argued against essentialist definitions of any kind (see *The Open Society and Its Enemies* 2002, 259–272).

prevent disease and manage risk." It is the risk management component, with all the complexity that entails,[4] that is so often underappreciated by politicians and the public, but which is essential for planning, preparedness and prevention, including against future pandemics.

History tells us that there have been crises before, and there will be crises again, and that learning is not guaranteed, even in the face of both recent and clearly foreseeable risk.[5] Historical experiences, including that of the 1918 influenza pandemic, in part create the expectations that in turn condition our attitudes to today's public health measures (Barry 2018).[6]

The emergence and spread of microorganisms are determined by biology and the mathematics of infectivity, as well as host and environmental factors, but effective control depends on the organization and consistency of the human response at a societal and local level. There are powerful social and economic determinants of health, and traditional public health strategies need to be attuned to these, so as to minimize any tendency to widen inequity and worsen outcomes for vulnerable groups.

As seen in the case study that follows, tailoring of the response can take place at a macro-level (e.g., provision of economic support) or at a micro-level that takes into account critical contingent factors (e.g., housing conditions for some low-income populations). The case study also highlights the importance of understanding both the changing aims, formalized or not, that have shaped the actions of governments everywhere in this crisis, as well as the administrative nuances of the expert processes that have underpinned the political decisions made.

Nothing threatens an open society (symbolically and practically) as much as the closing of borders; such closures are "instinctively" viewed by citizens as a harsh response by nation-states that threatens whatever one's view is of an open or ideal society and thus need to be justified accordingly.

Case Study of Covid-19 in Australia in 2020—A Stress Test for the Federation

Australia is an island-continent of 7.6 million km^2 and has a population of 26 million people. Since federation in 1901, the Commonwealth of Australia has consisted of nine main jurisdictions: six states, two territories, and the national

---

4 See, for example, Lupton (1999) for a sociological analysis of the emergence of the "risk society," with specific public health examples.
5 See, for example, the new preface (ix–xii) to Snowden (2020), where the author points to a "recurring pattern of societal amnesia" after outbreaks and quotes Nobel laureate Joshua Lederberg's argument that "in the contest between humans and microbes, the only defence humans possess is their wits."
6 In an afterword written after the 2009 flu pandemic, Barry reiterates the traditional view that closing borders would do little to slow the spread of influenza (456). This stance will need to be rethought given the effectiveness of border closures during the Covid-19 pandemic.

or Australian government. There are three levels of government—national, state or territory (hereafter referred to as "state"), and local government. Under the Constitution, the national government has responsibility for trade and commerce, international borders and quarantine, while health and public health services remain state responsibilities. Over time, a growing national government role in funding and regulation has effectively meant shared and overlapping responsibilities for health.

Covid-19 emerged in early 2020. Chinese authorities reported the identification of a new type of coronavirus on January 7, 2020. Australian Health Protection Principal Committee (AHPPC), the peak expert public health advisory body, comprised of chief health and medical officers (and other representatives and experts) from all jurisdictions, first discussed the matter on January 20, with frequent meetings thereafter.

The first case of Covid-19 in Australia in a returning traveler from Wuhan was confirmed on January 25. The World Health Organization declared the Covid-19 outbreak a Public Health Emergency of International Concern on January 30. Australia introduced international border restrictions on arrivals from China on February 1 and other selected countries from March 1; all international arrivals were required to self-isolate for fourteen days from 20 March.

The prime minister also announced the formation of a new governance mechanism on March 13, a National Cabinet that included political leaders from all states and the national government. States followed by enacting their own emergency powers legislation, either under emergency management or public health acts or both. Under such legislation, isolation and quarantine requirements were introduced, travel was restricted, and directions were given to limit non-essential business and community and sporting activities and to enhance social distancing. The exact measures differed from state to state, with the national government unable constitutionally to direct state decisions. Essentially, the new National Cabinet acted as a consultative and coordination mechanism in the federation, aiming for national consistency where desirable and where agreed.

In responding to the uncertainties of a new global pandemic, Australian politicians at all levels of government stated their desire to be driven in their decision-making by data, science and "the experts" (initially, and in the main, from public health and epidemiology). When National Cabinet was formed, AHPPC was elevated from its pre-Covid status and designated as a subcommittee.

In balancing health and economic costs, the clear and unified message was that the health response needed to be prioritized, and social and economic costs borne, so as to safeguard the health system, reduce transmission, and then return to some kind of normality as quickly as possible. The hard closure of the international border was reinforced by a National Cabinet decision on March 27 to require any returning citizens (who qualified for limited exemptions) to undergo fourteen days of hotel quarantine. As the economy contracted and businesses closed or laid off staff, the Australian government provided strong temporary financial support for workers and businesses.

Australia reached a thousand cases by March 23, 2020, with more than half imported from overseas or their direct contacts, and with seven deaths. An early major setback occurred in the state of New South Wales (NSW), where a failure in the public health risk assessment allowed disembarkation of passengers from the Ruby Princess cruise ship on March 19, prior to their Covid-19 test results being known, and contributed to over 700 cases and 28 deaths across the country over the next weeks and months.[7]

There were intense community and expert debates, common to all countries, about outbreak strategy (suppression vs. elimination), the need for business and school closures, mass gatherings, social distancing, and evidence for mask-wearing. By May 2020, the initial wave had subsided, the health services had capacity to spare, and Australia had every reason to believe that the measures taken had dealt with the health risk and that this would lead to a swift economic rebound. Though some borders, notably the West Australian border, remained closed, most other restrictions were being relaxed in a step-wise process, state by state. So effectively had transmission been suppressed, it was thought that elimination of the virus might be feasible.

Ironically, Victoria, the state that was most cautious in reopening after the first wave, was the site where a second and much larger wave of Covid-19 emerged. Case numbers started to rise in June 2020, and then rose rapidly in July and August, peaking at over 700 cases/day. This second wave originated from breaches in hotel quarantine of returned international travelers, with transmission into the community occurring quickly thereafter.[8] Contact tracing and outbreak management capacity was overwhelmed, and clusters appeared in health care and aged care settings, as well as households and worksites.

The state response to the second wave included restrictions of movements in selected Victorian suburbs, further movement restrictions across the whole of the state, mandating of mask-wearing, and finally a lockdown with night-time curfew in the metropolitan area. The Australian government provided a high level of support, including deploying thousands of Australian Defence Force personnel to Victoria.[9] The lengthy and restrictive lockdown in Melbourne, the second largest city in Australia, had major flow-on effects to all parts of Australia, as other states refused entry to residents of Victoria. Daily press conferences held by the political leaders and the chief health (or medical) officer in each state became mainstays, indeed rituals, of lockdown life.

There was a disproportionate effect on those most vulnerable in society, best illustrated by a sudden lockdown of public housing towers in Melbourne, accommodating a high proportion of low-income residents, many from non-English

---

7 See the Special Commission of Inquiry into the Ruby Princess (2020), available at https://www.rubyprincessinquiry.nsw.gov.au/report/.
8 See the COVID-19 Hotel Quarantine Inquiry (2020), available at https://www.quarantineinquiry.vic.gov.au/.
9 For a reflection on militarization of a public health response, prompted by the appointment of a general to head the National COVID-19 Vaccine Taskforce, see Anderson (2021).

speaking backgrounds. Though instigated for public health reasons, the impact on people's lives and livelihoods, mental as well as physical health, even in the short term, was substantial. Victoria constitutes 25% of the national economy, and the second wave derailed plans for a rapid national economic recovery. National GDP declined by 7% in the second quarter to June 2020.

This set of measures succeeded in controlling the second wave. Although the risk to other jurisdictions was reduced by internal border closures (used for the first time in more than 100 years), there was some spread of cases to other states including NSW and Queensland, which managed to contain outbreaks to low numbers of cases. By November 2020, Victoria had achieved complete suppression of community transmission with zero cases and zero deaths for twenty-eight consecutive days.

In effect, Covid-19 provided a stress test in 2020 for the Australian federation. Australia capitalized on its relative geographic isolation (which enhanced the effectiveness of its international border closure), economic standing, and the strengths of its health system. As at November 13, 2020, there had been 27,600 cases with 907 deaths. Australia's economic downturn was at the lower end of international comparisons, with a broad correlation between a country's success in controlling the virus and its success in protecting its economy.

However, the tensions first evident in the response in 2020 were heightened in Australia in 2021 as it experienced first Delta and then Omicron variant outbreaks. Though the different levels of government continued to cooperate in many areas, there was obvious tension in the federation over the rationale for border closures, the timing of border openings, the adequacy of the quarantine system, the speed of the vaccine rollout, the cessation of economic support, and other issues.

Expert committees, once lauded, came under fire from the prime minister in 2021, for their assessment of the risks and benefits of particular vaccines (Grattan 2021), and from academics and commentators for their lack of transparency. Even committee members shared their frustration publicly.[10] As in the UK, an independent expert group was formed to provide alternative consensus views to the public from that of the appointed expert committees.[11]

The National Cabinet process moved from uniformity and a common purpose in early 2020, to a grudging consensus at best later that year, and an outright blame game by 2021.[12]

Finally, in August 2021, the Federal Court, in its consideration of a freedom of information request, found that National Cabinet, despite its impressive name,

10 A committee member told a radio program: "It is a frustration of mine . . . We're all fighting the same enemy yet it feels like there are decisions being made without the basis for those decisions being entirely clear." See https://twitter.com/abcperth/status/1389022894970179585.
11 OzSAGE in Australia, Independent SAGE in UK.
12 See the frontpage "COVID Hotel Blame Game" in the *Sunday Times* April 25, 2021, reproduced at: https://www.croakey.org/airborne-transmission-of-covid-19-and-hotel-quarantine-lets-stop-going-round-in-circles/.

was not properly constituted so as to be considered part of Federal Cabinet, and therefore its documents were not protected from scrutiny. The wheels were coming loose on National Cabinet, formally and politically, though it has continued to meet up to the time of writing. The initial promise made in March 2020 of a "strong spirit of unity and cooperation" had not been sustained.

By early 2022, as the risk assessment changed, most of the country, with the exception of Western Australia, had abandoned strict suppression of transmission as a goal, with its associated public health control measures, in favor of just enough public health control measures to reduce demand on hospitals and intensive care units.

Such changes in policy became increasingly frequent and led to mixed messages from government to the public. Two years into the pandemic, public confidence and trust in government had declined substantially from the early months of 2020. Political leaders argued that the level of case numbers and deaths remained low by international comparisons. Notwithstanding this, and the fact that state and international borders were open by March 2022, many political commentators felt that the Australian federation had failed its stress test in part, as outcomes in vulnerable groups were much poorer, and Covid-19 continued to spread in a fractured national community.

A Libertarian Critique and Response

Governmental measures, such as the ones described above, have provoked a strong (mainly minority) reaction in many countries. In "The Open Society and Its New Enemies," philosopher Michael Esfeld (2021) plays on the title of Karl Popper's most famous work and offers a libertarian (my description, not his) critique of the societal (read governmental) response, suggesting that like after the Second World War, we stand "at a crossroads between the open society and totalitarianism" (no pagination). He asserts that challenges like Covid-19 or climate change are not unprecedented and have been mastered by societies in the past through "spontaneous adaptation of behaviour and technological innovation." The role of the state is, in his view, to protect fundamental rights, but not to direct society. The "new enemies" of an open society are those who "spotlight these challenges in such a way that they appear as existential crises" to justify an all-encompassing political strategy of "comprehensive control."

I find such an extreme critique unconvincing and unhelpful. In a restrained response, Christof Royer takes issue with Esfeld's interpretations of Popper's work, pointing out that nowhere in the original *Open Society and Its Enemies* "can be found an argument that freedom is an *absolute* value" (2021, no pagination). Royer criticizes Esfeld for an overreliance on the notion of dignity, a too simple reading of Popper, and for presenting a binary choice between freedom and totalitarianism. Royer stresses that the critical ethos in Popper's work, and therefore "at the very heart of the concept of Open Society," recognizes the "ambiguous character of human beings as well as the complex nature of the global problems we face today."

I would take this critique of Esfeld's article further. A global pandemic and climate change have not been made to "appear as existential crises" by the media and others, they *are* existential crises on any sensible reckoning. Philosophy and philosophers cannot simply wish away government or public health in favor of a society which, as Esfeld puts it, "gives people free rein to shape their social relations" (even as we live through a pandemic that has claimed millions of lives). Of course, there must be found a balancing point between government intervention and citizen's rights, but that is the case at all times for all interventions.

Public health practitioners are acutely aware of the need for such a balance, and modern public health law has multiple checks and balances, including rights of administrative review, that serve to safeguard individual rights. Historically, commercial forces (including tobacco, alcohol and gambling interests) frequently argue against any public health restrictions or regulations, by labeling government pejoratively as the "nanny state."[13] Such a rhetorical device is often effective and allows industry to maintain its own dominance and profits. Esfeld's article can be read as an extension of such "nanny state" views.

The point of government is not simply to find and justify a balancing of interests (citizen and commercial, health and economic), but to allow for that balance to be adjusted by its citizens over time. There are legitimate arguments for and against vaccine mandates, for example, but if the term "Open Society" is to have any meaning, both words need to do some work. Open cannot automatically mean "empty of intervention," otherwise society tends to anarchy.[14]

Royer's critique makes it clear that Popper's work and the "Open Society" concept is valuable as an entry into a "complex dialectic of openness and closure, inclusion and exclusion, and freedom and security." This seems preferable to reducing it to a calling card that could be misused by populist, right-wing libertarian movements, and the commercial forces that back them, as is possible if Esfeld's reading of Popper is accepted at face value.

Alternative Philosophical Lenses

So where else might we look for useful philosophical insights that might guide and inform expert advice and public health practice in the time of Covid-19?

Gramsci's well-known work on the Italian intelligentsia provides some fundamental (and cautionary) guardrails for experts in the political world.

---

13 See Moore et al. (2014) for a description of how industry uses fear and the "nanny as a threat to freedom" argument, and their alternative framing, based on the political philosophy of Philip Pettit, which stresses freedom from (commercial) dominance, as opposed to an individual's freedom from interference.
14 See, for example, Popper's "Statement about Serbia" in 1993 arguing for military intervention in the former Yugoslavia, in chapter 47 "Europe Now Exists" (Popper, 2012, 411–412).

His emphasis on the central role of politics, the possibility of domination by a hegemonic state, and the dangers of an expanding and unaccountable bureaucracy, have become widely acknowledged and indeed guarded against in liberal democracies (an outcome advocated for and welcomed by the full spectrum of libertarians and liberals).

But his broader "philosophy of praxis" approach has perhaps been less often realized (in practice), and his distinction between "intellectuals" and "functionaries" of the state should be read as a warning that experts can be subtly co-opted by the state in the service of "corporate hegemony."[15] This is a salutary warning for public health professionals, for whom the public sector is a major source of employment and underpins many a career in the administrative bureaucracy. Hence, their independence and ability to speak freely as a professional expert and/or public intellectual can potentially be constrained.

New work sheds some light on the social practices and decision-making processes of some of the leading public health figures in the Covid-19 crisis. MacAuley and colleagues (2022) have commenced an international study focused on the office of the chief health (or medical) officers in five countries, the office-holders, and "how different institutional and individual approaches impact what incumbents feel able to do, say and achieve."

When we stand back and reflect on the myriad, and sometimes contradictory, roles that experts and expert groups have been asked to play during Covid-19, it is unsurprising that they have found it hard to navigate at times and failed to meet some expectations (including their own[16]). If we stay with the group of chief health officers, who are the central figures in AHPPC, they have been asked to act simultaneously as senior administrators in government, statutory office-holders (responsible for far-reaching public health emergency legislation), members and chairs of expert committees, sources of independent advice, public spokespeople for government decisions, and commentators in the public domain. Quite a leap into visibility.

MacAuley and colleagues pose the question: "Can the same person who independently advises the government during non-crisis times also serve as its spokesperson without irrevocably straining the role and its public image?" They point to the contested nature of the roles and the trade-offs required as the office-holders try to do justice to their position as senior public servants as well as health professionals (thereby balancing "functionary" and "intellectual" roles as previously mentioned).

It is unsurprising in this context that many office-holders have focused on getting the technical part of the job done, up to and including dealing with the

---

15 See Hoare and Smith's introduction to Gramsci (1971, xxi–xxv) for a discussion of Gramsci's "philosophy of praxis," and the chapters "The Intellectuals" (3–23) and "On Bureaucracy" (185–190) of the same volume for Gramsci's explanation of the "intellectual-functionaries" distinction and other matters.
16 See the interview at: https://www.abc.net.au/news/2021-07-21/victoria-former-dcho-allen-cheng-on-covid-lockdowns/100310158.

media, but perhaps given less thought to the "communicative" aspects. The far-reaching work of Jürgen Habermas on communicative, as opposed to instrumental, rationality points to the dangers of such neglect, and is already being used as a basis for analysis of the Covid-19 response (see DeLanty 2020 and Verovšek 2022).

Boin and colleagues (2005), drawing lightly on Habermas's work, emphasize that threat, urgency, and deep uncertainty are common elements to any crisis and go on to define five leadership challenges or phases in crisis response. These are: (1) making sense of the crisis as it unfolds; (2) making decisions with limited information; (3) crafting the meaning of the crisis through political communication;[17] (4) terminating the crisis in the midst of blame and a desire for accountability; and (5) learning from the crisis (or not, as history shows). If this framework is applied to the Covid-19 crisis, the role of public health professionals (including chief health or medical officers as discussed above) becomes evident in each phase.

Lessons for Experts and Decision-Makers

So, if we acknowledge the difficulties in crisis management, what could politicians, public health professionals, and experts do differently?

The first is to acknowledge the difficulties when dealing with the public, particularly early on in a crisis. A four-part structure for government communication was used successfully in the 2009 H1N1 pandemic in Australia to "tell the public what we (the government) know, what we don't know, what we as government are doing, and what we're asking the public to do" (Weeramanthri et al 2010). It is the second part—this is what we don't know—that is most neglected but paradoxically is most important in building public trust.

The second is to dispense with the myth that politicians merely and simply "follow the health advice." That notion may have been a useful fiction at the beginning of the pandemic, but it has never actually been the case and should not be the case in a democracy. For example, in the case study provided, the decision by National Cabinet to introduce hotel quarantine was not based on health advice prior to the decision and not supported by AHPPC until some months afterwards.[18] We have also seen how chief health officers in Australia are not simply expert advisors but have a variety of potentially conflicting roles, including on key committees (e.g., AHPPC) that are themselves subcommittees of a political body (National Cabinet).

---

17 Luhmann's work on the real-world empirical basis of systems, resulting in dynamic meaning-making, and a society that is an "improbable result of contingent events" is relevant here (see Morgner and King, 2017).
18 See COVID-19 Hotel Quarantine Inquiry (2020), Final Report, volume 1, 102–104, available at https://www.quarantineinquiry.vic.gov.au/.

Obviously, in the midst of a pandemic, politicians should listen very carefully to the expert health advice, either from senior officials or an expert committee, but politicians must consider other factors and they remain accountable to the public for their decisions. Popper is again instructive in his warnings against a benign dictatorship of experts.[19]

Thirdly, and most obviously, transparency is critical to public trust, and data and expert advice that underpin crucial decisions should be released at the time of the decision. National Cabinet has come under frequent criticism for its lack of transparency, as have its expert committees. Contestability and transparency of advice should form part of the expert committee process, not be separate from it. Experts may well interpret the science differently from each other, but the splitting of experts into opposing camps, as happened in Australia, is unfortunate and avoidable.

Lastly, and less obviously, the structure and process of expert advice needs also to be more visible, and we must carefully dissect the interface between public servants, experts, expert committees, and elected politicians. This issue is often ignored when sociologists or political philosophers critique the administrative state as a whole, without distinguishing between its parts. But Covid-19 provides a wealth of empirical data, available in the public domain, that will shed light on such matters. Media and journalists should likewise focus more on asking how expert advice was arrived at, rather than simply asking experts to debate each other about various options.

The same interplay of technical and political issues that surface in the Australian case study is also evident at a global level and plays out in multilateral institutions like the World Health Organization (WHO), which is an expert technical body governed by its member states that also has normative, convening, and operational response roles.

For example, issues of global inequity are front and center when considering vaccine production, approval, distribution, and pricing. Overall, there has been insufficient global support for equity of access to vaccines, and pharmaceutical companies supported by some countries have not wanted to sign intellectual property waivers. WHO has sought to ensure fair access to vaccines and counter misinformation, but also to understand legitimate vaccine hesitancy. Vaccine mandates have sharpened preexisting social or cultural divisions in some countries, while opposition to mandates has played into populist agendas that are antithetical to an open society. WHO experts have been caught between these various agendas and come under fierce criticism even while trying to promote good science and policy and advocate for equitable access to vaccines for all countries.

Having arrived at this point, we can see the importance of a middle- or meso-level analysis to a comprehensive understanding of the Covid-19 response as a whole. It is not enough to simply point out the vulnerabilities of certain groups

---

19 Discussed, with respect to public health, in Weeramanthri (2019).

(for example, those from low-income backgrounds) or a profound inequity in outcomes, without such an analysis. Traditional disciplines (history, political philosophy, sociology) need to do their usual work on societal, structural, and social determinants of health and well-being, but this needs to be complemented by an analysis and detailed case studies of meso-level factors in the workings of government, commercial entities, and civil society institutions that mediate (either amplify or diminish) the effect of those factors on the outcomes that people experience.

We can ask the following with respect to border closures or lockdowns. What was the supporting technical or expert public health advice on which the decision was made? Who contributed to that advice and how? How were the needs of vulnerable groups taken into account? What else was considered, and how were all inputs weighed and balanced in the political process? And finally, can the measures be justified in an open society, and what safeguards have been put in place against potential overreach by the state?

Conclusion: Toward a More Open Society

Public health sits at multiple crossroads of science, evidence, policy, politics, and practice. They are difficult bedfellows in normal times, let alone in a pandemic. Boin and colleagues described specific phases in a complex crisis, and we can see public health involved in all of them, influencing and being influenced by a range of societal factors. Coggon reminded us that everyone has a stake in the contested space that is public health, and that it is not owned by any expert group. Tensions, contradictions, and trade-offs abound.

It is possible that open society enthusiasts (myself included) and theorists have relied too heavily on Popper when we look to understand public health through a lens of political philosophy. We may need to broaden the philosophical underpinnings of the concept and look to others. Perhaps too much emphasis has been placed on the points of difference between Popper and Habermas (see also Stokes 2016), for example, and too little on their shared defense of modernity (as an always incomplete but worthy project) and the value of free speech, open dialogue, and the criticizability of government in the democratic process.

Indeed, Habermas's distinction between system and lifeworld (1986), which are the counterparts of instrumental and communicative action previously mentioned, provides a useful conceptual framework to make sense of the Covid-19 response. The system side (power and money) is relatively easy to understand as including the administrative state and associated expertise. The lifeworld side includes the "public" part of "public health" and the more phenomenological aspects of professional life.

In a prolonged crisis like Covid-19, true communicative action and a strong civil society are potential remedies against "colonisation of the lifeworld" by the system. Government therefore needs to support or nurture spaces for civil society and the public to have meaningful input.[20] The lack of such spaces in Australia may partly explain why social media is on fire with criticism of governments and experts. This problem is deep-seated and will not be remedied quickly. Failures of communicative action are a recipe for political failure, and more importantly, lead to a decline in public trust, as seen in our case study. People can feel talked down to, colonized even. Such failure can then play into the hands of contemporary enemies of an open society, who use it as a justification to spread misinformation and entrench their power or commercial interests.

On a more mundane level, governments need to ensure that they deliver on the basics of transparency and accountability. Expert advice is never perfect, and risk assessments will change (especially as new variants arise), but transparency of data and reasoning from individual expert health committees will build trust amidst unavoidable uncertainty. That transparency should extend to the process and overall system of expert advice, and to its boundaries with political decision-making.

Though we must certainly guard against capture and misuse of the words "Open Society" by libertarians and others with populist agendas, is there any possibility of public health finding common ground with its critics? I believe there is if we agree there are dangers on both sides (not intervening vs. intervening), and that a balance is needed between governmental intervention and individual freedoms.

We may not be able to agree on where precisely that balance should lie, but we should be able to agree that any restrictive measures should be proportionate, time-limited,[21] and subject to review, and that the bar for effective communicative action must be set higher when government uses public health laws to mandate particular measures, particularly for disadvantaged or marginalized groups.[22]

We should remember that such laws are always made by nation-states within a specific governmental or constitutional context. In the case study presented, this was the Australian federation, and it is of note that Habermas presents his most recent views on the legitimacy of lockdown during Covid-19 with specific reference to the fundamental rights enshrined in the Basic Law of the Federal Republic of Germany (see Verovšek 2022).

In conclusion, this chapter suggests that the experience of public health during Covid-19 provides grounds and empirical data for scholars to explore further the continuing importance of a range of philosophers to the open society concept. Covid-19 is in many ways the most modern of morality tales, which

---

20 See Warren (1995) for a discussion of Habermas's emphasis on the importance of the "public sphere."
21 Agamben has colorfully highlighted the dangers of a "permanent state of exception"; see Silva and Higuera (2021).
22 Azmanova's "pandemic of precarity" describes the combination of massive economic insecurity with social vulnerability during the pandemic, features which she ascribes to the "constitutive logic" of contemporary capitalism in Biale et al. (2021).

should trigger self-reflection from all public health professionals and an opening up of the discipline beyond its roots in the biomedical establishment and toward an engagement with other disciplines, especially political philosophy and sociology. Covid-19 may even be of use to philosophers in further developing a philosophy of praxis, first as a lens through which to view rich empirical data and second as a mirror to assess the utility of one's favored theories and their applicability to a crisis.

Bibliography

Anderson, Warwick. 2021. "When the General Calls: Military Tactics Against COVID-19 in Australia." *Arena Quarterly*, December. https://arena.org.au/when-the-general-calls-military-tactics-against-covid-19-in-australia/.

Badiou, Alain. 2020. "On the Epidemic Situation [blog]." *Verso*, March 23. https://www.versobooks.com/blogs/4608-on-the-epidemic-situation.

Barry, John M. 2018. *The Great Influenza: The Epic Story of the Deadliest Pandemic in History*. New York: Penguin Books.

Biale, E., M. Stein, C. Vergara, B. McKean, and A. Azmanova. 2021. "Regaining Control over Precarity." *Contemporary Political Theory*, June 29: 1–27. https://doi.org/10.1057/s41296-021-00503-y.

Boin, A., P. t' Hart, E. Stern, and B. Sundelius. 2005. *The Politics of Crisis Management: Public Leadership Under Pressure*. Cambridge: Cambridge University Press.

Coggon, John. 2012. *What Makes Health Public? A Critical Evaluation of Moral, Legal and Political Claims in Public Health*. Cambridge: Cambridge University Press.

DeLanty, Gerard. 2020. *Six Political Philosophies in Search of a Virus: Critical Perspectives on the Coronavirus Pandemic*. LSE 'Europe in Question' Discussion Paper Series. LEQS Paper No. 156/2020, May. https://www.lse.ac.uk/european-institute/Assets/Documents/LEQS-Discussion-Papers/LEQSPaper156.pdf.

Esfeld, Michael. 2021. "The Open Society and Its New Enemies." *Euroscientist*, April. https://www.europeanscientist.com/en/features/the-open-society-and-its-new-enemies/.

Gramsci, Antonio. 1971. *Selections from the Prison Notebooks*. Edited by Quintin Hoare and Geoffrey Nowell Smith. London: Lawrence and Wishart Ltd.

Grattan, Michelle. 2021. "Scott Morrison's Attempt to Influence ATAGI Advice on AstraZeneca Vaccine is Misguided." July 2021. https://www.abc.net.au/news/2021-07-23/scott-morrison-atagi-vaccine-advice-astrazeneca/100316092.

Habermas, Jürgen. 1986. *The Theory of Communicative Action: Reason and the Rationalization of Society*. Cambridge: Polity Press.

Kennedy, Jonathan. 2019. "How Populists Spread Vaccine Fear." *Politico*. https://www.politico.eu/article/how-populists-spread-vaccine-fear/.

Lupton, Deborah. 1999. *Risk*. London: Routledge.

MacAulay M., Macintyre A., Yashadhana A., et al. 2022. "Under the Spotlight: Understanding the Role of the Chief Medical Officer in a Pandemic." *Journal of Epidemiology and Community Health* 76: 100–04.

Magee, Bryan.1973. *Popper*. Glasgow: Fontana.

McKenna, Maryn. 2019. "How the Rise of Right-Wing Nationalism is Jeopardizing the World's Health." *The New Republic*. https://newrepublic.com/article/153264/rise-right-wing-nationalism-jeopardizing-world-health.

Moore, M., H. Yeatman, and R. Davey. 2015. "Which Nanny – The State or Industry? Wowsers, Teetotallers and the Fun Police in Public Health Advocacy." *Public Health* 129 (8): 1030–37.
Morgner, C., and M. King. 2017. "Niklas Luhmann's Sociological Enlightenment and its Realization in *Trust* and *Power.*" In *Trust and Power*, edited by N. Luhmann, vii–xxiv. Cambridge: Polity Press.
Popper, Karl. 2002. *The Open Society and its Enemies*. Suffolk: Routledge & Kegan Paul Ltd.
Popper, Karl. 2012. *After the Open Society: Selected Social and Political Writings*. ed.ited by Jeremy Shearmur and Piers Norris Turner. Oxford: Routledge.
Roitman, Janet. 2021. "Framing the Crisis: COVID-19." *Arena Online*, November 12. https://arena.org.au/framing-the-crisis-covid-19/.
Royer, Christof. 2021. "The Critical Ethos of the Open Society: A Reply to Esfeld." *Euroscientist*. November 9. https://www.euroscientist.com/the-critical-ethos-of-the-open-society-a-reply-to-esfeld-1/.
Silva, D., G. Andrés, and C. Higuera. 2021. "Political Theology and COVID-19: Agamben's Critique of Science as a New 'Pandemic Religion'." *Open Theology* 7 (1): 501–13. https://doi.org/10.1515/opth-2020-0177.
Snowden, Frank M. 2020. *Epidemics and Society: From the Black Death to the Present*. New Haven: Yale University Press.
Soros, George. 2010. *The Soros Lectures at the Central European University*. New York: Public Affairs.
Stokes, Geoffrey. 2016. "Popper and Habermas: Convergent Arguments for a Postmetaphysical Universalism." In *The Cambridge Companion to Popper*, edited by Jeremy Shearmur and Geoffrey Stokes, 318–51. Cambridge: Cambridge University Press.
Verovšek, Peter. 2022. "Habermas on the Legitimacy of Lockdown." *Eurozine*, February 14. https://www.eurozine.com/habermas-on-the-legitimacy-of-lockdown/.
Warren, Mark. 1995. "The Self in Discursive Democracy." In *The Cambridge Companion to Habermas*, edited by Stephen White, 167–200. Cambridge: Cambridge University Press.
Weeramanthri, T. S. 2019. "Public Health in an Open Society: How Society and Language Shape Prevention (Gordon Oration)." *Australian and New Zealand Journal of Public Health* 43 (6): 510–15. https://doi.org/10.1111/1753-6405.12940.
Weeramanthri, T. S., A. Robertson, G. Dowse, et al. 2010. "Response to Pandemic (H1N1) 2009 Influenza in Australia: Lessons from a State Health Department Perspective." *Australian Health Review* 34: 477–86. https://doi.org/10.1071/AH10901.

List of Contributors

Rachid Boutayeb is Assistant Professor of Social Philosophy and Ethics at the Doha Institute for Graduate Studies. He worked as Lecturer in the disciplines of philosophy, anthropology, and Islamic studies at several German universities. He has written numerous research papers related to the ethics and social philosophy of migration. Most recently he published in German: *Tristesse oblige. Eine kleine Philosophie der Nachbarschaft* (Alibri, 2022).

Kenneth Ka-Lok Chan is Associate Professor at the Department of Government and International Studies and Director of the Comparative Governance and Policy Research Centre at Hong Kong Baptist University. His research interest includes European integration, communist and postcommunist politics, electoral integrity, as well as government and politics of Hong Kong. His work has been published in *Europe-Asia Studies, West European Politics, Electoral Studies, Central European Political Science Review, European Journal of East Asian Studies*, and *Asia-Europe Journal* and in edited books. He has held visiting positions at the University of Warsaw, Gdansk University, the University of Macau, and Sciences Po Bordeaux and has given papers on EU–China and EU–Hong Kong relations across the EU. He was an elected member of the Hong Kong Legislative Council during 2012–2016.

Gazela Pudar Draško is a political sociologist and Director of the Institute for Philosophy and Social Theory, University of Belgrade. Currently, she is engaged in the Volkswagen Stiftung-sponsored project "Cultures of Rejections in Europe" and Horizons 2020 project "Enlightened trust: An examination of trust and distrust in governance – conditions, effects and remedies." She serves as an Executive Board Member of the Institute for Democratic Engagement Southeast Europe (IDESE) and Coordinating Board Member of the Network for Academic Solidarity and Engagement (MASA). She writes on intellectual engagement, social movements, and gender.

Katalin Fábián is Professor of Government and Law at Lafayette College, Easton, PA. Her book *Contemporary Women's Movements in Hungary: Globalization, Democracy, and Gender Equality* (2009) analyzes the emergence and political significance of women's activism in Hungary. She contributed chapters to and edited *Globalization: Perspectives from Central and Eastern Europe* (2007) and *Domestic Violence in Postcommunist States: Local Activism, National Policies, and Global Forces* (2010). Her most recent publication is *The Routledge Handbook of Gender in Central-Eastern Europe and Eurasia* (2021), edited with Janet Elise Johnson and Mara Lazda.

Jean-Louis Fabiani is Professor of Sociology at the Central European University. Born in 1951 in Algiers (Algeria), he studied at Ecole normale supérieure and received his PhD in 1980 from École des hautes études en sciences sociales (EHESS) (Paris). From 1980 to 1988, he was agrégé-répétiteur and then maître-assistant at the Department of Social Sciences at Ecole normale supérieure. In 1988 he moved to the administration of culture, being appointed as Director of Cultural Affairs in Corsica. He went back to the academic world in 1991 when he joined EHESS, first in Marseille, and then in Paris in 2002. He is the author of twelve personal books. He was the Chairman of the board of the Mediterranean Youth Orchestra from 1998 to 2014.

Anna Grutza is currently an Open Society University Network (OSUN) Doctoral Fellow at the Democracy Institute and a PhD Candidate in Comparative History at Central European University where she works on her thesis "Imperial Laboratories of Governance in Disguise: Seeing Through the Grid of Cold War Information Analysis." In general, she is interested in the intersection of the history of the Cold War social science, the history of ignorance, social history, and the history of emotions. Her particular focus meanwhile lies on Cold War truth regimes, epistemologies, and enemy and affect cultures, especially in relation to propaganda and mass communication research as well as surveillance practices.

Predrag Krstić is Research Associate at the Institute for Philosophy and Social Theory, University of Belgrade, and PhD Professor at the Faculty of Media and Communications, Singidunum University, Belgrade. He specializes in critical theory, modern theory of the subject, philosophical anthropology, philosophy of Enlightenment, and philosophy of education. In addition to fourteen books and numerous articles, monographic studies, and editorial contributions in academic publications, he is also the author of one novel and two books of poetry.

Gregory Joseph Lobo teaches in the Departamento de Lenguas y Cultura at the Universidad de los Andes in Bogotá, Colombia. Much of his work focuses on language and power, and most specifically, on the nation. His research has been published in *Cultural Studies*, the *International Journal of Cultural Studies*, the *Revista de Estudios Sociales*, de *Revista de Estudios Colombianos*, the *Journal of Language and Politics*, and *Philosophy of the Social Sciences*, and other well-regarded journals. His current project seeks to understand identification as arising out of an ontological difficulty afflicting *homo sapiens*, with the hope that it will contribute to transcending current polarization.

List of Contributors

Liviu Matei is currently Head of the School of Education, Communication and Society at King's College London. Prior to joining King's College in March 2022, he was Professor of Higher Education Policy at Central European University (CEU), where he directed the Yehuda Elkana Center for Higher Education, a collaborative academic initiative promoting applied policy research and professional training in higher education.

Nwankwo Tony Nwaezeigwe is Senior Research Fellow at the Institute of African Studies at the University of Nigeria. He is a native of Ibusa, in Oshimili North Local Government Area of Delta State. He received his PhD in 2003 from the University of Nigeria, Nsukka.

Christof Royer, who holds a PhD from the University of St Andrews, is Assistant Professor of International Relations and Political Theory at Forward College (Paris) and the program leader of the 'Open Society Research Platform' at Central European University. In 2020, he published his first book *Evil as a Crime Against Humanity: Confronting Mass Atrocities in a Plural World*. He is currently working on a book that examines the question of limits to diversity and plurality in radical democratic theory and practice.

Thom Scott-Phillips is Ikerbasque Research Associate in Cognitive Science and Philosophy, at the University of the Basque Country. He has previously held research positions in Cognitive Science (CEU), Anthropology (Durham), and Linguistics (Edinburgh). He has authored many research papers linking evolutionary, cognitive, behavioral, and cultural levels of analysis, with a particular focus on communication and culture. His first book, *Speaking Our Minds*, about the evolutionary origins of human communication, was published in 2015.

Lubomir Terziev has taught British literature of the eighteenth century and romanticism, and creative writing at Sofia University's Department of English and American Studies for twenty years. Since 2016, he has been a full-time professor of Writing and Literature at American University in Bulgaria. His research is focused on the correlation between politics and esthetics in Romantic literature as well as on issues concerning literary education. Terziev is currently working on a monograph entitled *Subject and Event in William Blake's Poetry*.

Andrea Timár (PhD, Habil.) is Associate Professor of English Literature and Literary Theory at Eötvös Loránd University, Budapest, Hungary, where she is also the director of the Modern English and American Literature and Culture Doctoral Program. In 2019/2020, she was Senior Research Fellow at the Institute for Advanced Studies, Central European University. Her first monograph was A *Modern Coleridge. Cultivation, Addiction, Habits* (Palgrave Macmillan, 2015, paperback: 2017). Her recent publications include "Dehumanization in Literature and the Figure of the Perpetrator" (in *The Routledge Handbook of*

Dehumanization, 2020), and "Against Compassion: Post-traumatic Stories in Arendt, Benjamin, Melville, and Coleridge" (*Arendt Studies* 2022/6).

Piers Norris Turner is Associate Professor of Philosophy and Director of the Center for Ethics and Human Values at The Ohio State University (Columbus, Ohio, USA). His articles on the history of liberal theory, especially in the work of John Stuart Mill, have appeared in leading journals including *Ethics* and the *Journal of the History of Philosophy*. He is also Co-editor of a volume of Karl Popper's previously unpublished and uncollected political writings, *After the Open Society* (with Jeremy Shearmur; Routledge, 2008).

Tarun Weeramanthri is President of Public Health Association of Australia and Adjunct Professor at the University of Western Australia. He is a trained specialist in internal medicine and public health, and has a PhD in social medicine. He has extensive experience in disaster and emergency preparedness and response, and seeks to apply insights from political philosophy to reframe public health responses to complex societal challenges and crises.

Avery White received a PhD in Political Science from Ohio State University in 2019, with a dissertation entitled "An Open Society: Robert Nozick's Utopian Project." Avery also received a JD from Yale Law School in 2013. His research interests include libertarianism, utopian projects, the political implications of virtuality, the nature of guilt and responsibility, and the practical role of philosophy in daily life.

Index

9/11, 14

abortion, 121–23
abstractness, 46
abstract potential threat, 53
Achebe, Chinua, 165, 169
acquis communautaire, 121
ADF International, 123
Adorno, Theodor W., 38, 66, 183
adversarial systems, 25
aesthetic judgments, 98–101
"affect alien," 159–60
African societies, 162, 163, 167, 173. *See also* Igbo of Nigeria
Agamben, Giorgio, 15
Ahmed, Sara, 159
Akalaka (Destiny), 170
Alliance Defending Freedom (ADF), 123, 123n3
Althusser, Louis, 50
AmCham event, 138
Amoore, Louise, 185
Anarchy, State, and Utopia (Nozick), 83, 85
animal body, 50
animalism, 51n3
animality, 51, 52
anthropology, 32, 108; concepts, 109; French, 109
anti-colonialism, 127
anti-discrimination law, 121
anti-European Union, 118
Anti-Extradition Bill Movement, 140
Anti-Extradition Bill Movement: People's Public Sentiment Report, 140
anti-genderism, 118–20
anti-government movement (2019), 139
anti-Igbo riots, 163
anti-immigration, 118
anti-intellectualist orientation, 110

anti-national security law movement (2003), 139
anti-Semitism, 105
anti-sorosoids, 148, 151, 152, 159, 160
antitrust laws, 92
anxiety, 53
Apostolov, Vassil, 158
Arab Islam, 44, 45
Arendt, Hannah, 17, 57, 94, 98–100, 102, 103, 183; "The Crisis in Culture," 94; discussion of culture, 101; *The Human Condition*, 95; literature and classroom, 95–97; *The Origins of Totalitarianism*, 94; "Truth and Politics," 94
argumentation, 25
art and taste, 97–99
artificial intelligence, 2, 3, 56
artworks, 96, 97, 99
Asian Development Bank, 134
association, 85–87, 90–92
atheism, 77
atomization, 41
Atran, Scott, 55, 56
Australia, 191, 197, 200, 201, 203. *See also* Covid-19 pandemic; public health
Australian Defence Force, 195
Australian Health Protection Principal Committee (AHPPC), 194, 199, 200
authoritarianism, 10–11, 78, 104, 139, 191
Autocratic Functionalism, 11, 133, 136–38, 140, 142
autocratization, 133, 142

Bakhti, Mikhail, 103n9
bankruptcy of values, 106–8
"Baptist-burqa" network, 125
Barnes, Julian E., 177
Basden, G. T., 171
Basic Law, 132, 134, 137–38; Article 39, 134; of Federal Republic of Germany, 203

Beck, Ulrich, 112, 134
Beijing, 132, 133, 135–38, 141, 142
Belt and Road Initiative (BRI), 137
Benedict XVI, 120
Bergson, Henri, 4–7, 23, 105–13
Berlin, Isaiah, 181
Bessette, Joseph M., 59
Biden administration, 177
Bloch, Ernst, 174
Blutgemeinschaft, 42
Boin, A., 200
Bourassa, Alan, 154, 155
Bovens, Mark, 10
brain, 53
Brexit, 9, 191
Brown, Lawrence A., 164
Bulgarian Socialist Party, 148–49
Bulletin of Atomic Scientists and *Minerva*, 179
Butler, Samuel, 77

Camus, Albert, 113
capitalism, 1, 40, 43, 46, 65
Cartesianism, 24, 29
Catholic Church, 124
Central and Eastern European anti-gender movements, 11–12, 117–19, 128; EU integration, feminism and liberalism, 121–24; foreign policy, 124–26; relationship to globalization, 119–21; significance in, 126–27
Central Committee, of Bulgarian Communist Party, 151, 152
Central Intelligence Agency (CIA), 177, 178, 180, 181
Central Military Commission, 137
Central People's Government, 137
Chamoiseau, Patrick, 41
charismatic domination, 110, 111
Charlie Hebdo, 153
Chi (Personal Guardian Spirit), 170
China, 1, 194; Hong Kong's relations with, 132–38, 141
Chinese Communist regime, 135
Christian Democratic People's Party (*Kereszténydemokrata Néppárt*, KDNP), 117
Christian family, 149
Christianity, 105, 106, 152
"Christian women against Femen" (Facebook page), 119
Chukwu-Okike (God the Creator), 167, 170

churches, 111, 120, 123
CitizenGO, 121, 125
citizens diplomacy, 140
civilization, 62, 105–6, 108, 121
civilizing process, 105
civil peace, 76, 77
civil religion, 112
civil rights movement, 75
civil society, 11, 27, 135, 139, 142, 202–3
climate emergency, 113
closed morality, 110, 112
closed society, 4–10, 46, 48–50, 61, 105, 106, 108, 110, 112, 175
Coetzee, J. M., 102, 103
Coggon, John, 192
cognitive capacities, 26, 28
cognitive science, 3, 25, 32
cognitivist approaches, 59
coldness, 13, 38, 39, 41, 44, 46
Cold War, 125, 179; rationality, 183; security dilemma, 176
Coleman, James S., 163
collectivism, 49, 51, 54–56
color revolution, 156
Coman, Adrian, 124
communal life, 63
communism, 38, 74, 91
The Communist Manifesto (Marx and Engels), 38
community and society, 39–40, 44, 46
compassion, 100–102
conceptualized rights, 124
Conference of Bishops, Slovakia (2013), 119
confirmation bias, 24, 66
conscious fear, 52
consciousness, 52, 110
conservatism/conservatives, 33, 113, 120, 122, 125–27
conservative Christian networks, 125
conservative-nationalist political parties/politicians, 117, 122, 126, 128
Conservative Youth Club, 149
conspiracy theory, 29
conversations, 26–28
Cooper, Chester, 182
Cooper, Helene, 177
corporate hegemony, 199
Covid-19 pandemic, 2, 15, 161, 190, 202–4; expert advice, groups and decision-makers in, 190, 199–202; lockdown, 190, 191, 195, 202, 203;

stress test for Australia, 193–97. *See also* public health
"The Crisis in Culture" (Arendt), 94
crisis management, 190, 200
critical discussion, 49, 61, 72
critical rationalism, 6, 7, 9, 61–64, 67, 68, 73, 76, 77, 185
critical thinking, 103, 160
The Critique of Aesthetic Judgment (Kant), 94, 97
Croatia, 119
Crowley, Michael, 177
culture, 120; codes, 54; crisis, 121; pluralism, 46; wars, 125, 128

de Biran, Maine, 108
decision-making, 24, 29, 32, 33, 64; collective/group, 25, 28, 34, 72; legal, 25; political, 59, 190; process, 67, 199
decolonization, 113
defensive behaviors, 52, 53
Defoe, Daniel, 101–3
#DefundIPPF campaign, 123
Deleuze, Gilles, 5
deliberation, 7, 14, 25, 28, 31–33, 66, 67, 68
deliberative approaches, 31, 32
deliberative mini-publics (DMPs), 60, 66, 67
deliberative political theory, 59
deliberative system, 60n1
deliberative theory, 60, 61, 67
democracy, 4–5, 30, 41, 46, 92, 128, 140; citizenship, 94; culture, 46; deliberative, 3, 7, 59–61, 63–68; discursive, 59; liberal, 1, 2, 62, 63, 72, 84, 86, 91, 122, 152; movement, 133; neoliberal, 156; open, 32, 33, 61; participatory, 67; politics, 44, 118, 126; representative, 32, 66, 67; systems, 111
demographic decline, 120, 128
demographic nationalism, 118, 120
Derrida, Jacques, 44
Descartes, René, 24, 26
design device *vs.* filter device, 86–87, 90
Detarium senegalense, 167
Dewey, John, 74, 108
digital technology, 14–15
discourse ethics, 28
District Council election, 133, 141
Dnevnik, 153
dogmatism, 3, 17, 77, 78
Duration and Simultaneity (Einstein), 105

Durkheim, Èmile, 108, 109, 111
Dworkin, Ronald, 63, 66

economic crisis, 119
egalitarianism, 28–29
egalitarian society, 28
Eichmann, Adolf, 100
Eilam, D., 53
Eingedenken, 44
Einstein, Albert, 105
empathetic quality, 66
Engels, Friedrich, 38
enlarged mentality, 17, 99–102, 103n9
enlightened/enlightening approach, 159
Enlightenment, 105, 109, 159, 183–84
epistemic function, 60, 60n1, 66
epistemology, 30, 31
epistocracy, 64–67
Esfeld, Michael, 15, 197, 198
Estrela, Edite, 121, 122
Estrela Report, 121
EU Commission, 122, 123
Europe, 41, 43, 105
European citizens' initiative (ECI), 122, 123
European Conservatives and Reformists, 122
European Council, 149
European Court of Justice (ECJ), 124
European Dignity Watch, 121
European Parliament (EP), 121, 122
European People's Party (EPP) Working Group on Bioethics and Human Dignity, 123
European Union (EU), 119, 121–24
Evangelical Christians, 125
evolutionary conserved systems, 53
existential utopians, 89
experimental progress, 84, 85
extradition law, 139

Fabiani, Jean-Loius, 5
Facebook, 28, 32, 150
fallibilism/fallibility, 27, 60, 62, 73, 78, 80
falsification, 29, 30, 62, 185
family mainstreaming, 121
family relations, 126
Federal Court, 196
Federation of Catholic Family Associations in Europe (FAFCE), 122
feminism, 11–12, 117, 119, 121–25
Fidesz, 117

First World War, 108
Foe (Coetzee), 102–3
forebrain, 52, 53
foreign policy, 119, 124–26
Foucault, Michel, 50, 62, 108
France, 105
Francis (Pope), 120
Frankfurt School, 183
Frederick, Danny, 12
free criticism, 56, 57
freedom of association, 23, 33, 91, 92
free-market economy, 42
free participation, 26–27
French republican ideology, 109
French Revolutionary Terror, 96n2
Freud, Sigmund, 105, 106, 108
Fuller, Steve, 186
Functional Magnetic Resonance Imaging (fMRI) studies, 52

G20 Summit, 139
Gaddis, John Lewis, 178
game theory, 182, 185
Gaus, Gerald, 9, 72, 73; criticism of Popper, 74–76; Popper resisting criticism, 76–78
gay rights, 125
Gemeinschaft (community), 39, 150, 156
gender, 127; concept of, 122, 123, 126; definition, 149; discrimination, 121; equality, 119, 122, 126; ideology, 119, 121; progressive regulations, 121; relations, 126; Roman Catholic critique of, 120
Georgia, 177
Gerber, Burton, 177
German academic culture, 106
German sociology, 38, 40
Germany, 107
Germino, Dante, 106
Gesellschaft (society), 39, 150
Gestalt, 151, 159
Gigerenzer, Gerd, 185
Glissant, Edouard, 41
"Global Domestic Politics" (*Weltinnenpolitik*), 134
global economic policy, 57
globalization, 12, 119–21, 127, 128
Goezt, Andrew R., 164
good neighborhood, 38, 41
Gotz, Norbert, 1
governance, 24, 30–33, 34, 59, 186; collective, 23; democratic, 91, 92

Gramsci, Antonio, 15, 198–99
Granitski, Ivan, 149
Gray, John, 50
Grieves, Robert, 138
groundlessness, 46
group cohesiveness, 54
group existence, 56
Guangdong-Hong Kong-Macau Greater Bay Area (GBA) Development, 137
Gulliver's Travels (Swift), 150–51

H1N1 pandemic, 200
Habermas, Jürgen, 15, 26, 31, 40, 44, 59, 200, 202, 203
Harris, Shane, 177
Hausa-Fulani, 162
Havel, Václav, 77
Hayek, Friedrich, 4, 7–8, 73, 75, 76, 78, 181
Hayes, Calvin, 8
historical indeterminism, 63
Hitler, Adolf, 62
Hobfoll, Stevan E., 56
Homer, 100
Homo economicus, 26
homophobia, 122, 128
homo sapiens, 50, 52–53, 111
Hong Kong, 11, 132; Autocratic Functionalism, 137–38; autonomy, international ties and global-local nexus, 134–38, 140, 142; electoral systems, 133; open society, 140–41; resilience of Liberal Universalism, 138–40
Hong Kong Democracy and Human Rights Act, 140
Hong Kong Democratic Alliance of Overseas Postgraduates, 140
Hong Kong Higher Institutions International Affairs Delegation (HKHIIAD), 140
Hong Kong Police Force, 140
Hong Kong Public Opinion Research Institute, 140
Hong Kong Special Administrative Region (HKSAR), 132, 134–36, 141
Hong Kong Watch, 141
Honig, Bonnie, 94
Honneth, Axel, 41
Horkheimer, Max, 183
Horton, Robin, 165
Hosein, Ian, 14

Index

hotel quarantine, 194, 195, 200
The Human Condition (Arendt), 95
humaneness, 50, 51
humanity, 23, 33, 50, 84, 109, 112, 113, 121
human mind: as social minds, 23–26
humanoid, 153, 154
human(s): cognition, 30; evolution, 26; life, 95–97, 109; nature, 23, 32, 33; *vs.* orangutans, 25–26; as problem solvers, 23; rights, 101, 124, 126, 127, 139, 140; uniqueness, 95, 103
Hungarian Catholic Church, 119
Hungary, 117–19, 121, 126
Hunt, Lester H., 87
Hunt, Lynn, 101
hyper-rationalism, 9, 73

identity fusion, 55, 56
identity politics, 5, 13, 43, 49, 55–58, 103, 106, 113, 127
Igbo of Nigeria: cosmology, 3, 166–68; *vs.* Jews and Irish, 163; location, expansion and migration, 162–65; *Ofo, Ikenga*, political and economic powers, 167–72; *Ogu-ukwu* Igbo sub-group, 164; socio-political structure, sentimental attachment, spirit and adventurism, 165–67, 173
Ignatieff, Michael, 10, 12–13
Ikenga, 166–73
Ikenga-Oha, 171
illiberalism, 113
Ilogu, Edmund, 167
immigration/immigrants, 91–92, 148–50
imminent danger, 52
impartiality, 68
The Imperial Archive (Richards), 176
imperialistic utopians, 89–91
inalienable identity, 158
individual animals, 50–51
individual freedom, 55, 56, 62, 63, 65
individuality/individualism, 51, 55
individual responsibility, 48
informal conservatism, 125
information wars, 176–78
inquiry, 11, 108, 133, 136, 156, 174
institutional design, 25
insufficiency consciousness (*Insuffizienzbewusstsein*), 43
intelligence, 174–76; agencies, 175, 176, 178, 181, 186; data and interpretations, 178; human, 110; revolution, 186;

as scientific prophecy, 14, 181–84; services, 14, 176, 178, 182, 185, 186; Soviet, 179; US, 177–79
international border restrictions, 190, 193–95, 202
International Covenant on Civil and Political Rights (ICCPR), 134
International Covenant on Economic, Social and Cultural Rights (ICESCR), 134
international human rights, 119
International Human Rights Day, 122
Irish abortion referendum (2018), 31
irrational hypersensitivity, 180
irrationalism/antirationalism, 76, 77, 111
Islam: orthodox, 125; political, 42
Islam(ic): caliphate, 45; populists, 45; radicalism, 42
Islamophobia, 118
Istanbul Convention (2011), 123
Istanbul Convention on Violence against Women, 149
Izhar, R., 53

Jeffreys, M. D. W., 171
Jervis, Robert, 176, 184
Jewishness, 103
Jews, 105, 163, 166
jihadism, 45
Jobbik, 119
John Paul II, 120
Joint Declaration (1984), 134
Joseph, Tara, 138
justice, 1–2, 8, 63, 65, 72, 75, 113, 167, 184, 199

Kaebnick, Gregory, 179
Kamusella, Tomasz, 153
Kant, Immanuel, 94, 97, 99, 109, 159
Karsenti, Bruno, 107, 113
Kathibi, Abdelkebir, 44
Kent, Sherman, 181, 182
Komov, Alexey, 120
Krastev, Ivan, 153
Kuby, Sophia, 121

Lam, Carrie, 137, 138
Landemore, Helene, 61
Langer, William L., 181
Laqueur, Walter, 178
Law, Nathan, 141
Law and Justice Party (*Prawo i Sprawiedliwość*, PiS), 117

lawmaking, 33
leading culture (*Leitkultur*), 43
LeDoux Jospeh, E., 52
Lee, Everett S., 164
Lefort, Claude, 41, 42
Legislative Council (LegCo) election, 133, 141
Legutko, Ryszard, 122
lesbian, gay, transgender, trans, and queer (LGBTQ+) rights, 118, 122, 127
Leung Chun-ying, 137
Levine, Robert A., 163, 169
Levinson, Ronald, 191
L'Heuillet, Helene, 41
liberal community, 122, 149, 157, 158
liberalism, 2, 50, 62, 63, 72, 91, 119, 121–24; aristocratic, 65n3; political, 113
Liberal Universalism, 11, 133, 136, 138–40, 142
Lilla, Mark, 2, 12–13, 42, 44, 45
The Limits of Community (Plessner), 38, 40, 42
listener choice, 27
literary works, 101–3
literature, 101, 103
literature classroom, 94–97, 101, 103, 104
living together, 23–25
logical fallacies, 24
love of beauty, 97–98
Lozanov, Georgi, 151
Lukács, György, 46
Lunacek Report, 122
Luther, Martin, 42

MacAuley, Margaret, 199
Mannheim, Karl, 181
Manow, Philip, 43
Marklund, Carl, 1
marriage, 123; same-sex, 121, 124
Marxists, 106, 183
Marxist utopia, 86
Marx, Karl, 38, 52n4
Mauny, R., 165
Maxwell, Nicholas, 184
McInnes, Neil, 2, 13
Melbourne, 195
meta-utopia, 83, 85–92, 85n7
migration, 13, 40, 43, 126, 163–65
Mikolášik, Miroslav, 123
The Mild Voice of Reason (Bessette), 59
Mill, John Stuart, 74, 84, 86
minimal state, 85, 89, 91

Mishkoved, Mihail, 153
misogyny, 117, 118n2, 128
missionary utopians, 89
Mobbs, D., 52
modernity, 44, 109, 158, 182
modernization, 39
modern nation-state, 107
modern society, 40, 42, 46, 108, 111
monodemocratic policy, 43, 45
moral framework, 78
moral judgment, 99
Morgenthau, Hans, 76
Mort, J., 53
multiculturalism, 113
Mum, Dad & Kids: European Citizens' Initiative to Protect Marriage and Family, 123
Muslim diaspora, 44–45
mutatis mutandis, 150
mysticism, 112, 113

National Cabinet, 194, 196, 197, 200, 201
national exceptionalism, 126
national identity, 120, 128, 148
National Intelligence Estimates (NIEs), 181, 182
nationalism, 13, 38, 44, 49, 51, 54–56, 118
National People's Congress, 137
National Security Department, 141
National Security Law (NSL), 132, 133, 140, 141
nationhood, 157
natural law, 84
natural selection, 23
natural social order, 121
Nazi phenomenon, 111
negative utilitarianism, 61–64
neighborhood, 40, 46
neoconservatism/neoconservatives, 148–51, 154, 157
neo-Kantians, 106
neoliberalism, 8, 44, 84n3, 113, 127
neopatriarchy, 44
"neo-traditional," 126
neo-tribal barbarism, 51
Network DIPLO, 140
Neumann, Franz, 111
New South Wales (NSW), 195, 196
The New York Times, 176, 177
NGOization, 125
Nigeria, 162, 163
Ninova, Kornelia, 149

Index

Niskanen Center, 72
Niven, Sir Alex, 163
nomocracy, 8
nongovernmental organizations (NGOs), 120
"non-human," 154
nonimperialist utopians, 90
Nossal, Kim Richard, 135
nostalgia, 45
Notturno, Mark, 8, 17
Nozick, Robert, 83, 85–92, 85nn6, 7, 89n14
Nussbaum, Martha, 101
Nwaezeigwe, Nwankwo, 4

Oakeshott, Michael, 1, 181
objectivity, 100, 174, 181, 182. *See also* scientific objectivity
Office for Strategic Services (OSS), 180, 182
Office of National Estimates (ONE), 181
Ofo, 167–72
Okpala (*Diokpala*), 167, 169, 171, 172
"One Country, Two Systems" policy, 132, 137, 141
"One of Us" campaign, 123
On Liberty (Mill), 86
online discourse, 27
open access, 26
open discourse, 29
open engagement: within and between institutions, 29–33; minimal conditions of, 26–29
open morality, 110
open neighborhood, 38, 40–42, 46
open society, 23, 27, 29–31, 33, 41, 45, 46, 48–51, 56–57; belonging and identification in, 11–12; Bergson on, 4–5, 105–10, 112; concept of, 3, 6, 117, 162; critical rationalism of, 67–68; definition, 83–84; desiring, 89–91; Gaus on, 9, 73; Gaus's criticism of Popper, 74–76; Hayekian view of, 7–9, 73, 75, 76, 78; in Hong Kong, 136, 139–42; idea of, 3, 4, 72, 103–4, 117; institutions, 62; literary works to implementation of, 101–3; meta-utopia as, 85–89; at national and international security, 178–81; negative utilitarianism and, 61–64; neoconservatism and, 148–51; as oxymoron, 2; sectarian

defense/defenders of, 9, 74–76, 80; sustainability of, 79. *See also individual entries*
The Open Society and Its Complexities (Gaus), 9, 73, 75, 84n3
The Open Society and Its Enemies (Popper), 5–6, 48, 49, 54, 56–58, 72, 76, 78, 94, 138–39, 180, 183, 197
"The Open Society and its Friends" (Gaus), 74
Open Society Foundations, 72, 151
Open Society University Network, 72
orangutans, 25–26
Orbán, Viktor, 113
The Order of Public Reason (Gaus), 72
The Origins of Totalitarianism (Arendt), 94
Orthodox Church, 149
Ostrom, Elenor, 31
Ottenberg, Simon, 164, 166
oughtness (*Das Sollen*), 39
overconfident rationalism, 76

panhuman cognitive phenotype, 23
Parvin, Phil, 67
perceptible threat, 53
Perception and Misperception in International Politics (Jervis), 176
persuasion, 17, 89, 97, 98, 100
Pettit, Philip, 56
philosophy: anthropology, 38; in France, 108; political, 61, 62, 72, 80, 99; social, 38
"philosophy of praxis" approach, 199
piecemeal engineering approach, 7, 8, 60, 63, 65, 67, 73, 76, 77
Pitts, Andrea, 5, 12
place, concept of, 40
Planned Parenthood Federation (IPPF), 123
Plato, 33, 65, 88, 150
Plessner, Helmuth, 13, 38–46
pluralism, 43, 84–86, 88, 91, 120; reasonable, 84–86, 88, 90
pluralistic society, 79, 180
plurality, 95, 102–4, 174, 184
Poland, 117–19, 123, 126
Polanyi, Michael, 181
political decentralization, 165
political discourse, 31
political judgments, 98–101
political liberalism, 42, 79

political theory, 6, 29, 59, 61, 63
politics, 99, 120; culture and, 98; philosophy and, 97–99; right-wing, 125
Politzer, Georges, 105, 107
Pooley, Jefferson, 181
Popper, Karl, 23, 26, 29, 30, 38, 39, 41, 43, 45, 46, 181; conception of politics, 44; critical approach, 174, 184, 186; critical rationalism, 6, 7, 9, 61–64, 68, 73, 185; fallibilistic problem-solving, 9, 73; Gaus's criticism of, 74–76; historicism, criticism of, 174, 176, 181; idea of falsification, 185; on knowledge and ignorance, 184, 186; McInnes' criticism of, 2; on open society, 1, 6–10, 13–17, 50–51, 61, 62, 64, 65nn2, 3, 72–74, 76, 106, 136, 150, 160, 174, 175, 180, 191, 198; *The Open Society and Its Enemies*, 5–6, 48, 49, 54, 56–58, 72, 76, 78, 94, 138–39, 180, 183, 197; "paradox of tolerance," 79; philosophy of science, 180; piecemeal engineering approach, 7, 8, 60, 63, 65, 67, 73, 76, 77; political philosophy, 191; *The Poverty of Historicism*, 183; "Public Opinion and Liberal Principles," 78; on reasonableness, 78–80; resisting Gaus's criticism, 76–78; social scientific methods, criticism of, 14; "Towards a Rational Theory of Tradition," 77; tribalism, collectivism, and nationalism, criticisms of, 49, 54–56, 181; "Utopia and Violence," 78; view of politics, 65
"Popper's Return Engagement" (McInnes), 13
populism, 1, 43, 44, 191
populist radicals, 179, 180
positivism, 182–85
postmodernism, 42
The Poverty of Historicism (Popper), 183
The Practice of the "One Country, Two Systems" Policy in the Hong Kong Special Administrative Region, 137
prejudices, 43
primitive mentality, 109
The Principle of Hope (Bloch), 174
probability, 175, 176, 182–85
Prodanov, Vassil, 156
prodemocracy movement, 135, 142
pro-family movement, 120
Project Citizens Foundation, 140

Prokopiev, Ivo, 153
pseudo-crisis, 180
public announcement, 27
public discourse, 1, 14, 72, 120, 125, 153, 160
public emergencies, 10, 14–15
public health, 202; law, 198; measures, 190, 191, 193, 197; in open society, 191–93; and political philosophy, 198–200; practitioners, 192, 198; risk assessment, 195, 197
Public Health Emergency of International Concern, 194
public institutions, 31, 59
publicity, 179, 180
"Public Opinion and Liberal Principles" (Popper), 78
public policy, 65
public sphere, 27, 31, 41, 42, 44, 59, 96, 101
public things, 94
public university, 94
Putin, Vladimir, 161, 177, 178

Queensland, 196

racism, 1, 113
radical openness, 176–78, 186
Rashidov, Vezhdi, 153
rational choice theory, 182, 185
rationalism, 160, 161
rationality, 26, 29, 30, 32, 62, 108
rationalization, 67
rational-legal domination, 111
rational unity, 55
Rawls, John, 78, 79, 88
reality, 2, 3, 39, 40, 43, 88, 95
reasonableness, 78–80
reason/reasoning, 24–26, 28, 32, 66, 76, 160; collective/group, 60, 66; critical, 59; human, 24, 25, 27; irrational, 159, 161
reflexive modernity, 112
religion, 74, 75, 77, 92, 107, 109, 110, 112, 120, 124; dynamic, 112; fundamentalism, 44; right, 121; static, 110–12
religious religions, 112
Renminbi (RMB), 137
Report on Sexual and Reproductive Health and Rights, 121
representative thinking, 17, 99–102
reproductive rights, 120, 122, 125–27

Republic (Plato), 33, 88
reputational effects, 27, 28
"*ressaisissement*," 107
revolt against freedom: cultural form, 54–56; evolutionary nature, 51–54; as against humanity, 50–51
Rezvani, David A., 137
Richards, Thomas, 176
Robinson Crusoe (Defoe), 101–2
Roma minority, 148, 155, 156
Romania, 124
Romanian Constitutional Court, 124
Ronson, Jon, 24
Rorty, Richard, 101
Royer, Christof, 197, 198
Russia, 1, 117–19, 120, 125, 176, 177. *See also* Soviet Union
Russophilia, 160

Sachgemeinschaft, 42
Sanger, David E., 178
Sassen, Saskia, 134
Schmitt, Carl, 15
Schulddemokratie, 44
science, 29, 30, 62, 100, 180; evolutionary, 25
scientific ethics, 186
scientific knowledge, 29
scientific method, 14, 62, 65, 174, 180, 183, 184
scientific objectivity, 180
scientific practice, 175
scientific prediction, 183
scientific progress, 84
scientific research, 180
scientific thinking, 111
Second World War, 46, 178–80, 182, 197
secrecy, 14, 174–76, 179, 180, 186
secret: information, 179; services, 175, 181
secularism, 120
secular law, 33
security motivation system, 53
security services, 178
Serbia, 66, 67
sex education, 121, 122, 125
sexism, 1, 118n2
sexual minorities, 119, 124, 126
Sharabi, Hicham, 44
Sharia law, 45
Shils, Edward, 14, 176, 180–82, 186
Shklar, Judith, 5
Shkvarek, Kristiyan, 151

Simmel, Georg, 39
slavery, 135
slave trade/transportation, 164, 165
Slovenia, 119
Smart, R. N., 64
social class, 40
social competence, 32
social distancing, 194, 195
social diversity, 3, 9, 16, 25, 72–74, 78, 80
social ecology, 26, 27, 29
social engineering, 65
social interaction, 26, 27, 31
social media, 27–28, 203
social morality, 9, 73, 74, 75, 78, 79, 107–10
social progress, 62, 175
social radicalism, 38, 41, 42–46; Muslim diaspora and its challenges, 44–45
social relations, 41, 46
social sciences, 10, 16, 62, 76, 77, 109, 111, 182–84
societal norms, 127
sociology, 108, 204; German, 38, 40; of knowledge, 180
Socrates, 50, 51, 150
Sohm, Rudolf, 111
Šojdrová, Michaela, 123
solidarity, 100, 101, 103, 104, 113
Song Ruan, 138
Sonne, Paul, 177
Soros, George, 153
sorosoids in Bulgaria, 11; animalistic semiotics *vs.* human semantics, 155–56; assertion of values of open society, 159–60; definition, 151–52; dehumanizing potential of inflection, 152–54; divinity, 157–58; figure of machine, 156–57; neoconservatism and open society, 148–51; role of supporters of open society, 160–61
Soviet Union, 178, 179. *See also* Russia
Spain, 119
stable association, 90
Starshel, 153
state interventionism, 64, 65
stateless societies, 165
state system, 165
storytelling, 96, 100, 103
Streeck, Wolfgang, 46
sufferings, 64, 102
suicide bomber, 43
superstition, 74, 75, 111
supra-intellectuality, 110, 112, 113

surveillance, 14, 182
Swift, Jonathan, 150
Szechtman, H., 53

taboos, 48
temptation of community, 46
Thalmann, Katharina, 185
A Theory of Justice (Rawls), 88
Things Fall Apart (Achebe), 165, 169–70
Thomas, L.V., 165
Thunberg, Greta, 112
Tiananmen Square crackdown (1989), 135, 140
tolerance/intolerance, 7, 28, 42, 63, 68, 73, 76, 79, 128
Tönnies, Ferdinand, 39, 40, 149, 150
The Torment of Secrecy (Shils), 179, 180
totalitarianism, 41, 78, 96n2, 138, 152, 181–84, 197
totalitarian society, 46
totalitarian thinking, 39, 103
"Towards a Rational Theory of Tradition" (Popper), 77
tradition, 44; liberal, 74, 80; open society, 83, 84, 88, 92
traditional belief system, 162
traditional family, 123
traditionalism, 44
transcendental homelessness (*Transzendentale Obdachlosigkeit*), 46
"Transforming Travel and Border Controls: Checkpoints in the Open Society" (Hosein), 14
transnational mobilization, 125
transnational social networks, 119, 120
transnational World Youth Alliance-Europe, 122
transparency, 14, 16, 27, 28, 178, 190, 196, 201, 203
trial and error, 6, 62, 186
tribalism, 9, 11, 43, 45n1, 49, 51, 54–56, 61, 78, 79, 181
tribal unity, 54
tribe, 152
Trud, 151
Trump, Donald, 9, 149, 191
trust, 33, 67, 76, 179, 182, 186, 190–91, 197, 200, 201, 203
truth, 24–26, 43, 52, 98–100, 150, 156–58, 160, 181
"Truth and Politics" (Arendt), 94
Tsang, Jasper, 137, 138

Twitter, 28
two-party systems, 29
The Two Sources of Morality and Religion (Bergson), 4, 105, 106, 108
The Tyranny of the Ideal (Gaus), 72, 74, 77

Ukraine, 1, 157, 158, 176, 177
Ukrainian refugees, 160
Umbrella Movement (2014), 139
United Nations High Commission for Refugees, 126
United Nations Human Rights Council, 139
United Russia Party, 117
United States, 72, 107, 121, 125, 176, 177
United States-Hong Kong Policy Act (1992), 135
universalism, 5, 105, 106, 113
Universal Periodic Review on Hong Kong (2018), 139
US Christian Right, 125
US Supreme Court, 75
utopia, 83, 86, 90, 91
"Utopia and Violence" (Popper), 78
utopian challenges, 88–89
utopianism, 5, 7, 76

vaccine mandates, 198, 201
Valéry, Paul, 108
Vansina, Jan, 165
Vatican, 120, 124, 125
Victoria, 195–96
Villa, Dana, 95
violence, 44, 46, 78, 79, 85, 98, 128
Virilio, Paul, 40
Voegelin, Eric, 5

Wahhabism, 42
Warren Court, 75
war(s), 105, 106; culture, 125; information, 176–78; writings, 106–7
The Washington Post, 176, 177
Weber, Max, 39, 110, 111
Western civilization, 125
Western populists, 45
Western universalism, 5
Westmoreland, Mark, 5, 12
white supremacy, 56
Wikipedia, 28, 32
Women for the Nation (*Kobiety dla Narody*), 119
women's rights, 120, 127
Wonder Woman (2017), 54

Woody, E. Z., 53
World Congress of Families (WCF), 120–21, 125
World Health Organization (WHO), 192, 194, 201
A World of Secrets: The Uses and Limits of Intelligence (Laqueur), 178
Worms, Frédéric, 113

xenophobia, 128
Xi Jinping, 138

Yoruba, 162

Záborská, Anna, 122
Zelensky, Volodymyr, 178
Ziobro, Zbigniew, 122

*For Product Safety Concerns and Information please contact
our EU representative GPSR@taylorandfrancis.com Taylor & Francis
Verlag GmbH, Kaufingerstraße 24, 80331 München, Germany*

T - #0021 - 200326 - C0 - 229/152/13 - PB - 9789633865897 - Matt Lamination